The
Blandys
of Madeira

1811–2011

The lower garden at Quinta do Palheiro which was acquired by John Burden Blandy in 1885

The Blandys of Madeira

1811–2011

Marcus Binney

F

FRANCES LINCOLN LIMITED
PUBLISHERS

Frances Lincoln Ltd
4 Torriano Mews
Torriano Avenue
London NW5 2RZ
www.franceslincoln.com

Contents

Foreword
by Adam Blandy

Two hundred years ago, when John Blandy set up a business in Madeira, he wrote all his correspondence with a goose's quill. In fine copperplate he and his clerks filled ledger columns with details of shipments of wine and other goods. Letters in longhand from my great, great, great grandfather went by the regular sailing vessels, known then as packets, to his agents and his family in England. With a following wind they would have been delivered within a week. The world beyond Madeira was a distant place – even though he would have been reminded of the turmoil on the Continent by the presence of the British garrison on the island.

When he arrived, there were already a number of established British wine exporters and traders on the island and more were to become established in the 19th century. Those businesses have since been sold, faltered or faded away. We have managed to keep going. Over generations we have been lucky to have produced firstborn sons temperamentally suited to taking over from their fathers and who have wished to make their lives in Madeira. In one case the generation changeover was highly charged, with father-son strife and talk of betrayal. But the business survived and led to greater fortune. There have been family rifts. The first John Blandy was tight-fisted, which led to complaints from his sisters, and one or two members have left in a huff never to return. But on the whole peace has prevailed and the lawyers have gone hungry. Luckily, the Blandys have not lived extravagantly. They have looked after their inheritances as trustees. They have not been big gamblers. John Burden, my great grandfather, toured the grander spa and casino towns of Europe with his second wife. But we should forgive him the extravagances of his retirement. He had already bought Quinta do Palheiro at a knockdown price and built a fine house – which has been in the family ever since and where I've been lucky to live.

In his twenties my grandfather, John Ernest, wagered the odd sovereign at poker. But he was not the type to have blown his winnings on horses. His only vice was French literature, a passion he picked up as a young man in Rheims, the Champagne area of France.

I regret to admit it but we Blandys have been dull dogs: not bad at business and management but not much else – except sport. We did produce one good amateur artist, Raleigh, who had an unrequited love affair. Letters from his beloved have only recently come to light. But for the rest it has been work and attention to business. We also managed to keep our enterprises going (or at least most of them) in the face of riots and revolutions.

In business the English on Madeira and the *Madeirenses* have a common purpose but there are differences in how we all go about it. The English favour a formal approach to meetings. Our Portuguese colleagues prefer a less structured approach and the word *desenrascar* is often used. This essentially means solving a problem immediately with an unplanned solution which with luck will become permanent. Another phrase used is *para inglês ver*, or for English to see. That expression arises from the longstanding tradition of English tourists being shown the best of a product and not the less desirable!

But we do have a lot in common. We're both suspicious of the metropolitan outsider, whether he comes from London or Lisbon. They may laugh at our Madeira accent and we may seem insular to them, even old-fashioned. Not all of us are on Facebook or Twitter. Yes, we are islanders and we have our own ways. But we have the mountains, the ocean and a kind climate, which are recompense enough. And when we are away from the island we have *saudades* and long to return.

In the course of helping the author Marcus Binney with this book, letters and photographs have been fished from drawers, attics explored and archives dusted down. Old Blandys and their wives have come to life again, forgotten stories have been unearthed and new insights gained into the company's ups and downs over the past 200 years. The experience has brought us closer to our ancestors and it has also made us realise how fortunate the Blandys have been. We have had business disasters and failures, family strains and stresses. In recent years the lives of Edward and Richard Blandy have been cut brutally short by cancer. But in the main we have been lucky. Michael, my cousin, with his indomitable spirit has taken over the driving seat and my son Christopher has been appointed to the Board.

The island of Madeira has given us much. Its incomparable landscape, its productive earth and rich seas are a daily reminder of how blessed we are. Across the centuries and days, we have made many good friends at work and at play. We value particularly those Madeira people who have worked for Blandy companies. Their loyalty, hard work and enduring spirit have ensured the lasting success of Blandy's.

The businesses have changed hugely. We are no longer in the Canary Islands and no doubt will continue to adapt to changing circumstances. We have chosen to be involved in hotels, tourism, wine and media. We are unlikely again to want to sell boots to the French army, educational books to West Africa, fumigation lamps to India or risk imprisonment in Siberia. These are uncertain times but then so it was in 1811, when much of the continent of Europe was ravaged by war. Our offices and working lives would astound earlier generations of Blandys but our guiding business principles remain much the same. Our families are still here, our homes are here and on this island we hope to stay, where that first John Blandy, a young man in search of advancement, started trading and contributing to the island's development.

We asked Marcus Binney to tell the story of the 200 years of the family and our businesses in a readable way as well as setting it in the context of history. I very much hope you will enjoy the book.

Adam Blandy was Blandy's Chairman from 1975 to 1985

Introduction

The Man with the Big Cigar

Churchill was driven to Reid's in
Graham Blandy's Buick sitting on the
folded- down roof and acknowledging
the cheers of the crowd.

On the evening of 1 January 1950, a short stocky figure in a dark blue overcoat and black felt hat walked slowly up the town pier at Funchal, cigar in hand. A large crowd watched in awed silence. Finally there was a cry of 'Viva Churchill' and cheering and clapping began.

From the start the Blandys had been closely involved in the visit of Britain's wartime leader. They were the agents for the Union Castle Line and owners of Reid's, Madeira's internationally known hotel, which they had acquired in 1937 and promptly had to close as war broke out in 1939. Madeira, though part of neutral Portugal, had suffered considerable hardship in the war years and the economy was slow to pick up amidst the austerity of the late 1940s. Churchill's visit was a coup of the first order both for the island and the Blandys.

Churchill liked to travel south in winter – often to the French Riviera. The idea of inviting the Churchills for a winter holiday in Madeira was formed one August day while Graham and Mildred Blandy were talking to Bryce Nairn, the British consul, and his wife. Margaret Nairn was an artist of some talent who had accompanied Churchill on painting expeditions in Marrakesh during the war.

Reid's Hotel was due to reopen in December 1949 and in those days of restricted travel and strict

Winston Churchill, cigar in hand, with his wife Clementine on the terrace of their suite at Reid's in January 1950

foreign exchange allowances for tourists it was far from certain that the venture would be successful. The Nairns said they would write to the Churchills suggesting a holiday on the island for bathing and painting. The reply was positive and telegrams were exchanged with London about a 'former naval person'. Walter Blandy and Douglas 'Hopper' Read (the accountant of the Blandy London office; he was a former Test cricketer once regarded as the fastest bowler in England, whose nickname came from his distinctive hopping run) visited Churchill and showed him the Reid's wine list.

Through a Mr Valentine of Cook's, who made Churchill's travel arrangements, the Blandys learnt that Churchill always liked to sleep in a double bed. As none was available at the hotel, Graham's brother, John Reeder Blandy, lent his own. Churchill was put in the ground-floor suite occupied by Lloyd George, the great First World War leader. Furniture came from Blandy houses while pictures were supplied by Elia Monier-Vinard, John Reeder's mother-in-law, who lived at the handsome Quinta da Achada, set in a large garden overlooking Funchal Bay.

Reid's Hotel with the panoramic Garden Wing added under Blandy ownership in the 1960s

Churchill was driven to Reid's in Graham Blandy's Buick sitting on the folded-down roof and acknowledging the cheers of the crowd. 'I have been greeted by many people in the world for whom I have done something,' he remarked laconically, 'but never in my whole life been greeted with such enthusiasm by people for whom I have never done anything.'

The Churchills had embarked at Southampton on the *Durban Castle* – one of the smartest of the Union Castle liners – on the evening of 29 December 1949. She was late sailing as, just after Churchill left Chartwell, his home in Kent, he remembered he had not fed his favourite black swans and promptly ordered the driver to turn back.

The Churchill party consisted of Colonel Bill Deakin, two secretaries, a valet and two detectives. Deakin was an Oxford don with a distinguished war record in Yugoslavia who was assisting with Churchill's war memoirs.

The extravagance of Funchal's New Year's Eve fireworks is always a heart-stopping spectacle. Mildred Blandy described the splendour of the scene which was repeated twenty-four hours later as Churchill's ship sailed in. 'A wonderful night, the whole island brilliantly illuminated with millions of lights, and huge setpieces on the hillside. As the *Durban Castle* came round the Brazen Head people started letting off fireworks. Blandy's office had a huge V in triple lights which could be seen for miles out to sea. Thousands of people in the streets and on the pier, and the local guard of honour all lined up.'

The *Durban Castle* entered the bay at 18.45 to the sound of sirens from the other ships in the port. The welcome party greeting the Churchills sailed out in the Blandy steam launch, the Mosquito. The party included Bryce and Margaret Nairn, Graham and Mildred Blandy, and the general manager of Blandy Brothers, Major Rupert Mullins.

Later that evening Winston and Clementine received a standing ovation as they entered the dining room at Reid's. The manager John Paquot made a speech of welcome asking other guests to respect the Churchills' desire for a quiet holiday.

Churchill, initially rather silent, opened up when the champagne was served. 'He was excited at seeing a side of beef (England still had a meat ration) and insisted on having cold beef as his main dish,' recalled Mildred. She described Churchill as being 'in amazing form. Astonishing as you would have expected him to be exhausted after a four day voyage of bad weather, all the fuss of landing etc …'

Graham Blandy describes how towards the end of dinner Churchill 'asked me what was the best Madeira on the list, to which I replied I believed it was the 1792 Blandy Solera'. When it arrived at the table Churchill said, 'I must do honour to this,' and stood up, put his napkin over his elbow and poured the wine for each of the guests. Then he sat down and talked of the year 1792, three years after the French Revolution, when Louis XVI and Marie Antoinette were still alive. The bottle came from a pipe (105 gallons) taken on board *HMS Northumberland* as it sailed south carrying Napoleon to exile in St Helena. The emperor had not drunk the wine and, as it had never been paid for, the pipe returned to Madeira.

Mildred and Graham Blandy see Lady Churchill on to a liner at the end of her return visit to Madeira in 1970

Churchill's keen sense of humour was in evidence throughout his visit. The Nairns hosted a reception for the Churchills to meet local people. The day before, the weekly Union Castle boat had again been, most unusually, six hours late, due to bad weather. Digging Rupert Mullins in the ribs, Churchill quipped: 'Can't blame me this time because your ship was late, can you?' Later, when Mullins took Churchill's senior detective on a mountain walk, Churchill called out to the detective in mock irritation: 'I shall be painting tomorrow at Câmara de Lobos – if you are available.'

When in bed Churchill liked to have the light coming in over his right shoulder. Another requirement was for plenty of pillows. A local resident gave Churchill's valet a bottle of anti-mosquito ointment but when Churchill saw it he is reputed to have exclaimed: 'Mosquito bites. Why, the little buggers would freeze to death in this climate.'

The welcome boost provided by Churchill was reported in the *London Evening Standard* on 18 January 1950: 'Mr Churchill's painting holiday has put the Portuguese Island back on the tourist map. Travel agencies report a big increase in bookings and enquiries since his visit. Many insist on booking at the hotel where Mr Churchill stayed.' In an instant Reid's was back in fashion, continuing to prosper in Blandy ownership for four decades.

Old Master: Churchill paints at the fishing village of Câmara de Lobos, where a plaque still records the event

1. A Poor Young Man
In Search of a Fortune

'It seems the most extraordinary thing
that ever happened: what can induce John
to act so — never was a man so changed.'

The first John Blandy as a young man in fashionable English Regency dress with cravat, white waistcoat and dark frock coat

The early 1800s – like the first decade of this century – were tumultuous times. Napoleonic tyranny was sweeping the Continent and, at one point, 90,000 French soldiers were poised at Boulogne ready to mount an invasion across the Channel. Republican ferment was unsettling the drawing rooms and palaces of Europe. In Britain agricultural mechanisation and the enforced enclosures of fields were driving poor farmers off the land and into the growing cities, where the Industrial Revolution was creating huge and often miserable urban populations. Villages were being deserted, food was often scarce and prices high, and legal costs could weigh heavily on hard-pressed farmers. For many it was not Merry England.

In Dorset a previously prosperous farming family was struggling. Charles Blandy, who was born at Lambourn in Berkshire in 1755 and had married Elizabeth Davis in 1782, had acquired in 1794 the lease of a farm at Piddletrenthide. The terms of the lease were harsh – they included the requirement that he should supply the landlord with regular loads of coal – and Charles and Elizabeth had six boys and three girls to feed. After the death of their father in 1803, the family were placed in highly straitened circumstances. That may have propelled John, the eldest son, to set sail in 1808 aged twenty-four and seek his fortune in the island of Madeira, to

A merchantman flying the Red Ensign enters Funchal Bay from the South, 1852

be joined later by his brothers Thomas, Robert and George.

Let us pass quickly over the rigours of the sea voyage that the young Dorset countryman had to endure; the gales in the Channel, the pitching and rolling deck across the Bay of Biscay, the slops and the cramped sleeping quarters shared with strangers. His destination was the island where, in the late fifteenth century, Christopher Columbus had met his wife, Filipa de Moniz, daughter of the first governor. They were married in Lisbon in 1478.

At last, after ten days, the sun would have warmed the sea air and the prevailing north-easterly pushed John Blandy's packet past Porto Santo and on to

'Several fast-sailing vessels, built expressly for the trade between England and Madeira, commanded by experienced seamen, and fitted up with every regard to the accommodation and comfort of passengers, leave Southampton at stated intervals direct for Madeira, and accomplish the voyage, under ordinary circumstances, in from eight to twelve days. These are ... the brigs Brilliant, Comet and Dart ... The first of these vessels was originally intended for a pleasure yacht; has a flush deck, and accommodation for fifty-four passengers ... The others have raised quarterdecks, sail fast, and have accommodation for about forty-five passengers each ... These packets are all fitted up with family and double-berthed cabins, well ventilated, with good bedding, and even the luxury of a bath-cabin. The attendance on board is truly excellent, and the table is most liberally and plentifully supplied, including wines, porter, ale, etc ... Opportunities of reaching the island by East and West India merchant ships, sailing from London, Liverpool or Glasgow, and touching at Madeira on their outward voyage, frequently offer during the autumn ... the comforts are by no means equal, and the passenger is required to furnish his own bedding.'

Madeira, Robert White, 1851

Ponta de São Lourenço, at the eastern end of Madeira, where an ugly surf breaks over submerged rocks two or three cable-lengths from the Ilhéu de Fora, the lighthouse island. Those rocks, on which several incautious masters have driven their vessels, were later known as Blandy's Reef because of the lucrative salvage and insurance work that came the firm's way. To port the diversely shaped Desertas – flat, whale-backed and saw-toothed – would have gradually assumed their distinctive profile lined across the southern horizon. Surrounded by skimming shearwaters and flurries of flying fish, with distant blue mountains peeping through their cloud caps to landward, the passengers got their first view of Madeira. Progress would then have slowed, especially as their vessel rounded Cabo Garajau, or the Brazen Head, and into the lee of Funchal Bay.

The gigantic amphitheatre behind Funchal scored by two deep

John Blandy's first house pictured in 1941 showing the lookout tower from which he could check shipping movements. The office of the British Consul is marked by the coat of arms and flag over the doorway

*E*arly on the morning of Christmas Eve 1807, just weeks before John Blandy arrived in Madeira, a large British convoy sailed into the bay of Funchal with orders to take the island. The governor, Pedro Fagundes Bacelar, was given just half an hour to agree to the landing of British troops and by dark the forts were in the hands of General William Beresford. The eight warships and fifteen troop carriers brought a force of 3,658 soldiers. On the following day Bacelar received 'surrender terms' which stipulated that Madeira should hand over to the commanders of the British forces the rights, privileges and jurisdiction of the Portuguese crown. Britain would respect public and private property but Madeira was to become a British possession in all but name.

The British occupation was prompted by Napoleon's military triumphs on the Continent. When Napoleon and Czar Alexander met on a raft moored on the River Niemen to sign the Treaty of Tilsit in July 1807, they agreed that they would instruct Denmark, Sweden and Portugal to close their ports to British shipping. Soon after Napoleon sent an ultimatum to Prince João, the Regent of Portugal, demanding that Portugal, England's oldest ally, should declare war on Britain, seize British property, and detain all British residents as hostages. The regent was forced to agree to these terms though he delayed carrying them out till the British had left with what goods they wished.

Marshal Junot, who invaded Portugal from Salamanca, entered Lisbon in November 1807, increasing the potential threat to sea routes. Madeira was an important victualling station on the route round the Cape to India and across the Atlantic to the Americas. Britain could not allow Madeira to fall into French hands. To preclude a surrender of Portuguese sovereign power to the French, the British offered to provide a naval squadron to escort the regent

ravines, or *ribeiras*, is an impressive sight to any sea traveller, then or now. Early prints show a single road flanked by a few white-walled houses leading straight up to the Monte church. A huge grey military fort glowers over the town, as it still does.

In an often quoted passage, Captain Frederick Marryat, the Victorian pioneer of the sea novel, who had visited Madeira on an Admiralty mission in 1828 to search for shoals around the island and the Canaries, noted: 'I do not know a spot on the globe that so astonishes and delights upon first arrival, as the island of Madeira … Winter has become summer; the naked trees which [the traveller] had left are exchanged for the luxuriant and varied foliage … a bright blue sky; a glowing sun; hills covered with vines; a deep blue sea; a picturesque and novel costume; all meet and delight the eye, just at the precise moment when to have landed on a barren

The main front of John Blandy's house with balconies to the main reception rooms on the upper floor

and his government to Brazil. Under intense pressure from both the French and the British, the regent finally set sail on 29 November for Rio de Janeiro which was declared the new capital of Portugal and its far-flung empire.

The British occupied the old Jesuit college and other buildings in town. General Beresford established himself at the Quinta da Achada above Funchal which years later would belong to the Blandys. Under instructions from the Foreign Office, Beresford made an inventory of military equipment and provisions and established contact with leading British merchants and the British consul. He was told to sound out leading local figures including 'João de Carvalhal, a gentleman of most excellent character and a very large fortune'.

Beresford set about improving the island's defences and increased the salaries of the Portuguese militia. In March 1808 a new treaty was signed by the British and Portuguese foreign ministers annulling the 'surrender terms'. Madeira was restored to the crown of Portugal but Portuguese troops were to remain under the control of the occupying force. Civil powers were largely restored, allowing Beresford to concentrate on military matters as well, including the inspection of all ships visiting the port. The treaty was to stay in force until the conclusion of definitive peace between Britain and France. Beresford was replaced by General Robert Meade in August 1808. For the next few years the main external threat was from corsairs and privateers, Moroccan and Algerian, which preyed on merchant shipping and were a source of constant worry to families like the Blandys who regularly travelled between England and Madeira. The occupation finally ended in September 1814, seven months after Allied forces had taken Paris and Napoleon had been exiled to Elba.

Food and drink at Santo António da Serra Inn, 1843

island would have been considered a luxury.'

His vessel having dropped anchor and the shipboard hubbub of arrival abated, the sounds of the island would have assailed him as John landed on *terra firma* – the barking of dogs, the crowing of cocks, the cries of children, the banging of stone breakers, blacksmiths and carpenters, the rushing of water, and the slapping of washing against rocks. Here and there would have been peasants selling vegetables. Did John perhaps pass a unit of soldiers from the British garrison?

John Blandy is one of hundreds of young men who left Britain in search of fortune. In the East and the West Indies, as well as America, India and Africa, many such fortunes were made, but in most cases later generations wanted to enjoy the fruits of success rather than attend to business. The story of the Blandys over the past 200 years is that they have survived drastic reverses, whether caused by wars, depressions, family upheavals or commercial failures. It is the more impressive as their businesses have been principally based not in a British colony but in Madeira where they have remained, speaking Portuguese but retaining strong English ties.

Maintaining a family business and fortune over generations depends on finding members of the family who are not only hardworking and dedicated but also have good management skills and a talent for figures and finance. Survival in Madeira has meant endurance not just through two world wars, the great depression of the 1930s, and the successive economic cycles which have brought down so many businesses or caused them to be sold. It has also meant keeping control of the equity and avoiding its dilution. In addition there have been Portugal's own ups and downs – serious unrest in the 1930s followed by the Fascist takeover and all the difficulties of living under a dictatorship, even if a relatively benign one. Madeira, too, has had its own island crises and setbacks – famine in the

When John Blandy arrived in Madeira British trade was already well established in the island. 'The merchant community of Funchal was cosmopolitan in origin, international and transatlantic in outlook, and maintained agents, factors and correspondents in the seaports of four continents.' So wrote Thomas Bentley Duncan of Madeira at the end of the seventeenth century in his absorbing book, Atlantic Islands. In the late 1680s the leading English merchants in the island were Obadiah Allen (the English vice-consul), Henry Criton, George Fryer, Lawrence Gay, Samuel Hutchins, Matthew Matson and Richard Miles.

A number of people of English, Scottish and Irish extraction had lived in Madeira since the fifteenth century, including the Scotsman John Drummond of Perth said to have been the nephew of King Robert III of Scotland, whose descendants spread to the Azores. The pioneer English merchant was Robert Willoughby who arrived at Funchal as a young man about 1590. He was a staunch Catholic, and much in favour in Lisbon and Madrid and was buried at the Franciscan convent in Funchal. More important was William Ray who in 1620 paid more duty for goods exported from Funchal than any other merchant – though it needs to be remembered that Portuguese merchants exporting goods in Portuguese ships were not subject to duty. During the middle years of the seventeenth century the principal merchant was Richard Pickford, active from 1638 to 1682, above all in the wine trade. The best known is William Bolton whose extensive correspondence has been published in The Bolton Letters (1928).

By the mid-seventeenth century Catholic émigrés had been joined by Protestant adventurers. 'The English merchants – Catholic, Anglican, Presbyterian

1840s on an almost Irish scale, vineyards devastated by phylloxera and, before that, another almost equally devastating plague, the oïdium, a powdery mildew which attacks the leaves of vines.

During the American Civil War Blandy's profited from British neutrality and supplied coal to both Yankees and Confederates. But it left them with huge quantities of worthless Confederate cash and bonds which the Federal Government had no inclination to honour. In the 1970s the Communist revolution threatened confiscation of businesses, especially foreign-owned ones. Avoiding political confrontation was all the more tricky as the family firm has long owned the principal local newspaper.

Above all, there is providence and sheer human frailty. One generation holds on to the reins too long, while another dies young, thrusting responsibility on family members who had never been brought up to run the business. In recent times two of the leading talents in the family succumbed to cancer.

The continuing success of the Blandys is due to adaptability. Successive

generations have shown a remarkable eye for new business opportunities, taking the firm of Blandy Brothers successively into Madeira wine, general trading, and the coaling, supplying and watering of passing ships. Blandy's have been agents for leading shipping lines, acted as Lloyd's agents in the insurance business, and founded their own bank. In the 1980s Blandy's made good money in car dealerships in the Canary Islands. Then, to almost universal surprise and bafflement, they sold their most famous asset, Reid's Hotel, only to return to the hotel business, in Madeira and now in mainland Portugal and Brazil, and soon, it seems, in major cities in Europe. They have ventured into tourism,

19th-century view of Funchal harbour with the Loo Rock on the left

and Independent — were men of true "Atlantic" outlook, at home on two or three continents. They sent their ships to the farthest shores of Africa and of North, Central, and South America,' wrote Duncan approvingly. He continues sternly: 'The unbroken history of the English commercial community at Funchal, from the 1620s ... speaks eloquently of the Anglo-Saxon power to accommodate, to compromise, to persuade, and to persist. The Protestant merchant had to bear the weight of legislative discrimination, and official disapproval; he had to endure public obloquy and petty insults; he was a pariah beyond the pale of decent Catholic society.'

British merchants not only traded in wine and sugar cane. The island also needed to import food, notably meat, potatoes, maize and cereals — in 1757 the governor estimated the population at 80,000 persons, an impressive figure for a small island, and at a time when the population of London was estimated at 700,000. Recurrent wheat shortages had to be met by imports which could not come from Portugal, itself heavily dependent on imports. For Madeira, the best hope of relief from recurrent food shortages came from the English colonies in North America. In 1700 Bolton noted seven shiploads of provisions arriving from the colonies at Funchal. These included a brigantine from Boston laden with wheat and Indian corn and three brigantines from New England, one from New York and one from Virginia — all in Funchal during February 1700 with cargoes of wheat, Indian corn, pease and other products. In September 1700 a ketch arrived from Pennsylvania with 3,600 bushels of Pennsylvania wheat. In return Madeira had little to offer but wine and more wine. By the end of the seventeenth century Madeira wine accounted for 90 per cent of the value of all exports.

opening the Blandy wine lodge in Funchal on the site of an old monastery, and set up the ambitious Madeira Story Centre on the Funchal waterfront. But it has not been success all the way. A venture into country-house hotels in England was a costly reverse due to unfortunate timing. An investment in marble businesses in Portugal produced a substantial loss. The Canary Island car dealerships could have been sold at the top of the market. But they yielded such plum revenues that the Blandys decided to retain them, only to see competition erode sales and drastically reduce the value of the company. Then there is the sheer difficulty of selling certain quite valuable assets in a small island marketplace, success depending on lateral thinking and the ability to devise ingenious means of splitting assets or attracting new investors. Today many of their businesses are jointly owned: the Madeira wine with the Symington family in Oporto, the hotels with a syndicate of dynamic Madeiran investors.

The other visible sign of Blandy's long connection with Madeira lies with their handsome properties: town houses in Funchal and *quintas*, notably Quinta da Achada and Quinta Santa Luzia, pretty country houses combining beautiful gardens with farms and sometimes vineyards too. The great estate at Palheiro with its ten gardeners is open to the public five days a week. Adjoining farmland and pine woods have been transformed first into a beautifully landscaped golf course, followed by a series of substantial villas and now a complete village dramatically constructed on a plunging hillside providing every house with an uninterrupted view of the ocean. Easier perhaps when you have your own land to build on but not so easy when completion coincides with the most savage property recession for many decades.

As the Blandy business celebrates its 200th anniversary, the younger members of the family are more involved than ever – in managing the shipping and travel agencies, a golf course, big-game sports fishing, and learning the hotel trade.

When John Blandy set up in Madeira 200 years ago it was not the isolated Atlantic island it might seem, a distant outpost of Europe 300 miles off the coast of Africa. Madeira sat astride one of the world's great shipping lanes – the route from England to the Cape and on round to India and the Far East. Increasingly the island became an important stop on the route to the newly liberated states of South America. Earlier Madeira had prospered as the sole European port with which the American colonists could trade directly. Under an Act of Parliament only British ships could carry imported goods to the American colonies and tea, wine and brandy all had to come via British ports. This was a prime cause of the American War of Independence

---

John Blandy's letter of introduction to Messrs Newton, Gordon, Murdoch took him straight to one of the island's leading British shippers. Francis Newton had a large share of the American market and had been joined in 1758 by his younger brother Thomas, and then by Thomas Gordon, who was to receive the freedom of the Scottish burghs of Dumfries, Glasgow and Dundee while he was abroad. In 1791 Thomas Murdoch's name was added to the firm, followed by Thomas Gordon's son James in 1802. Another Scotsman, Robert Scott, became a partner in 1805. Meanwhile Francis Newton retired to live in London in 1800 and was given by his grateful partners 'five pipes of Best London Particular Madeira per annum' to keep him comfortable in his old age. This was equal to 2,700 bottles a year, evidence of the island's flourishing wine trade during the Napoleonic Wars.

'There being no roads in Madeira fit for wheeled vehicles, those who are unable to ride on horseback, and ladies in visiting, usually employ the palanquin, a kind of settee suspended from a long pole, which, when carried, hangs about 12 inches from the ground. It is partly covered with an awning and curtains, the seat is low, and the attitude rather cramped. These vehicles are carried on the shoulders of two men, one preceding the other, who are paid 7½ pence each per hour … Many of the furnished houses provide a conveyance of this description. On account of the greater weight of

manifest in the Boston Tea party. Madeira, because it was off the coast of Africa rather than Europe, was outside these controls.

It has long been said that John Blandy, the founder of the family business, arrived in Madeira in 1807 aged twenty-three as a quartermaster to General Beresford, commander of the British garrison (see page 10-11). A British fleet had been sent to Madeira as a precaution against French successes in the Peninsular War which threatened the takeover of Portugal and the island's loss as a victualling port for British ships. Yet prolonged research among army lists yielded no mention of a John Blandy serving in Madeira.

The truth was found instead by the Madeira wine lover and expert Emmanuel 'Mannie' Berk. Mr Berk has long traded in fine Madeira vintages in the United States and his extensive researches led him to write a delightful book on the Madeira wine parties in America a century ago. In August 2006 he found a letter of introduction sent from London to Messrs Newton, Gordon, Murdoch & Scott, wine merchants in Madeira, which immediately solved the family mystery: 'Sirs! At the desire of our particular friend, Richard Fuller Esq., Banker in this City, we beg leave to introduce Mr John Blandy, who visits your Island on account of ill health, and wishes to obtain Employment in a Counting House.

The letter of introduction brought by John Blandy to Madeira

We shall be obliged if you can promote his views, and accordingly recommend him to your attention.' The letter is dated 23 December 1807, implying that John Blandy arrived in the island early in 1808 rather than with British forces some months before.

A vivid picture is provided by an early guidebook,

the palanquin, and the rugged nature of the country roads, hammocks are usually made use of by invalids for any lengthened excursion ... the Madeira hammock is generally made of strongly woven hempen threads, of various colours, with a deep netted fringe; it is suspended from a long pole and carried as the palanquin, but the elevation from the ground is considerably greater, and the position much more agreeable.'

Madeira, Robert White, 1851

'The appearance of the island is very beautiful and we saw it this morning to the best advantage as we steamed slowly along its Southern Shore and from our ship could see Every house, field & garden Which seemed to Cling to every little ledge along the Steep Mountain Sides and in the Small valleys that furrow its steep sides. All these were bright and green with patches of sugar Cane which grew like a Close Corn field, only the Colour is a brighter green. The town of Funchal is old-fashioned Enough but as seen from the ship it looks like a Close Cluster of White Stone houses with red-tiled roofs with an old Fort overhanging it and sundry houses, churches and Convents perched high on the hills behind.'

W.T. Sherman, US Wabash, 5 December 1871

An Account of the Island of Madeira, by an Edinburgh doctor, N.C. Pitta, living on the island. It was published in 1812, the year after John Blandy established his business. 'A packet regularly sails from Portsmouth for Madeira at the beginning of every month, and affords the safest mode of conveyance and the best accommodation,' writes Pitta. 'In all cases those who apply earliest have the choice of cabins.' He continues: 'Almost everywhere, the island presents the most picturesque and

Early 20th century view of the rooftops of Funchal looking west towards the Pico do Forte

According to longstanding legend, the island of Madeira was first discovered by an English knight Robert Machin or Machim. The story of his elopement from Bristol, with his beloved Anne d'Arfet, is a fourteenth-century precursor of Romeo and Juliet. It finds the young lovers driven to the island by a fierce storm, only for Anne to die of exhaustion within days.

The entry on Robert Machin in the Oxford Dictionary of National Biography by Felipe Fernández-Armesto describes the origin of the legend. The earliest version appears in a Descripção de Ceuta e norte de África, apparently dating from 1507. Here Machin is said to be an exiled English knight, bound for Spain with his unnamed mistress and blown to the island of Porto Santo, where he sights Madeira to the south-west. While he explores the island, most of his crew, fearful of the thickly wooded and mysterious mountains, sail away. Shipwrecked on the African mainland the survivors are enslaved. When his lover dies Machin builds an oratory over her grave and escapes with his remaining crew in a boat they have built. They too are wrecked and enslaved on the African coast, and when they encounter their old shipmates they promptly attack them. The Moors separate them, upbraiding Christians for fighting each other, and hear their story, which is related to the king of Fez. Machin is sent on to the court of King Juan of Castile, where he dies.

António Galvão included an almost identical story in his Tratado dos Descobrimentos, published after his death in 1563. He dated Machin's

enchanting appearance: in some places, huge perpendicular rocks and lofty precipices, contrasted with deep excavations and chasms; in others, prominent ridges and beautiful valleys blended with deep ghylls and ravines, containing immense torrents of water and innumerable cascades, afford a highly varied and sublime picture of nature.'

Dr Pitta enthuses about the many exotic plants and trees, natives of both the East and West Indies, to be found in Funchal and the gardens around the town – the banana, the guava, the pomegranate and the fig, as well as recent introductions such as the mango and pineapple. Flowers which in England could only be nursed in greenhouses here grew wild. Myrtles, lilies, lupins, violet and balsam sprang up in the fields 'forming 1,000 natural parterres of embroidery'.

Pitta found the people of Madeira to be very musical. 'No night passes at Funchal or in the country without serenades of guitars,' he wrote. 'The women are also remarkable for their delicate and beautiful works in wax and in artificial flowers, which are not easily distinguishable from those of nature.'

A notable feature of the island was that it was without wheeled traffic of any kind – neither carts, coaches nor carriages. The richer classes were conveyed quaintly in chairs and palanquins. The grape pressings were brought to town in goatskins, carried on the shoulders of the workmen who often illicitly quenched their thirst on the way (the origin, some say, of the expression 'having a skinful').

In his *Guide to Madeira*, published in 1801, Dr Joseph Adams observes: 'The character of the Portuguese is universally polite … No one meets a well-dressed stranger without taking off his hat, and feels offended if his salute is not returned … Among the poor, a seaman who pleads that he has been left by his ship, and that, in consequence, he is without money and clothes, never fails to be kindly received.'

Adams also noted that English dress and manners were increasingly in fashion. 'The cocked hat, sword and buckles have gradually given way to the shoe-string and round hat, except in visits of ceremony, or among officers of the revenue, who are obliged, even to the custom-house clerk, to appear on duty in full dress.' Many of the labouring mechanics still continued to wear long cloaks, principally to hide their tools as they considered it demeaning to be seen carrying anything in their hands. This was something of a shock to English ladies arriving on the island for the first time, who 'from the custom of dressing assassins on our English stage in long cloaks … suspect a dagger under every *capote*'.

Funchal derived its name from *funcho*, the Portuguese word for fennel which grew in

---

voyage and discovery of the island to 1344, claiming that a Castilian expedition of 1393 was inspired 'by the information which Machin gave of this island'. Thanks to a translation published by Richard Hakluyt in 1601, Galvão's version later became well known to English readers.

A second tradition derives from a work said to have been written by a squire of the household of the Portuguese prince Henry the Navigator (1394–1460), variously called Francisco de Alcoforado or Gonçalo Aires Ferreira. Two seventeenth-century manuscripts of the work survive, and it is first cited in 1579. In this version, the hero, a good knight called Machim, and his lover Ana de Arfet or Harfet, both die on Madeira. The survivors tell their story to a Castilian fellow captive in Morocco called Juan Damores, who, after his ransom, falls into Portuguese hands and inspires Dom Henrique to mount an expedition in search of the island around 1419.

Most later writings on the subject combined the two stories. According to Felipe Fernández-Armesto, 'Elements of these traditions are common in late-medieval chivalric fiction: the amorous imbroglio, the seaborne setting, the interventions of the wind, the romantic island, the changes of fortune, the interplay of treachery and fidelity, the exemplary conduct of the model knight, the generous Moors. The historical discovery of Madeira is undocumented, but the island appears recognisably in sea charts dated from 1339 onwards.'

profusion on the natural rock. In 1800 it was a town of some 30,000 inhabitants. The streets were mostly irregular but kept clean by fast-running water. The most conspicuous buildings were the cathedral and the churches – ablaze with fine tapestries, gold altar cloths embroidered with precious stones and soaring solid-silver candlesticks.

'The best houses in this island are very high,' wrote Pitta, 'and from their elevated turrets the inhabitants, by the help of spyglasses, observe distant vessels, and conjecture their destination ...' The ground floors of the houses were occupied by wine stores and shops. The older ones had plain plaster walls and wooden ceilings – only lately had stucco been introduced which was good enough to adhere to horizontal surfaces. Thanks to rising prosperity, almost all the houses in the town now had glass windows instead of lattices. These were sashes, like English ones, as is usual in Portugal, though without sash cords.

The young John Blandy would have been given a warm welcome. 'The British merchants ... are remarkable for their hospitality to strangers; and their houses are open on the slightest recommendation for the reception of travellers on the island, or passengers who stop there, for refreshments,' wrote Dr Pitta.

By 1780 there were more than 70 British merchant houses in Madeira, most trading in

The house John Blandy built at Santo Antonio da Serra

Madeira wine. In Funchal there was a chamber of commerce, known as the British Factory, like the larger ones in Lisbon and Oporto. By means of levies on shipments the British Factory was to build an English Church, burial ground and hospital as well as a capstan to pull up lighters on to the beach and load wine.

The enormous popularity of Madeira wine was due to the fact that it not only travelled well but

The author of Parkinson's Law, the famous satire of bumbling bureaucracy, noted the prodigious consumption of Madeira wine in the Indies. Young men in India, Parkinson observed, had a tendency to overindulge themselves, ruining their livers with vast quantities of alcohol. 'The supply of Madeira ... was on a scale hardly conducive to the health of the English community in Bengal ... in 1805, for instance, 6,260 pipes of this wine were imported to India, at a cost of about £44 each pipe ... An annual wine bill which includes the cost of over 3 million bottles of one wine is not unimpressive, considering the comparatively small number of people in a position to drink wine at all.'

Many of the East India Company's fast sailing cutters called at Madeira on their outward voyage to take on water, fresh fruit and vegetables and, mainly, wine. 'Madeira was then fashionable and expensive ... It had come into prominence as the drink of the "Nabob" – the man who returned to England after shaking the pagoda tree,' wrote Parkinson. Not all the wine purchased in Madeira was destined for India; some of it was brought back to England, having matured on the long voyage.

The army in India also took considerable quantities. An expedition preparing in 1800, in which two battalions were to embark, had to allow for eight pipes of Madeira and 144 dozen of port for the officers.

Cyril Northcote Parkinson, Trade in the Eastern Seas, 1937

could stand the hot climates of Britain's far-flung colonies in North America, the Caribbean and the Indies. Christoper Jefferson of the island of St Kitts in the West Indies wrote: 'There is no commodity better drunk in these parts than Madeira wines. They are so generally and so plentifully drunk, being the only strong drink that is natural here, except brandy and rum, which are too hot.' It was a taste he acquired in 1676 after his ship had been chased into Funchal by a Turkish privateer.

John Blandy's letter of introduction notes that he had come to the island on account of ill health. Poor health was one of the scourges of Georgian England, with numerous young people as well as old suffering from chest complaints, coughs and prolonged colds. Many took regular cures at spas such as Bath and Buxton, but others sought escape from cold, damp winters. With Napoleon's continental blockade there was no prospect of travelling to the Mediterranean and Madeira was one of the few places enjoying a milder winter climate which was within reach of England. Sir James Clark, Queen Victoria's doctor, wrote extensively on climate and health, observing that Madeira 'is warmer during the winter, and cooler during the summer; there is less difference between the temperature of the day and that of the night, between one season and another, and between successive days; it is almost exempt from keen, cold winds; and enjoys a general steadiness of weather.'

In his book *Madeira* (1851), Robert White writes: 'A fact well known to medical men, and to most of the English residents who have reared families in the island, is the remarkable exemption enjoyed here from most of the complaints to which children are exposed in England during the early years of life, and the ease with which infants get over the period of teething – a time of great anxiety for mothers in general.' Children, he said, of healthy constitution, brought up in Madeira, were more robust in later life. Whatever the prevailing perception of the age, the Blandy children were to show the opposite was sometimes true, their health improving when they returned to England.

With the mild and warm climate came the opportunity of a better standard of living. All visitors to Madeira remarked on the number of pretty houses and gardens in and around Funchal overlooking the sea. There was an abundance of fresh fruit, vegetables and fish, even if there were shortages of meat and flour – which John Blandy was quick to address.

John Blandy returned to England in 1810 and married Jennet Burden at St Andrew's Holborn, returning to Madeira the next year with his brothers Thomas and George to found the family firm in 1811.

The story is taken up in a vivid series of letters mainly between Thomas and his four sisters, but from their mother and cousins too. The letters provide a window on a world like that of a Jane Austen novel, with constant concerns about suitors and prospects of marriage, places to live, good and bad investments, worries about health (with visits to Bath and Madeira in search of better air). Though some branches of the family had estates, houses and an income, others, including several of the girls, had to work and could only ever aspire to rent a house or a cottage not to buy one. The letters are remarkable too for the amount different members of the family knew about each others' finances. Often the women are arranging funds and even investing their 'modicum', as well as soliciting and passing on orders for wine. They also illustrate an astounding reach for a young man who had landed on the island in 1808 to work on the accounts of a wine merchant. By his death in 1855 John Blandy had established a business that was trading across much of the western world – from Russia and Holland to the West Indies and the Americas. He crossed the Atlantic and several times it even seemed that this restless man might move permanently to America or back to England. But Madeira had a hold on him, for which succeeding generations can be thankful.

The first letter, from John Blandy to a Robert Pattison in Dorchester, is dated 17 April 1811, soon after his return to the island. It was brought to England by his brother Thomas and is evidence that the brothers were already trading together in wine. John enquires of Pattison 'Have never had the pleasure of hearing how your wine … turned out', adding 'shall be thankful for a renewal of the orders and any others you can help my brother to'.

The business was evidently prospering as John suggests that Thomas could have a share in the concern if his friend would advance him between £2,000 and £2,500, a sum which would 'give us both good bread'.

Two months later John wrote to Thomas expressing delight at 'the success that has attended your West Indies voyage', concerned only that his brother had omitted to say anything about being paid. If the bill was on a safe house, he said, 'we shall be in a better state than we have ever been in before'. They had also saved a substantial amount by omitting to insure the cargo, though he says with an eye to the future 'it was too great a risk to run on so large an amount'.

The day before a brig, the *Ocean*, had brought in ninety-nine pipes of brandy and forty-three of gin which he reckoned to be worth at least £1,700. John had also been advised of another vessel due from the same place with 100 pipes of gin, 4,000 Dutch cheeses and 300 barrels of Dutch butter, 'likewise to be consigned to us'.

He counsels Thomas: 'You will naturally take some time in England to see all our friends … and apologise for my not writing as often as I wish on account of my being a good deal occupied and no one to help me except Robert [a younger brother] who is poor help.' While in London, Thomas is 'to get respectable letters of introduction and credit to Lisbon, Cadiz, Gibraltar, Newfoundland and to some port or ports in the Mediterranean where oil and brandy is exported — it appears to me that a good deal is to be done with oil both olive and fish — being very troublesome, many people decline having anything to do with them.'

John also requests 'some smoked and pickled herring and if the butter has not been shipped by Houghton & Co. I wish 50 or 100 barrels either from them or Morgan & Kieves'. Glass, he said, was 'tumbling in from Holland … some large dishes are wanted in all colours'.

On 30 June 1811 Anna, the eldest of John and Thomas's sisters, wrote from Bath enclosing a bond for £1,000 'which we sincerely hope will enable [John] to give you a share in his business'. Though it was less than John had suggested, she touchingly hopes it will provide enough to keep Thomas in food and clothes, and that he will get more by degrees. The greater part of the bond was from their Aunt Martha 'who has such a smallish income' that it will be best if the interest is paid half yearly. Anna reminds Thomas of an offer of funds from their

John Blandy's enthusiasm for building houses in Madeira was frowned on by relatives at home who would have liked him to build a handsome house in England. It may well have been inspired, nonetheless, by the remarkable building activities of Henry Veitch, the much-loved British consul in Madeira.

According to Noel Cossart's rather colourful accounts, the genial Veitch built houses in a Georgian style 'in most of the villages. He furnished each house with one or more girlfriends and, in due course, all the villages where he had a residence were populated with fair-haired children whose descendants are distinguishable to this day'.

Veitch was an 'amateur' architect of considerable accomplishment, clearly with a library of architectural pattern books and a good knowledge of the latest architectural fashions, in Britain and continental Europe. His best-known building is the English Church in Funchal. Though it was described by one incumbent as the ugliest building he had ever worshipped in, the church is a sophisticated neoclassical design with a circular domed interior set neatly within square outside walls. Three decades after its completion Robert White properly recognised its quality. 'The building was designed, and its erection superintended, by the late consul Mr Veitch … of the pure Ionic order, exceedingly chaste and neat, and, in all its internal arrangements, well suited to the climate.'

He also observes that it was 'no doubt inspired by the temple erected over the Holy Sepulchre in Jerusalem — the model for all round churches' and

kinsman, a William Blandy – John ought now to apply to him as he may not assume to offer a second time, 'thinking it may be pushing'. She is also worried to hear that Madeira wine is 90 shillings a pipe higher this year as she had told people in Bath the price John had given her when he was in England.

The family in England were also alarmed at John's new ventures in the United States, with good reason as became apparent years later. 'I hope John is perfectly acquainted with the character of the people he intends doing business with in America as in England they do not bear good names by any means,' Anna says, adding, 'My aunts and mother wish you to give him a caution on the subject … there are so many dishonest people that there is no knowing anyone.'

The first of John Blandy's children, Charles Ridpath, was born in 1812, to be followed two years later by Jennet and then Anne. The next to survive into adulthood was Alfred, born in 1812, followed two years later by Frederick and then by Elizabeth in 1826.

The rapid growth of business is apparent in a letter dated 17 May 1812 from John Blandy in Madeira to Thomas in England. A schooner, the *Anson*, had arrived from Portsmouth, New Hampshire, and John had promptly purchased a quarter of the cargo 'which is likely to turn out a favourable spec'. His share included 32 pounds of flour, 50 pounds of beef, 16 pounds of pork, about 500 pounds of butter and 1,000 of lard.

John continues: 'I intend shipping Rocher & Co. five pipes of wine by one of the vessels direct'. He is awaiting a cargo of 'butter, candles and cheese, which I think are the best articles for the retail store' and expects more opportunities the same week, with the *Anson* sailing for Boston and another ship for Tenerife and New York.

Meanwhile Thomas received a charming letter from his sister Eliza dated 23 July 1813. She was now established at Crewkerne – a very quiet dull town, she said. Her house was close to the church and only one storey high. 'I am sure if the wind is very high during the winter it cannot stand … I sit down to take my meals with 3 old maids … the most complete old virgins I ever saw in my life … my salary is £20 a year which will make up for many inconveniences till I hear of something more advantageous.' With this letter she is sending seven shirts she has made for Thomas. She adds that she has just seen John who was in good spirits and anxious to return to Madeira. Here there is talk of a school – possibly in Crewkerne or Dorchester – that was run by the female members of the family.

Four months later, she wrote of John's arrival back

mentions (like all later writers) a Portuguese law 'which prohibited Protestant places of worship from assuming the external semblance of a church As a result, he evolved an edifice suggestive rather of a library, a senate house, or lecture hall.'
Neoclassical churches with domes rather than spires, however, are found all over the Christian world from America to Russia and the English architect James Gibbs included a plan for a circular church adapted specifically for Protestant worship in his widely used Book of Architecture (1728). The other distinctive feature of Veitch's design is the portico in muris, a recessed portico fronted with paired Ionic columns. These are Roman Ionic rather than the Greek Ionic which was more fashionable by this time.
The site was bought in 1810 by the British contingent in Madeira after a fund had been opened to finance the purchase of land and building. The amount required was £10,000 and the lengthy subscription list contained the names of King George III, King Leopold I of Belgium, the Duke of Wellington, the Duchess of Bedford, the family of Lord Nelson, and many ships, with the British traders contributing some £400 per year, financed by levying a supplement on the sale of each pipe (about 500 litres) of Madeira wine.
According to his tombstone Henry Veitch served as 'H[is] B[ritannic] Majesty's Agent and Consul General from 1809 to 1836'. The journal of Elizabeth Macquarie describes her arrival in Madeira on 12 June 1809. 'We landed in the afternoon at the Town of Funchal, and went by invitation to reside at the House of Henry Veitch Esq., British Consul at Madeira; we were received and entertain'd with much hospitality by Mr &

in England: 'He is looking very well, I think, and his spirits are very good.' He seemed anxious to return to Madeira, she said, adding, 'I hope please God he may get safe back' – even after Trafalgar there were dangers of privateers preying on merchant shipping.

Eliza the school mistress had now been joined by her sister Anna who wrote to Thomas on 15 August 1813: 'I shall be a stiff Madam Governante sitting as prim as any of my sect in Christendom.' Anna, then aged thirty-one, intended (though it was not to be for long) to assign herself to the 'honourable sisterhood called Old Maids' and if she by chance came across a male creature on her walks 'though he be the handsomest being which ever visited these lower regions, I intend to shun him as much as I would a serpent'.

Orders for Madeira wine were now surging in from the West Indies. Twelve pipes (each the equivalent of 600 bottles) had been sent to John Thompson Esq. of Kingston, Jamaica. Three pipes had been shipped to Smith and Rise of St Croix (in the Virgin Islands), for J. M. Heyliger Esq. Many more orders of course go unmentioned.

A severe shortage of butter had arisen. Fresh butter was a luxury much in demand and shipped through Madeira even in June. John wrote: 'For the last fourteen days we have had no butter in any merchant's hand and what little there was in the Huxter's shop sold at 600, 700 and 800 sh[illings]', a huge price. He continued, 'I should suppose the price will decline in Ireland on account of the opening of the Dutch ports and more particularly when governments give up their demands for supplies.' The same he believed would apply to beef and pork.

Madeira was not dependent on a weekly packet boat. Ships called in almost daily. One letter remarks: 'Yesterday a ship from St Domingo looked in here – and as I presume her cargo is speculative – she will in all probability land a part of it here.'

John wrote again to Thomas on 15 July 1814: 'The vessel with butter etc is not come to hand. If nothing has been shipped from Cork …twill be well to send fifty barrels from Liverpool or London.' He also seeks large quantities of china including forty dozen green-edged eight-inch plates, forty-two dozen matching flat dishes and six dozen matching salad bowls. Similar quantities of blue-edged flat dishes were required as well as plates and soup dishes.

John had also given instructions that no shipment was to be made unless the freight was paid in wines. If no vessel was available from Cork, Thomas should consider taking on a small one and loading her with potatoes, butter, lard and bacon. If the price of beef and pork had fallen he was to ship some of these

Mrs Veitch …' Veitch's handsome town residence, prominently sited by the Ribeira de Santa Luzia is now the seat of the Madeira Wine Institute. It takes the form of an unusually tall Palladian villa, with the added flourish of a different treatment to each of the four facades – one has a full-height curving bay and another a central pediment. On the roof is a temple-like pavilion, or mirador, presumably serving as a lookout for ships arriving in the harbour. Behind the house was a still taller tower which old engravings suggest had a tweaked Chinesey roof. Towards the river the villa was extended by a terrace with broad arches supporting a trellis roof providing shade from the sun.
Veitch's principal country house, the Quinta do Jardim da Serra, is a bright and startling pink following very extensive refurbishment but retains a number of distinctive features, notably curving bays on three sides, one inset with a Venetian window on each of the three floors.

too as they had none in Madeira. But this depended wholly on war continuing with America. 'If there be a peace there do not touch provisions of any kind,' he counselled. He also thinks herring will sell well this year, as not much fish was expected from Newfoundland, where prices were very high. Thomas was to bear in mind the idea of another trip to the West Indies, returning via Newfoundland which John thought would pay well.

He wants good flour from London or Cork, which will sell all the better if war continues. The latest consignment from London was very new and of excellent quality. Five hundred more barrels of flour and some wheat were needed for outward shipment to the West Indies. John was also trading in fabrics, reporting the Paisley patterns were much liked in Madeira and suggesting Thomas should order sixty dozen women's white cotton hose and white cotton lace.

He is also keen that Thomas should return to Madeira and help run the business. 'Tis certain that you would be very useful here – for my books are going sadly behind.' In a postscript he asks for all insurance to be done in future by Mr William Cox and adds that candles are needed for the shop – if Thomas paid cash he would get a good discount.

A letter of 9 November 1816 from William Turnbull in New York to Thomas describes Blandy's now extensive trade in America. Forty pipes of brandy have gone but wine continued very dull and low. Turnbull is sending a fine barrel of cranberries. He has recommended the Blandy house to a Mr Harbach, saying that when American prices permit he will procure some valuable consignments. He requests 'a few of your largest onions by way of curiosity'.

From Madeira, George, the youngest of the four brothers, had written saying how he was busy in the counting house at five o'clock every other morning while John's time was taken up in his different stores. He was also due to go to the north of the island to collect tithes which were due to him, evidence of an expansion into landed property. Vintages were good and it was thought wines would be much cheaper the next year.

On 14 October 1819 Mary Blandy, the youngest sister, writes to her brother Thomas saying she is back in England and comfortably settled in Dorset.. She speaks warmly of Anna's fiancé, Mr Furber, who generally comes down twice a week. 'What a good generous man he is. Anna I think is very fortunate for she has certainly very bright prospects before her. I wish Eliza had as good but I fear she has not for I do not find Adam is likely to get into anything, indeed I do not know what he is capable of undertaking excepting a farm and that he has

Buildings were in his blood: left, the British Consul Henry Veitch's imposing town house with lookout tower and elevated terrace by the Ribeira da Santa Luzia; right, the Quinta do Jardim da Serra, the country house he also designed for himself

Quinta Revoredo, John Blandy's house overlooking the sea at Santa Cruz. It is now a cultural centre

Christmas. 'I shall then want my little money. I am now so much in debt to Aunt Eliza [Elizabeth, a sister of John Blandy's father Charles] that it makes me feel rather uncomfortable.'

Before Mary left Madeira, John had said he would pay her expenses at Lisbon and from thence to England, but after that she must pay her own. Here is the first evidence that John's attitude of the hard man of business extended to family matters. Mary continues, 'I thanked him but felt hurt as I thought he ought to have paid all my travelling to Dorsetshire but was deceived in my opinion of his liberality. Well he neglected writing to Merle and Co. to desire them to pay my draft on them.' Mary had been forced to borrow £50 from her sisters Anna and Eliza to discharge her debts and had written to John 'begging him to tell me in what manner I was to get at my money' but had not heard from him since she left Madeira. 'I am quite at a loss what I am to do. My poor little modicum

not the means to do.' Mary chides Thomas, asking why he wishes 'to get us all off before you intend marrying? I would not advise you to wait longer than you might wish for as there is always one Old Maid in the family, of course, I am to be that one'. Eliza was to take Anna's place at the school after

'An ox sledge was waiting for us … it is a machine very much like the swings used at fairs in England, mounted on a sledge, with cushions, and curtains to it, and drawn by two of the small, dun, beautiful oxen of the country. All the streets in Funchal are paved with stones, mostly sharp ones, and there is no causeway, so that walking is neither clean nor agreeable, and as almost all the streets are either up or down hill, it is a most fatiguing operation … The oxen do not go beyond a walk; they wear bells on their necks … besides the driver, each sledge is accompanied by a boy, who runs before the oxen with a bit of old sacking in his hand, which he dips in every stream or puddle he sees and then throws it under the sledge to make it run easier … The idea of using these sledges for personal conveyance is quite a modern improvement, having been introduced by a Major Bulkeley about four or five years ago. Before that the only conveyance for ladies, or invalids, was the palanquin, borne by two men. Sledges drawn by oxen have been in use ever since the island has been inhabited for the conveyance of goods too heavy for a man's head, or a mule's back, but were never thought of as carriages to ride in … the usual mode of coming down from

will be reduced to almost nothing with one thing and another. When Anna leaves us, I shall want all my money to pay off her share in the house – it seems to be of no use to write to John about it as no one can get an answer from him. He is as you say so completely wrapped up in business that he can think of nothing else … I really quite dread his having a great deal of business, he is so anxious about it, and if he is to be so ungenerous, I think him better without much money.'

The next year on 15 March 1820 Anna wrote to Thomas announcing she had 'been a wife seventeen days and I am as happy as mortal can be … my good husband has I am sure a most tender affection for me … I could wish for more of his company, but that rigid business will not permit – I am therefore content, knowing it is as great a punishment to him as to myself. My mother is still with me. Eliza and Mary have been up for two or three days …'

The same letter brought news of the bombshell Thomas had just received. John was unilaterally severing their partnership. John had hinted at a change in their affairs at the end of the year, but the break surprised friends and family alike. 'It seems the most extraordinary thing that ever happened: what can induce John to act so – never was a man so changed.' Their Uncle Ridpath had counselled that John could not annul the partnership of his own

Grapes being trod in a traditional wine press or lagar

accord. 'You have a right to use any of the money on your own account if you enter into a different way of business,' Anna tells Thomas.

John was also playing the wounded party and had hinted to a friend that he had some thoughts of going to the Cape. If so, Anna tells Thomas, 'I hope you would return to Madeira. You have been very fortunate there and you and George could carry on the business there as well as John has done it. If he remains there, you must fix your tent elsewhere: America seems to agree with your health, but I am afraid farming would not.'

Thomas had mentioned that he had some thoughts of establishing himself as a wine merchant in Baltimore. Sisterly advice poured forth. 'You have

the Mount is in a carriage [resembling] a very short sofa, made of basketwork, nicely stuffed and cushioned, which is fixed on a sledge, to which ropes are attached, and two men give the sledge a push, when by its own weight it runs down the hill, at a pace that is of course accelerated every moment, while the two men holding the ropes, and running at the top of their speed, keep pulling with all their might to prevent the sledge from going too fast. It is exactly like being shot down a spout, the velocity with which you go is inconceivable, and how it is the men manage to run so far and so fast, is to me a perfect puzzle. They have absolute command over the sledge, so that they can slaken or accelerate the pace at pleasure'

Isabella de França, Journal, 1853

Tough going for an ox sledge taking visitors to the Monte and, opposite, a quick return by sledge. From Isabella de França's Journal of 1853-1854

always fixed your mind on a farm and one without so ornamental and useful a piece of furniture as a wife would not contribute much to your domestic happiness. You seem to be surrounded with nice and good girls, therefore I hope most sincerely you will fix your heart on one likely to make you forever more comfortable.'

Eliza's fiancé, Adam, writes to Thomas on 2 January 1820 about his ever-troubled prospects. 'You will have heard of my wishing to get into a brewery … after obtaining a thorough knowledge of the business there might be an opportunity of taking [over] a concern or entering into partnership, provided I can get a friend to advance some money.'

Now came more disturbing news of family break-ups, this time on the female side. 'I know you will be very vexed to find my sisters are disunited – a dissolution of partnership has taken place and Anna has left Salisbury but what she means to do I cannot ask,' writes Adam. 'I am very sorry for them and think them very silly girls for not being more united. They had a comfortable home and made both ends meet very well. There are some folks that do not know when they are well off.'

On 29 December 1820, Anna writes to Thomas reversing her earlier counsel and strongly advising him not to take a wife until he had 'fixed in some business … to have a wife and young family about you … with no means of providing for them, would, I am sure, render you very miserable: love in a cottage makes a very pretty tale, but as the old proverb says, If poverty comes in at the door, love will soon go out of the window.'

Two years later, in 1822, John was back in England. Eliza reports to Thomas: 'John, Jennet and family also joined us rather unexpectedly as we did not hear of their leaving Madeira until they stopped at our door. They landed at Weymouth after fifteen days passage with Jennet and Anne very ill, the former from fatigue in attending the little girl who had been very ill thirteen days from a disordered stomach … she however soon recovered … as did Jennet from fatigue. They spent a month with us jaunting about for the recovery of health and left us all well except Jennet who was tolerable considering that she expects to be confined sometime in the month and they have for that purpose taken a house in an airy part of London … most likely for the winter. Heavy expenses for our dear John but life is sweet … They have some sweet children.' There was Jennet, who had her mother's name, 'a short, heavy but clever child'. Charles was 'a beautiful boy but I think not very fond of learning at present and his height makes him appear very deficient. Anne is a very fine girl, much taller than Jennet and quiet and thoughtful. The youngest, Charlotte, is a little sylph

The sun rose in a blaze of golden clouds that made the waves look like a sea of fire, and by degrees tinted every peak and headland with a soft yellow light, while those parts which were in shadow presented every gradual hue of purple, lilac, grey, yellow, rose colour and white. These varied and beautiful colours seemed to play on the rocks, like the prismatic hues of crystal in the sun… by degrees as the sun rose higher, the loftiest peaks were tinged with gold, and the yellow light spread softly and gradually over the mountains. The dark green pine forests, and chestnut woods, and the bright sunny green of the canes, now showed themselves; the increasing light revealing at the same time the deep dense fissures formed by the ravines which radiate all over the Island; one by one the white quintas, or country houses, came peeping out from their little green nooks, as if to welcome the sunshine. Sometimes a grey mist would partially conceal one of the thousand peaks of which the Island is composed, and then melt away and leave them all revealed in their mountain beauty, crag above crag, broken into ridges, covered with forests of chestnut, laurel, pine, and many other trees, or with their bleak and barren summits towering beyond the clouds. Within the bay, lay the city of Funchal, looking beautifully clean from the sea, with its white houses, and green gardens, now flowering with oleander, heliotrope, blue hydrangea, the white blossom of the coffee tree, and a thousand other flowers new to an English eye.

Isabella de França Journal 1853

John Blandy approaching old age. He died in 1855

her mind the following spring. 'He had repeated colds and for the last ten days that he was here he was very unwell which added much to distress at parting from him … Mr Furber's business is thriving above all expectations – he will doubtless – if his life is spared – provide well for his dear wife and children – I wish that John would make up his mind to leave Madeira for that is the place, I think, for George … John should come to England, leave his wife some distance from London and have himself something to carry on with George … in Madeira,' she wrote to Thomas on 21 April.

From 1826 there is a gap of fourteen years in the correspondence which is taken up in 1840 with news of George, whose business in Brazil had not prospered. Mary tells her brother Thomas, 'He had been unfortunate and we can but own imprudent.' Even so George was hoping to hand on a family legacy to her [from a Mrs Graham] but she says: 'John will not allow me to have it. He is determined to have it himself or not let others have it … in John's last letter to me he says: "I do not know what George owes you neither is it necessary to know" … I think the money would be of more value to me than it could be to John. It appears that the more money people have the more desirous are they to have more. Charles Blandy tells me his father's property has greatly increased since he took him into partnership.'

Charles, she says, was in England, looking well and 'in good spirits. The share he has of the Madeira business supports him and his family and leaves an over plus. He told me the business is capable of being extended.' But she had further criticism of John's treatment of his large family. 'I really thinks

– the most elegant lively little thing you ever beheld … Robert is, we find, an active man of business …'

Soon after, Anna sends more news. 'John was very well and in very good spirits; when he first came over he talked a good deal of removing from Madeira to the Cape or to New South Wales but, after the arrival of your letter when he found you were fixed in America, that idea seemed entirely abandoned and I think he has now settled in Madeira till he has made his fortune.'

On 21 November 1823 Eliza writes to Thomas's wife saying their brother George's 'continued indisposition is the cause of much anxiety to all of us', adding 'Our dear Anna … now has two fine boys'. George's continuing bad health was still on

Looking north up the Ribeira de Santa Luzia, a 19th century print

John trifles too much with his children. There is Frederick [the youngest of the three boys], a very nice lad but what is he fit for? He has no education.'

Two years later, in 1842, Anna sends more news of the family business to Thomas: 'Our nephew, Fred Blandy, is with us. You have no doubt heard of his departure from Madeira on 1 June in the *Vernon* for St Petersburg. They took wine and were to take back boards and flax but the vessel, being mortgaged to some people in London, they did not choose that she should return to Madeira, so poor Fred was obliged to come to England without cargo. He arrived here on the 5th, just sick of Russia and the Baltic … he is a nice amiable youth and I wish he could get into some employment as I suspect there are too many in Madeira.' The good news was that George had sent Mary 'all orders to receive Mrs Graham's legacy'.

Various members of the family were now travelling to Madeira, often in the hope of improving their health. In November 1842 Mary reports to Thomas that Anna's daughter, Anne Furber, 'has been advised to try the climate of Madeira and she went out on the 8th just with her brother Charles who was going out to Mexico and Frederick Blandy who was returning home after a

very unsuccessful trip – at least as regards to business. Perhaps his health may have improved. We heard on last Sunday of their safe arrival but I regret to say, I had a most unfavourable account of dear Anne. The doctors there say she has no hope that that climate or any other can restore her to health. John wishes either Anna or myself to go out immediately … I cannot leave my school at a few days' notice.'

Worse was to come. In February 1843 Mary writes to Thomas: 'You will long since have received news from Madeira. I had hoped the climate would have proved healing to our sister's child as it had done to our brothers … she was too far gone before she left England … I was with her [mother] when the fatal news arrived from Madeira … she certainly was a beautiful rosebud, so tall, but so weak she could not support herself – she was almost double and Margaret is almost as bad. Anne's complexion was fair and had she been spared a few years longer, would have been, I think, very beautiful. She was by far the best looking of Anna's children.' Days later there is better news. Charles Ridpath's wife was expecting. 'What a large family,' Mary exclaims.

In 1845 John and his family were back in England again. In August Anna reported: 'All the Madeira party left us this day fortnight for a boarding house, 34 Bafford Place, Russell Square … they are consulting an aurist, Mr Toynbee, for poor Jennet's hearing which is very much worse than it used to be and her health is by no means good. Indeed, poor thing, she is much afflicted and Dr Renton has given it as his opinion that the climate of Madeira does not agree with her, in consequence, Anne wrote me word last week that she and Jennet are to remain in England for the present … I am quite sure they all require a change of climate and scene. Poor Anne looks old and careworn added to which Mr Burden will not take no for an answer and, as her father does not forbid him, intrudes himself at all times at Santa Cruz or the Serra [Santo da Serra]. I suspect her affections are fixed on a Mr Bayman who is in Mr Marche's house and not considered eligible for Anne by any of her family in Madeira. John himself, I am convinced, would be much better for a change if he could be brought to think so. He lives alone at the Serra 'till he seems to care for no one else. I dare say it is only his manner, but it is very trying to everyone's feelings and as it has pleased God to give him a family, he ought, I think, to live amongst them … I have tried all I can to persuade him to go to America but to no purpose. Fred is a fine young man and to me appears in very good health now but Anne tells me he was very ill for some time and that he will never think himself well in Madeira. I suppose that the anguish of this is that he and Charles do not pull together in business. Charles perhaps forgets that Fred is no longer a child.' This is early evidence that Charles Ridpath like his father was extremely domineering.

In October John arrived with Jennet, Anne and Fred to stay at Cheltenham with their Aunt Ridpath. Anna reports: 'John said he only wanted to return to Madeira if his daughters would … decide where they were to remain … I told him, I shall be very happy to have them if they would put up with the accommodations I could offer them. They immediately accepted my offer but John who has allowed two opportunities to pass without his leaving England … is most undecided and certainly not in good health … He said he did not like doctors.'

By the end of the month John was back in Madeira, having embarked on the West India steamer *Trent* which took just a week to reach the island. By contrast Fred who had sailed from Southampton in the *Grace Darling* took two weeks. Anna reported: 'We, or rather our nieces, got a nice long letter from their father. I am glad to be able to tell you that the trip has done him good and that he had a comfortable house and occupation, he should not have been in such a hurry to leave England. We all wish he had not built so many houses in Madeira as then perhaps he might have had one in England which would have pleased us all much better.'

In March 1846 Anna writes with news of another baby expected in Madeira. 'Poor Charles with such a family will, I fear, get old before his time … as for Fred his trip to England and elsewhere seems to have inspired him with new life and spirits'.

John had spent his Christmas in Rua São Francisco and wrote in good spirits. He was returning to the Serra to attend to the planting of trees and shrubs carried out by the *Grace Darling*. His tenants at St Luzia seem to give great satisfaction ... if he could see Jennet now, just come in from a walk, having had a good blow in a March south-west wind, he would think that England agreed with her better than Madeira. Everyone who sees her says how much better and younger she looks. When she came she looked such a little old woman. She is now in high glee at the thought of going to Bath someday this week.'

By April John was in worse spirits. 'He says his sons all look ill as also Charles's children. He will begin to think Madeira does not agree so well with them as he used to think it did.' By contrast there was now good news of George in Brazil, from two captains of merchant vessels who had seen a good deal of him in the last year. 'They both speak very highly of him and say he ought to do well …

Funchal from the south: how 19th century sailors would have seen the island

they say that George's present wife is one of four sisters, three of whom are married and live very near each other. One to a German, another to a Genoise … he keeps two horses and appears to live very comfortably … One of these captains was the one who went to Russia with Frederick (Captain Thompson). When he landed at Balua, he went into a store where he saw a boy whom he at once pronounced to be a Blandy and it proved to be George's son. He says that all three of the children are Europeans – not at all like Brazilians, but they cannot speak English.'

John, never much of a correspondent with his sisters, is now writing lively letters to his daughter Jennet. 'I came from the Serra last evening … I have been enjoying myself – planting potatoes and cabbages. Masons at work, carpenter promised me he would go up but, instead of that, he enjoyed himself by running away to Demara – leaving wife and children to enjoy themselves in Madeira … I may put some doors to the Serra house and do a few other things that, I hope, will make it a little more comfortable … we have had very cold winds which have destroyed all the tender shoots of trees – just the same as the frost often does in England. I should be very glad to see my horse chestnut trees in flower but I do not expect that will ever be the case in my days … my cows and sheep are much improved by my personal attention but I can't make cheese till the dairymaid arrives – then I hope to make some that will astonish the natives.'

Later that year John set out for America, where he would visit his younger brother Thomas. The trip was not a happy one. Thomas's wife writes that they had received a letter from John on Monday in Louisville and he was 'sick, confined to his room with intermittent fever'. But the doctor was going to give him quinine pills and, as John was anxious to get on, he was expected every day. She continues: 'He is very homesick and says if ever he gets back to his home, he will never leave it … He has never made a remark as to like, or dislike, of the south-west but I am sure he does not like it or indeed, America … The fact is he has lost so much money in America that I would not wonder if he was prejudiced against everybody and everything.'

John returned to Madeira to live with his large family for another seven years, until his death in 1855. Given that he came to Madeira, at least in part because of poor health, he had prospered extraordinarily, establishing himself as both leading wine merchant and general trader. Here was the beginning of a western counterpart of the great family trading houses of the Far East. The sense of dynasty was also to become evident in the names given to children. The family name of John's wife Jennet was to be given to his grandson John Burden, just as Ridpath had been given to his son, and Reeder was to be given to his great-great grandson, marking inheritances and marriages which were alliances as much as love matches.

2. Rich Harvest, Bitter Legacy

Charles Ridpath's reckless purchases of
wine proved, with surprising speed, to be
a major boon for the family business

Charles Ridpath Blandy retained his distinctive features into old age, here with Victorian stiff collar and sideburns, lapels edged in braid and matching waistcoat, pince-nez glasses and chain and fob

Today Charles Ridpath Blandy is seen as the man whose vision and determination formed the cornerstone of the firm's lasting prosperity. To his sons, Graham John and John Burden, the picture was very different. They saw their father's reckless behaviour as the road to ruin. In 1862 Charles Ridpath had agreed to steadily hand over the running of the business to them. This had not happened, precipitating a family crisis that came to a climax with their father's death in 1879 when the two sons discovered they had been cut out of their father's will.

Charles's talents were evident from an early age. In 1823 his Aunt Eliza had written: 'Charles is without exception the finest boy I ever saw.' He had married into one of the English families in Madeira. His bride, Mary-Anne Symonds, was born on the island in 1808 (and was to die there in 1891). The wedding took place in London in 1835 by which time Charles was trading in wine on his own account in both London and Funchal.

A picture of his growing family is provided in the letters of Mary-Anne's sister Eliza to her brother Richard in Australia. On 27 July 1844 she writes from London: 'Mary-Anne and their tribe of children are staying at St António, not near the Serra but much nearer town. Mary-Anne says there is a good road the whole way there so Charles rides backwards & forwards morning and evening which is good for his health & very pleasant for the family to have him amongst them. Mary-Anne says the house is a nice large one with plenty of rooms for them all & a nice garden for the children. Mary-Anne has had a nursery governess for the girls, who is now leaving much to her regret and Charles too.'

Two years later she writes elatedly from Madeira: 'I really am in our native place again ... since Papa's death Mary-Anne has sent oft-repeated invitations and at last Charles has joined in them so that I was induced to accept one and this visit may last several years.' Though she cannot 'quite understand anyone liking Madeira life' the idea of a 'respectable home with persons who are interested in me' had persuaded her.

In March 1847 she writes that Charles and Mary-Anne's boys seem 'very fine children. The youngest who is christened Charles Frederick Raleigh, the reason for this fine name I will tell you later, is really the admiration of everyone. Ladies and gentlemen stop daily in the street [to talk] to him, to ask to whom the beautiful child belongs, and I believe you will seldom see so fine a family when they are together.'

These were difficult times in Madeira. The island, she continues, 'is in a deplorable state at present. The supply of provisions is so low, that unless some ships arrive with some or other food, disturbances will undoubtedly be the result.' The letter also brings news of the growing schism in the Anglican Church in Madeira, in which Charles was to play a dominant role. 'There are great discussions in the Church here, owing to the chaplain holding High Church principles, closely bordering on Catholicism. Charles Blandy is one of the party who has set his face against these proceedings, and consequently avoids connection with the chaplain ... This made him apply to the chaplain of the frigate *Raleigh* which came in here to christen his child and accounts for the last of the three names.'

On 26 June 1845 Charles Blandy had presented the chaplain Richard Thomas Lowe with an indictment which has been described as 'one of the most extraordinary ever drawn up by members

The English church built to the design of Consul Veitch was riven by disputes over high church practices

The English church's circular interior is crowned by a dome and cupola

his High Church leanings increasingly disturbed and offended many of his congregation. The nine complaints against the minister included 'Praying with his back to the people', 'Preaching in the surplice instead of the black gown', 'Reading every Sunday the exhortation to the Communion', introducing a weekly collection 'instead of restricting the offertory to those occasions when Holy Communion was celebrated', 'Dismissing without a blessing those members of the congregation who did not stay for the sacrament', 'Singing the anthem and the Gloria in Excelsis in the sacramental service', and 'Proceeding with funeral processions to the church and from there to the burial ground in the surplice and bare headed'.

Eliza Symonds became steadily more absorbed in the large family of her brother-in-law Charles. On 30 January 1848 she writes, 'Mary-Anne and her family of seven children all continue well. She is a picture of health herself and so are her children.' But Charles looked 'very delicate and I believe works too hard for his health but not for the children he has to support. He requires a voyage to recoup his strength but it is doubtful if he will get it this year … ' She was 'now very busy in the teaching business' attending to her eldest nieces Eliza and Fanny who were eleven and ten years of age and 'backward in their education'.

of a Church of England congregation against their pastor'. Lowe, who had taken up his post on the island in 1828, was a brilliant naturalist who wrote major studies of the fish and flora of Madeira but

RALEIGH BLANDY Blandy was the third of Charles Ridpath Blandy's sons whose talent for drawing and interest in the sea led him to study engineering in Glasgow. In 1870 Laird Brothers certified that 'Mr Charles F. R. Blandy has been studying marine engineering at our establishment for five years', testifying to his 'ability as a draughtsman' and adding that he 'now leaves to take a situation on board a steamer, to gain practical experience afloat'.

This is followed by a letter from the White Star Line in Liverpool dated 16 May 1873 stating he has been in the employ of the Oceanic Steam Navigation Company for one year and five months, serving as third engineer on the SS Tropic to 'entire satisfaction … he leaves this service to better his position, and entirely at his own request'.

A year later he is described by the director of the Telegraph Construction Co., Rear Admiral Sherard Osborne, as 'a marine engineer of high promise'. And from the Wilson Line of steamers in Hull came letters saying that he had served as second engineer and then chief engineer of the Rinaldo, conducting himself 'entirely to our satisfaction'.

Raleigh returned to Madeira to look after Blandy's engineering business and repairs to the Blandy tugs, steamers, coal lighters and water barges.

The same letter also brought news of the visit of Queen Adelaide, the dowager widow of King William IV of Britain, and a large party of her relations, to Madeira for the winter. 'The young people delight in dancing and they have been the occasion of several balls being given, one by thirty English bachelors … It was a very nice ball and the princes and princesses danced very amiably with the plebeians. Another ball is to be given by the Portuguese bachelors to which the royal party have accepted an invitation …'

On 17 February 1848 a new Anglican minister, Thomas Kenworthy Brown, arrived. Charles Blandy met him at the beach landing stage and

This photograph was taken before 1889, when the town pier was built. The present Blandy offices stand on the site of the verandahed building to the right. On the left the imposing Palacio de São Lourenço once the seat of the Governor and now occupied by military authorities and the minister for the Republic

Water-colour by Raleigh Blandy who trained as an engineer

was immediately reassured. Brown, a plumpish, rather unctuous man in his mid-thirties, introduced himself with a somewhat lengthy homily in which he extolled his mission as a 'peacemaker'.

Three months later Eliza Symonds reports to Richard, 'Mary-Anne and all her family are well and it is possible to look at it as a miracle how after so many years spent in this enervating climate she keeps her good looks. Charles is very well but he looks more like a corpse than anyone I ever met with walking about … It is several years since he has been out of the island, a longer time than usual.'

They were preparing to go into the country at

He was a prolific painter in watercolours and a number of his sketches are housed in the Museum of Natural History in Funchal. He lived at the staff house in Rua S. Francisco — and at Quinta de Revoredo at Santa Cruz. The tiled roofs of Santa Cruz were said to be the result of the wages paid to the coal labourers by Blandy's. These labourers came to Funchal every morning in the Falcão, when the coaling trade was at its height. Raleigh was buried in the Santa Cruz cemetery; all the firm's tugs and steamers — Gavião, Falcão, Prompt and Lobo — brought people from Funchal to the funeral.

Raleigh Blandy water-colour of the church and Blandy stables at Santo da Serra

the beginning of June. Charles 'had taken a house at Campanário for three years, it is … beautifully situated and I should expect having beautiful rides and walks in the neighbourhood. We are to spend a long summer without any neighbours there so we must be prepared with books and occupations … Mary-Anne's new governess gets on pretty well. She is very attentive to the children and does her best. She is however so young with so few ideas that the children can only learn from books and nothing from conversation. She has no talking powers and is certainly rather an uninteresting girl … It is a very difficult matter to meet with just the right person.'

There was also news of the growing financial difficulties of other English traders which Charles was able to weather. 'You remember the Lewis here one of the oldest established families … John Lewis has failed lately. Everyone sympathises very much with them, they are universally respected. Three sisters here and one in England are dependent on their brother John. It is said that there will be sufficient to pay everyone but when all is wound up and all debts paid, the difficulty is to know then what they are to do.'

Meanwhile Aunt Penfold had sailed for England looking 'wonderfully well', taking one of her old manservants with her. She was presumably Clara, the widow of William Penfold who died in Madeira in 1835 aged fifty-nine. Her house, the Achada, later to become one of the Blandy quintas, was 'to be painted during her absence' while 'her other servants remain there doing nothing until her

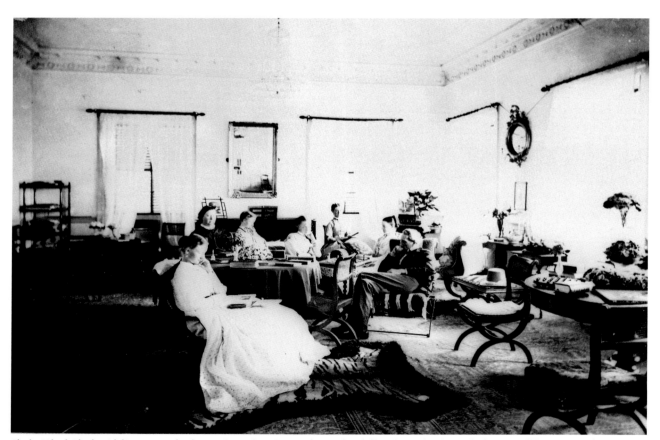

Charles Ridpath Blandy with his grown-up daughters at Quinta Santa Luzia, a photograph probably taken in the 1860s. The furniture still has a Regency elegance, though Victorian tastes are evident in the tiger skin and objects crowding the table tops. Mary Anne Symonds, whom Charles Ridpath, the languid figure on the right, married in 1835, is second from left, wearing a dark dress

return'. They had sailed 'in a beautiful brig called the Brilliant, belonging to her son-in-law Mr Mathews'.

In December Eliza writes with news of 'the birth of another niece just two months old now. She is a sweet baby, dark blue eyes, not promising to be very fair and as … merry as so young a baby ever was'. As the family had been staying at Campanário, 'far from all medical and neighbourly advice', it was thought better that Mary-Anne should return to Funchal for the confinement. This illustrates the acute difficulties of travelling in Madeira's mountainous terrain for Campanário was just 12 miles to the west of the city. Mary-Anne did not see her younger children till they returned to town two months later. By now they were 'much improved and grown and Raleigh such a talker. He is a splendid child but a perfect little tyrant in temper.'

Eliza speaks delightedly of 'the pleasure of jumping into the cares of housekeeping and seven children all at once'. There was also Frederick: 'very good looking and rather delicate' who was in the family counting house but thinking of leaving. The three sisters were at home: Jennet 'blind, deaf and good natured as ever', Anne 'very ladylike' but unmarried and Lizzie, 'a pretty and clever and very little girl' of twenty-one years of age engaged to a Mr Frank Freeman, a gentleman who had spent the winter in the island.

Later Eliza became ever more involved in looking after the large family, writing to Richard on 8 May 1849: 'Mary-Anne has been ailing the whole winter, a thing very unusual with her'. The children were 'pretty well, some recovering from accidents which are constantly happening in large families such as a sprained foot from a fall from a pony'. The youngest boy, 'a splendid fellow', had 'pinched his fingers in the door', spurting blood, while Mary, the third girl, had slipped her foot into a can of boiling water. There must, says Eliza, be an 'especial Providence watching over children or how could they live through the numberless accidents they encounter'.

Mary-Anne and Charles had had two governesses, 'the first left because she was wholly incompetent for the task', the second had been there three months but was to leave in a fortnight. 'She is competent but she is the most ill-tempered, ill-mannered, ill-looking person that I ever saw. The servants, children, the whole house dislike her.' If no replacement appeared, Eliza continues, 'I shall make myself their governess for the summer months. It is an arduous task for there are already five in the schoolroom'.

Charles Ridpath was thirty-two when he became head of the firm on his father's death in 1855, which continued as John Blandy & Sons, though the London office and the Madeira wine business

'In 1941 Blandy Brothers were supplying the best-quality Welsh and Durham coal. When the coal arrived in Madeira, the coal bags were placed in lighters which were towed ashore and lifted by jetty cranes in slings of ten and taken by overhead transporters to the coal stores. The process was reversed when ships arrived to take on coal which could be fed into ships' bunkers at a rate of up to 100 tons per hour. At night operations continued with the help of powerful arc lights.

The coal lighters were equipped with willow fenders to prevent collision damage. Blandy's had a squad of men continually employed in the production of these fenders. Madeira was noted for the first-class quality of drinking water. Blandy's stored the water in large underground tanks and steel water barges. Up to 2,000 tons could be loaded over twenty-four hours.'

Article in the Syren and Shipping, 16 July 1941

were in the name of C. R. Blandy. By this time the firm had extended interests beyond wine and were engaged in ships' agency business and coal-bunkering. They continued as general merchants importing and exporting. A banking business was starting to operate in a small way by the cashing of travellers' Letters of Credit for visitors who came to Madeira hoping to improve their health. A business of discounting merchants' bills had also commenced.

Charles Blandy traded with both sides during the American Civil War. At the outbreak of war the Confederate States had fitted out cruisers to attack Northern merchant shipping. The Northern States correctly deduced that war materials had been purchased by the South in England and held that the British Government should have taken active steps to prevent this as it was contrary to Britain's much-trumpeted neutrality. Blandy company records show that 147 tons of coal were discreetly taken out on 17 October 1864 to the Confederate cruiser *Shenandoah* at the Desertas islands. The *Shenandoah* had been launched

Patio at Blandy Wine Lodge

in Glasgow the year before as a civilian steamer, the *Sea King*. She had been bought in secret by the Confederate Navy and had rendezvoused off Madeira with a ship bringing Confederate Navy officers, crew and heavy guns to refit her as a warship.

War at sea: This 1875 painting by Zanthus Russell Smith 1875 shows the rebel Confederate Navy sloop Alabama being sunk off Cherbourg in 1864 by the US Navy's Kearsage. Blandy's supplied coal to the Kearsage in 1862

Renamed after the Shenandoah Valley in northern Virginia, she had sailed on to the Indian Ocean and Pacific, taking and sinking Yankee merchant ships even after Confederate collapse, news of which had not reached her. The firm's books show that the following American cruisers were coaled by Blandy's: the *Kearsage* (Yankee) on 31 May 1862, the *Merrimac* (Confederate) on 11 August 1862 and the *Phoebe* (Confederate) on 1 February 1865.

Ultimately the British government paid no less than £6 million to the USA to compensate for the losses occasioned by the Northern States and other nations by these cruisers. British owners also claimed to be paid out of this fund. The Northern States admitted the claims of all nations except the British. By 1885 the US had about £600,000 left in hand. The British government asked to have this sum returned and the USA refused, but after further pressure consented to entertain British claims for losses. The Blandy's heirs were able to claim a net sum of £1,572.

During the oïdium plague of 1852 Charles Blandy had bought up the great proportion of the wine stock of British merchants who decided to leave the island. His renowned collection of Madeira vintages bore the name of the Blandy Madeiras. At his death in 1879 the firm's stock was estimated at 5,000 pipes (the equivalent of 3 million bottles), with a value exceeding £200,000.

According to Graham Blandy, his great-grandson, Charles Ridpath 'was intent on purchasing large stocks of wine for which he had no regular market of any magnitude and was doing so by borrowing monies at interest to make this for investment in doubtful transactions'. The position became so dangerous that in 1862 his two elder sons Graham John and John Burden formed the firm of Blandy Brothers & Co. for the purpose of taking over their father's business.

Charles Ridpath undertook to retire first from the coal, ship and steamer business during the year 1862, from the foreign bank and commission business in 1863, from the foreign import trade in 1864, from the island trade in merchandise in 1865, from the island trade in bills and discount

Graham John Blandy, brother and partner of John Burden

in 1866, from the wine trade for export in 1867, from the wine trade for sale in the island in 1868, and from all commercial business in Madeira in 1869. The sum for goodwill was 38,000 *milreis* (about £7,500). Apparently Blandy Brothers & Co. carried out their share of the bargain but Charles Ridpath Blandy did not, and continued in the businesses in spite of the agreement.

His father's reckless behaviour prompted John Burden to give notice of his retirement from the firm on 19 April 1865 and to sail for Durban with his bride Margarette Faber whom he had married in Oxford that year. Here he was joined by his brother Graham John.

The South African adventure was far from a success and by 1876 both brothers had returned to Madeira and were in partnership again. Their father's affairs were now in such a predicament that the brothers signed a second agreement with him by which Blandy Brothers & Co. pledged to take over his business for £75,000, payable over seven years. The assets included wines, casks, etc to the

Laden Blandy coal lighters south of the Loo Rock

value of 577,675 milreis – a vast sum.

Despite these furious quarrels Charles Ridpath continued as a man of business to the very end. Testimony of this comes in the support he gave to the great explorer H. M. Stanley on his second African expedition. A telegram received on 16 September 1877 from Stanley to the *Daily Telegraph* was sent via Blandy's telegram agency at Madeira. Stanley wrote doggedly: '… it is necessary that you inform me by telegraph care [of] Charles Blandy Madeira what you will do with expedition people are sick and weak and over twenty down with ulcers and it is too much to expect them to recross Africa cannot you induce Lords Admiralty order small gunboat convey expedition to Zanzibar …'

The telegram was forwarded by Blandy by submarine cable, via Falmouth, his expenses being £29 15s 5d. Blandy also wrote to the managing proprietor of the *Telegraph*, the expedition's sponsor, detailing the arrangements for shipping Stanley's followers to Zanzibar (involving a much shorter journey to the coast). Charles Blandy said he had taken it on himself to send an expensive telegram to them on Stanley's behalf for which he would pay. '… I will willingly throw in my mite in the cause of African exploration by Stanley …'

Charles Ridpath's reckless purchases of wine proved, with surprising speed, to be a major

boon for the family business. A high award had been given to Blandy wines at the Philadelphia Centennial Exhibition in 1876. Blandys were by then agents for Hooper Bros, Oporto; Vegas & Co., Jerez; Henriot, Rheims; Yriate, Port St Mary; Meyer & Coblenz, Bingen-on-the-Rhine; Dubois Frères, Bordeaux; and Big Tree California wine.

André Simon, the great wine connoisseur, held that two Englishmen had made outstanding contributions to Madeira wine: Thomas Leacock in viticulture and Charles Blandy in the wine trade. Charles Ridpath, he said, was a man 'with great common sense, extraordinary business flair and ability, and possessed of an imperturbable confidence in himself, his country and the future. If there are still splendid examples of pre-phylloxera and … pre-oïdium wines left in Madeira, it is chiefly due to the foresight and courage of Charles Blandy. It was, to a very large extent, due to him that there was no panic, no hasty realisations of stocks to stave off the financial ruin which threatened Madeira merchants, when the island's vineyards were destroyed … Charles Blandy built up stocks of fine Madeiras during those troubled years, when so many of his weaker brethren have lost all faith in the future of the wine trade of Madeira.

Stocks which have proved since of the utmost value not only to his descendants and his own firm … but to the reputation of Madeira.'

Two of the many ancient vintages at the Blandy wine lodge

3. Crisis Turned to Grand Advantage

In 1885 John Burden Blandy acquired one of Madeira's grandest estates, the Quinta do Palheiro, from the spendthrift 2nd Conde de Carvalhal

John Burden Blandy
with stiff collar and
Windsor knot in his tie,
tweed jacket and spotted waistcoat

Rarely have the prospects of Blandy Brothers looked more dire than at the end of 1879. Charles Ridpath's lonely death at the Great Western Hotel in Paddington had been followed rapidly by that of his second son Graham John. The eldest brother John Burden was immediately plunged into still more serious difficulties as in addition to discharging the liabilities under the 1878 agreement with his father, he had to pay, out of Blandy Brothers & Co., the share due to the heirs of his brother.

His father's will brought more bad news. Both John Burden and Graham John had been disinherited. The estate was instead divided between his other eight children.

Loading wine barrels on Calheta Beach

The family plate was left to Richard Ridpath, the family china and glass to Anne Mary Furber (later Cossart). The extensive cellar of bottled wines went to Mary-Anne Grabham – the origin of her husband Dr Grabham's famous cellar. Quinta Santa Luzia and its furniture were to be sold at public auction. So were the extensive wine premises at Rua S. Francisco.

John Burden, seeking relief from this desperate situation, had addressed a letter dated the day before his brother died to his brothers and sisters. Their father, he said, had 'systematically appropriated' Graham John's earnings, resulting in the collapse of Graham John's health. In addition their father 'was taking up monies at high rates of interest for investing in doubtful transactions and in Madeira

wine for which he had no regular sale of any magnitude'. The situation was so bad, contended John Burden, 'his financial transactions were such, that the slightest contretemps in business might have brought on a catastrophe, that had he died suddenly, while his affairs were in the state described, the immediate cash calls on it were of such magnitude that an absolute sacrifice of the whole of his assets would barely have sufficed to meet his liabilities.'

The sons had seen two options. The first was to cut off relations with their father's London office and demand payment. This, they calculated, 'would have caused the bankruptcy of a man much respected in this island; you will doubtless all concur in considering such a step impossible'. The second was to accept any terms they could extricate to end the rift. This was exceedingly undesirable – though 'our father imagined that his stock of wine represented untold wealth', it was simply not the case in their view.

John Burden wanted to put the matter to a jury of the other brothers and sisters, asking them to 'consider our just and equitable claims' rather

Richard Ridpath, younger brother of John Burden Blandy

than 'compel me to lay the matter before a jury of strangers'. He appealed to them to 'join together to save the honour of our father's name'. To this end both brothers were prepared to make a sacrifice but John Burden emphasised that he could not and would not allow his own family to be reduced to the status of dependants. If legal action had to be taken he would put a claim on his father's assets which were almost entirely in Portugal and Madeira. They would petition 'the court to appoint competent accountants to prepare a statement of our father's affairs … and to account for the stewardship of the different branches of business'.

Though some of the family were sympathetic,

Charles Ridpath Blandy's daughter Mary Anne married Dr Michael Grabham and inherited many of her father's choicest wines

Brunel's Great Eastern, anchored in Funchal Bay while laying the first transatlantic cable

he obtained little relief, except in terms of time to pay off his liabilities. Some seventy years later John Burden's grandson Graham recalled, 'It was Dr Michael Grabham and his wife who opposed the reasonable pretensions of JBB: the two men never spoke for over twenty years, until the banquet

Launched in 1853, the clipper *Red Jacket* set a speed record in January 1854 for sailing ships that has never been broken, crossing the Atlantic from New York to Liverpool in thirteen days, one hour and twenty-five minutes. There are only nine recorded occasions when clippers sailed 400 miles or more in a day and three of these were achieved by *Red Jacket* in 1854.

Thirty years later, in 1883, she was sold to Blandy Brothers as a coal hulk and stripped of her masts and rigging. In a storm on 15 December 1885, she parted from her moorings and was wrecked ashore by heavy seas. One of the fragments saved from the wreckage was the splendid carved figurehead.

Red Jacket was named after a Native American chief of the Seneca tribe from upstate New York. He earned his name from the red coat he

for D. Carlos took place at Palheiro in 1901 and JBB, hearing that Dr Grabham naturally wished to be asked, sent him an invitation.' Another theory was that the break between the two men was due principally to the death of Margarette, John Burden's first wife, from typhoid in 1877. John Burden blamed Dr Grabham for this, believing he could have saved her.

There is no record of what happened to Quinta Santa Luzia and the furniture but presumably John Burden was able to buy the property as he went to live there while his mother, Mary-Anne Blandy, ended her days at Quinta da Levada, after Graham John's widow had left for England. Remarkably John Burden also appears to have been able to buy up the premises at Rua S. Francisco and they

Coal lighter and temporary jetty

continue to this day as the firm's property.

John Burden's survival was testimony to both his skills as a manager and his eye for commercial opportunities. The year 1879 saw a deal which was to restore the family business to lasting prosperity. Blandy Brothers obtained a virtual monopoly of coal bunkering in Madeira with the purchase of the Quinta Grant, site of the coal stores, later converted to a grain silo, opposite the road to the Pontinha. Tradition has it that Krohn Brothers sold the Pontinha property and the Quinta Grant (which was close to their own store) because they did not like the exacting work of attending to ships that came in at all hours of the day and night requiring coal. It may have been a dirty business but it paid.

These were the years in which steam steadily took over from sail. Coal was supplied in shore lighters which were pulled up on the beach to discharge or be loaded by men using baskets. 'These lighters only held about 10 to 15 tons each,' according to Graham. 'Putting coal ashore from big lighters of 100 to 200 tons only became possible when our coaling quay was made at the Pontinha in 1901–2, and this had steam cranes for lifting out the bags full of coal. The coal store had transporters operated by steam for piling up the coal. In addition, the firm had at least one, and sometimes two, coal hulks anchored in the bay to supplement the coal

was given by a British officer in appreciation of his support during the American War of Independence. He later made peace with the new government and was awarded a medal by George Washington in recognition of his resolute defence of the interests of his tribe.

The figurehead was carved by the shipwrights of Rockland, Maine where the ship was built and launched before being towed to New York for masting and rigging. She was fitted with sails made of premium southern cotton canvas.

After standing for years in a garden in Funchal, the figurehead is now in the Cruzes museum awaiting restoration. Its splendid colouring survives largely undamaged, with a crimson red cloak and sash over a blue tunic.

Wood salvaged from Red Jacket was used for the main stair of Quinta Santa Luzia, and the staircase (still existing) in the old Blandy office at Rua de Alfandega. The Rockland local newspaper described the clipper's aft cabin as being 'veneered with Rosewood, Mahogany, Satin, Zebra and Black walnut finished in highest style'.

stores ashore. The most famous of these hulks was the *Red Jacket*. Another was the *European*. These held 3,000 to 4,000 tons each.'

John Burden also decided to strengthen the firm by inviting his brother-in-law, Maurice Faber, to join him. Maurice arrived with his beautiful wife Georgina (von Keller), the daughter of an Austrian general. They initially occupied the Quinta das Abóboras, just below the flagstaff at Quinta Santa Luzia. Later they bought the Quinta S. João, sold after the First World War.

The urbane and charming Maurice Faber became a partner in 1880 with Raleigh Blandy and was John Burden's right-hand man till he suffered a stroke and had to retire. 'He was largely responsible for the important German connection which the firm had, which included the agencies of the Woermann Line,' wrote Graham.

Graham remembered his grandfather John Burden as 'a tall man with a short white beard' and 'an impressive personality ... I was eight when he died, I was always frightened of him.' He

The Austrian Margarette Faber, John Burden Blandy's first wife

Among the most poignant items in the Blandy archives are the love letters between Raleigh Blandy and Floss Berrington — forced apart by her family's determined opposition to their marriage. They had met when Floss came to Madeira in the spring of 1891.

Back in Wales a distraught Floss wrote on 5 May, 'My own dear Ral, I hardly know where to begin to tell you about everything ... I am in despair and very miserable because, dear Raleigh, both Papa and Mama say they will never give their consent to our marriage ... I think our only chance is for you to come over if you can, my dearest, and try to make them alter their minds. You can do nothing by writing if you are a million miles off.'

Raleigh had a skin infection, the more tragic as he remained an extremely good-looking man. He wrote on 9 July 1891, 'As to my cursed skin disease I have suffered too much to wish to hand it down to posterity and I had thought a great deal about that. I don't believe it is hereditary, but some say it is and others not. I have applied to the Royal College of Physicians here and now have the names of some of the specialists in that line and it will be some satisfaction to have their opinion although it will be no good to us now ... I must tell you that this is the last letter I may write to you. Raleigh.'

Floss would not give up so easily and wrote two days later from the family home at Pant y Goitre, Abergavenny: 'I will marry you without anybody's consent because you are the only man I ever have or ever shall love and if you refuse it will mean that we must both be unhappy ... It is not wrong to marry without one's parents' consent — they won't die of misery and the only person in the whole world I should be sorry about is my dear mother ...

describes how John Burden 'ruled the firm with a rod of iron'. His copy books (he copied every letter he wrote) contained many very firm reproofs to the London manager, J. C. Turner, to Mr Charles Wigg, the first manager at Las Palmas, as well as to his sons and nephews. He wrote strongly to Dudley Oliveira Davies, who had recently joined the firm in the Canaries, condemning his engagement 'to the daughter of a hotel keeper' in Las Palmas. The marriage was called off.

Yet at home he enjoyed bridge (or whist as it was then called) with friends and even produced a small roulette wheel at Quinta Santa Luzia when he had house guests. One of these was Sir Donald Currie, the first chairman of the recently amalgamated Union Castle Line, but the canny Scot would never venture more than a few shillings.

Graham recalled how on Sunday mornings he would walk down with his father from Quinta Favila, first of all to the wine office at Rua S. Francisco, and then to the lower office at Rua de Alfândega. Here John Burden would be 'reviewing any cables which had come in about our large shipping and coal business'. Notice of impending arrivals came either from the shipowners or from the agents on the

John Burden Blandy and his young family: John Ernest, centre, Percy George, Emily Margarette, Charles Maurice, Frances Duff, Graham Frederick

If I could see you, Ral, you would be convinced in a minute. Please do not let us be unhappy all our lives — just because my father does not like it. I am quite old enough to know what I mean — I shall be twenty-four this year and I mean every word I have said.'

Raleigh, however, had concluded that caution should prevail for on 9 August 1891 Floss wrote again, 'My dearest, I agree with you that it would be better to wait for a bit and see how things turn out ... I had a talk with my father about it the other day and he was most decidedly against everything ... It is most horrid ... more especially as Papa is most alarming and says he will go to law about it if you write me any more letters ... Your last letter came by a second post and one of the servants happened to go to Abergavenny and brought it and gave it to me. Otherwise I would never have got it.'

The anxiety and the troubles in corresponding began to take their toll and Raleigh wrote to Floss on 21 August: 'I knew you would think my letter cold or unkind, but I wrote half a dozen times before I made up my mind to send it ... I have quite decided that it is best for us both to give it up. As you say "it was one of my unhappy days", but they have all been unhappy lately and I can't bear them any longer ... I hope you may find someone who will be thought more worthy of you by your parents.'

A hive of activity at the Blandy Wine Lodge. The first John Blandy's house is on the left This, and the two engravings opposite are from Vizetelly's 1880 book on Port and Madeira

St Vincent island of Cape Verde, though very often ships from the south would put in without notice, short of coal, to bunker.

John Burden had a very difficult time after his first wife Margarette Faber died in 1877 leaving him with six young children to bring up and educate: John Ernest, Percy George, Emily Margarette, Charles Maurice, Frances Duff and Graham Frederick. In 1882 he married Alice Gwendolen Berrington, sister to Floss (see page 46), with whom he had three more children: Florence Alice, Hugh Berrington (who died aged nine months) and Geoffrey Kelvin. According to Graham, Alice 'was a tall distinguished

woman, who had a very soft voice. She made my grandfather a magnificent wife, as he entertained lavishly at Santa Luzia and at Palheiro; the visitors' book of the early 1900s being filled with illustrious names ... British, Portuguese, American, German; Cecil Rhodes is there, and so are the admirals of the various fleets, Lord Charles Beresford [the renowned naval figure] and others.'

An intensely vivid picture of the Blandy wine cellars, just as John Burden inherited, was provided by a remarkable journalist, Henry Vizetelly, who had worked on the *Illustrated London News* as the magazine's Paris correspondent, transferring in 1872 to Berlin. His travels led to a keen interest in wine and he wrote two highly informative volumes: *Facts about Champagne* in 1879 and *Facts about Port and Madeira* the next year.

His excitement in exploring the Blandy cellars rivalled that of an Egyptologist in the Valley of the Kings. 'You pass out of the offices in the Rua São Francisco — a street running in the direction of the sea — into a small courtyard surrounded by quaint irregular buildings.' A ground-floor cellar was the ancient store containing the most venerable wines. 'It is a long, dim apartment, lighted by small square windows protected by iron bars, and paved with

In 1807, the French army invaded Portugal. The Prince Regent (and future King João VI) ordered the transfer of the Portuguese royal court to Brazil before he could be deposed by Napoleon. They set sail on 29 November under the protection of the British Royal Navy. In 1808 the capital of the kingdom of Portugal was established in Rio de Janeiro, serving as the seat of government for the entire Portuguese Empire. In 1815, during the Congress of Vienna, Prince João created a United Kingdom of Portugal and Brazil, giving Brazil equal status to Portugal. When he returned with the royal family as King João VI to Portugal in 1821, his heir Prince Pedro remained in Brazil and was crowned emperor in Rio on 7 September 1822, ending colonial rule which had begun 322 years before.

flagstones. Here, ranged in rows, are some thirty or forty huge butts, all more or less antique-looking, and many bearing the brands of once-famous Madeira firms, now defunct.' Each of these butts held from 620 to 670 gallons. All contained 'wines of rare flavour and aroma, although generally too concentrated and too powerful to be drunk by themselves'. Their chief purpose was to give character to younger growths.

Here they tasted a blended Cama de Lobos 'of great vinosity and pleasant subdued pungency of flavour', and a 'powerful choice old Reserve from the same district, the solera of which was founded as far back as 1792'. Next came a fine old concentrated wine from the Torre Bella vineyard, marvellously round and soft; then a remarkable Sercial, vintaged half a century

Workers bring the grape pressings down from the hills in goatskins

Barrels of maturing Madeira are shifted in the lofts of the Blandy Wine Lodge

ago, and 'emitting a wonderful aroma, and having a marked though pleasant pungent flavour'. During the first twenty years of its life this wine, he was told, was far too harsh to be at all palatable. Another venerable wine was a Malvasia velhíssimo, 'a Malmsey of exceeding softness combined with a seductive sub-bitterness of flavour'.

Next to this vinous museum stood the old theatre of Funchal, which Charles Ridpath Blandy had acquired and converted into a wine store. Here a series of wide arches led to a succession of courtyards 'girt round with buildings filled with pipes upon pipes of wine'. In the old theatre, where wines in double pipes were stored, 'trabalhadores were busy fining wines with white of egg, while in a kind

of open store a blend of fifty pipes was being made'. This blend, with an average age of eight years, proved an agreeable and not over-spirituous wine, fairly brilliant in colour.

Next they ascended a staircase to a platform with an apparatus for raising and lowering casks. This gave access to several roomy stores, each containing 200 or 300 pipes, laid out in rows in one room, stacked one above the other in the next.

'Here were some of the pleasant light northern growths, which ... occasionally developed the *mycoderma vina*, or so-called flowers of wine, so anxiously watched for and valued by the rearers of sherry.' Further wine stores, connected by numerous courts or landings, were 'like so many Clapham Junctions' containing the 1865 to 1875 vintages. Here they sampled a Cama de Lobos, 1868, which had received just 2 gallons of spirit, and been matured in a warm store at a temperature of 95 degrees. On a subsequent occasion they tasted a rare São Martinho Verdelho 'boasting a wonderful perfume, and already more than half a century old. This was one of the most perfect old Madeiras we ever tasted, far surpassing in flavour ... a wine of the year 1760' which though but a phantom of its former self 'had not in the slightest degree turned acid'.

Vizetelly provided an equally vivid picture of the vineyards. 'The pickers here are all men, black-bearded, barefooted, and in ragged raiment, with their skins almost as brown as their mahogany-coloured breeches. They cut off the grapes and fling them into round open baskets with handles, emptying these afterwards into a larger basket similar in shape, and known as the *cesto de vindima*. The latter holds above a hundredweight of grapes, about sufficient to produce a barrel of *mosto* [grape pressings], equivalent to a trifle over 9 imperial gallons. The *casa do lagar*, or pressing house, was in the centre of the vineyard.'

Blandy's Las Palmas firm, started in 1886, was another initiative of John Burden's. He had seen an opportunity of establishing a second coal-bunkering business there. He had some wooden coal lighters built in Madeira and sent them down to Las Palmas. He also dispatched some of his trusted Portuguese clerks to manage the business in its early days. The coaling and slipway concessions were obtained by a certain Señor J.B. Carlo. Before long John Burden began to feel uneasy about this gentleman who had granted himself, in the deeds of the Las Palmas properties and concessions, the title of 'partner in Blandy Brothers & Co.', whereas his position was evidently that of joint manager. He held this with Charles Wigg, who later established his own firm in a number of South American ports.

Carlo left the firm in 1888 or 1889, and John Burden asked his son Percy George to go to Las Palmas and take charge. 'Percy George, being tall, fair and a good games player, was popular and, despite strong opposition from our competitors, did very well till he was struck down by a hideous crime,' wrote Graham. In those days Las Palmas town and port were completely separate, and the 2 miles between them had to be covered on foot, horseback or by *tartana*, a two-wheeled gig pulled by a horse. Percy George was walking back one night from the port when he was set upon by three men who overpowered him, took his watch and money and then proceeded to kick him almost to death. His life

The launching of the Falcão, Blandy's first coastal vessel, on June 3, 1893, with Raleigh Blandy and ladies at the stern

was saved by some Spanish seamen who happened to be passing and stopped the assault, but he never fully recovered and died from tuberculosis at Davos in 1902.

He was succeeded as head of the Las Palmas firm by John Burden's third son, Charles Maurice, who was later joined by his first cousin, Dudley Oliveira Davies. These two were in charge of the Las Palmas firm until the start of the Second World War when they both died.

In Las Palmas Blandy's main competitors were Miller's, but by 1902 Elder Dempster & Co. had established themselves there under the name of the Grand Canary Coaling Co. Cory Brothers, Hull Blyth and Wilsons had a share of the market too. Cory Brothers were also Blandy's competitors in Madeira. In November 1902 the firms signed an agreement intended to stabilise prices, to pool the business with penalties for those exceeding their agreed percentages, and of course to keep out

The Cory was a working Blandy tug. She was also used in the 1950s to take occasional family fishing parties to the Desertas

The Second Conde de Carvalhal, owner of Quinta do Palheiro, enjoys a picnic on his estate

competitors. The percentages applied (covering the ports of Madeira, Las Palmas, Tenerife and St Vincent, Cape Verde) were Cory's 33½ per cent, Elder's 18 per cent, Blandy's 16½ per cent and Hull Blyth and Wilsons the same. In Graham's orotund words, 'The agreement signed by distinguished and far-seeing gentlemen was in the main honoured, though there were many disputes …'

The turnover of the British firms was enormous. In four and a half years between 1903–7 they supplied 601,047 tons of coal in Madeira, 1,009, 718 tons in Tenerife; 1,305,470 tons in Las Palmas; and 1,317,080 tons in St Vincent – an average of nearly 1 million tons per annum. Blandy's, wrote Graham, 'held their own quite well at Las Palmas until the important and powerful firms of Lamberts, Mann George and William Cory purchased the firm of Miller & Co. and then diverted their big coaling contracts with a large number of owners, from Blandy's who they had previously supported, to Miller's.'

The coal service was just the beginning of a fleet of small vessels – tugs, lighters, launches and coastal steamers serving towns along the coast before usable roads were built. The first coasting vessel was the *Falcão*, wooden and copper sheathed with compound engines that came out to Madeira on 21 February 1881.

Under John Burden the firm took an interest in the flour-milling business which was protected by the Government. 'Our flour mill was the Fábrica dos Lavradores, but there were competitors in the shape of the Pelourinho Mill … Fábrica da Ponte Nova bought by Blandy Brothers & Co. and sold to William Hinton & Sons in the late 1920s and the Fábrica Progresso also bought by Blandy's.'

In spite of his early difficulties John Burden was progressively able to pay off the liabilities. In 1885 he acquired one of Madeira's grandest estates, the Quinta do Palheiro, from the spendthrift 2nd Conde de Carvalhal. The beauty of this estate was noted by numerous early visitors to Madeira. Emily Smith in

1841 enthused about 'the lovely silver pheasants and doves' which she watched while dining under the trees.

The 1st Count, one of the largest landowners in Portugal, had built the handsome hunting lodge that is today known as the Casa Velha Hotel. Tradition has it that in the laying out of the quinta in about 1801 a French landscape gardener was employed. The magnificent plane-tree avenue, stretching down from the old house, is 100 trees in length but no wider than the carriage drive which it shaded.

According to Graham, 'Tradition also has it that many of the rare specimens of trees of considerable age were given to the first Conde by Dom João VI (John the Runaway) who was King of Portugal at the time the quinta was begun. There are many fine specimens of Brazilian trees – for example, the huge *Araucaria brasiliensis* – and it seems possible that they were sent to Madeira during Dom João VI's stay in Brazil during the Peninsular Wars.'

The Madeiran chronicle, *Elucidário Madeirense*, relates that during the Miguelite Wars of 1828–34 over the Royal Succession, the first Conde, whose sympathies were on the liberal side, had to seek refuge on the English corvette *Alligator* on 22 August 1828 when the island was occupied by the Miguelite troops. According to the English novelist, Fanny Burney, writing in 1839, the troops ransacked the 'splendid house, destroyed the costly furniture, his valuable old wine, injured and cut the trees, shrubs, etc.'

He returned to the island in 1834 and was made Conde de Carvalhal, dying three years later on 11 November 1837 when he was laid to rest in the chapel at the quinta. In spite of his great wealth, the 1st Count lived without luxury or ostentation, and did much during periods of economic crises to alleviate the sufferings of the poor. On various occasions he sustained the price of the *mosto* (grape pressings) against the wine exporters who had an interest in driving down prices.

Robert White described the estate in 1851 as 'situated at an elevation of 1,800 feet above the sea. The ascent occupies about an hour, but the road is good. The grounds are somewhat in the style of an English park; the garden however is small but contains many curious plants, among which are several kinds of cacti, and some enormous trees of the *Camellia japonica*, bearing flowers of great beauty and variety of colour. The house is small, and almost hid from view by the lofty trees which surround it.'

The 1st Count had no male heirs and the title and properties passed to his nephew who was then just six years old. Graham continues: 'History relates that personally [the 2nd Count] was extremely agreeable and charming and a typical aristocrat. However, little time was spent in Madeira, but Paris, Madrid and

Fanny Blandy, the second of Charles Ridpath's daughters, was a radiant girl who enchanted all who met her. She married Sir William Thomson, later Lord Kelvin, the greatest physicist of the age. In 1873 he sailed into Funchal on a mission to lay a cable to Brazil. Due to a fault in the cable the ship was detained at Madeira for sixteen days when he attempted to teach the Blandy daughters the art of flag signalling. Fanny was the only one quick enough to learn and when he returned a year later aboard his own 126-ton schooner-rigged yacht, the Lalla Rookh, he hoisted flags carrying the message 'will you marry me'. Yes, she promptly signalled back from the Belvedere at Santa Luzia.

Around the middle of July the newly wedded couple set sail for Cowes in the Lalla Rookh, arriving in the Clyde towards the end of the year. Soon after Thomson bought a small estate to the north of Largs where he built his bride a country house, Netherhall, which was fitted with all kinds of engineering devices and gadgets. During the next thirty-three years the couple were rarely separated, Fanny accompanying her husband to nearly every public meeting and festive occasion.

Fanny carried on a considerable part of Kelvin's correspondence, writing to Sir George Darwin in 1881 that he had set up a tide gauge in the Clyde. 'He is very busy on electric light just now — also telephone companies'. Kelvin's wealth derived from his key role in laying the first cable across the Atlantic, but Fanny inherited a fortune too, 'enabling her husband to maintain his position as a peer in fitting style' according to an obituary.

Lisbon saw much of this example of *jeunesse dorée*

Enormous *festas* and entertainments were given at Palheiro on many occasions, particularly when the Infante, afterwards Dom Luis, visited the island … In 1866 the Count became engaged to an English girl, a Miss Nugent, for whom he commenced building the Quinta do Til. When the building was half completed the engagement was broken off by Miss Nugent and the house was left incomplete … The eastern wing was destined for a great ballroom which was only finished in 1936 by Cecil Miles who had acquired the property when he married three years before.'

The 2nd Count constructed a small house in 1858 on higher ground at Palheiro, consisting of two floors only, colour-washed pink like the old house, the chapel and the other buildings in the *quinta*.

John Burden acquired Palheiro in 1885 through a mortgage. He explained two years later to a Mr Rawes, his financial adviser in Lisbon: 'My father had lent Carvalhal money and in order to get some kind of security for it, I lent him some £500 and £600 more … I had either to buy the property or lose my money.' He had had to pay out more than he anticipated, adding, 'If I had known all this I should have probably forfeited the money and had nothing to do with Palheiro.' His family and business partners thought it was a white elephant and John Burden evidently agreed some of the time. But he persevered and steadily bought up more of the surrounding estate.

In 1889 he embarked on an ambitious new house

Illuminated address presented to Dom Carlos by British citizens on the King's visit to Palheiro in 1901

to the designs of the architect George Somers Clarke Junior (1841–1926) on the site of the 1858 house. Somers Clarke was the architect of the new Reid's Hotel, then being built by the sons of William Reid. He and his partner John Thomas Micklethwaite (1843–1906) were both pupils of Sir George Gilbert Scott, architect of the Foreign Office in London, the Albert Memorial and St Pancras Station Hotel. Somers Clarke was also a leading Egyptologist who wrote a number of books and designed the celebrated Shepheard's Hotel in Cairo, which was burnt down by an anti-British mob in January 1952.

Somers Clarke's house for John Burden could stand equally in a hill station in India or Malaya and is a wonderful embodiment of the romance of far-flung Empire. Clarke conceived the house as a series of pavilions with cascading roofs, encircling

At the foot of the Loo rock is Lord's Kelvin's device for measuring the tides, known by the Blandys as Uncle William's breeches

Guests gather for the banquet at Palheiro in 1901 held in honour of the King of Portugal, Dom Carlos

colonnades and clusters of soaring chimneys. The entrance hall stands forward from the rest of the house lit by lunette windows – a distant echo of one of the most enchanting buildings of the Italian Renaissance, the Pazzi Chapel. It represents the very best of nineteenth-century eclecticism, conjured up from many memories and influences but a highly original and unusual composition.

John Burden moved into his new house in 1891. The lawn in front surveys a grand series of garden terraces and also commands a majestic and beautifully framed panorama of the whole bay of Funchal. From here, John Burden had a view of every ship approaching the harbour. He could see his fleet of coasting vessels and watch the Blandy coal and water lighters hurrying out to refuel ships anchored in the bay.

A decade later John Burden received the ultimate honour of a visit from Dom Carlos and his Queen Donna Maria Amelia. Carlos, a cultured and sophisticated monarch whose interests included oceanography, was like Edward VII, a man with indulgent tastes. His incompetence was compounded by his own extreme extravagance and wastefulness; Portugal was declared bankrupt during his reign in 1892 and 1902. But what might have caused an extra frisson to spread among the Blandy womenfolk was talk of his extramarital affairs. Carlos's controversial rule ended dramatically with his assassination in 1908 when both he and his heir, Prince Luis Filipe, were shot while riding back to the palace in Lisbon in an open carriage.

John Burden arranged a huge picnic banquet for the king and queen in front of the old house at

Palheiro and invited a number of British residents. The king rode up on horseback while the queen came in a bullock sledge. Everything had been thought of except one thing – toothpicks. A guest deftly whittled down a match for the king who after lunch played a game of tennis in his waistcoat smoking a cigar with John Burden as his partner, playing in elegantly stockinged feet. On the other side of the net were Harry Hinton and the vivacious Fanny Blandy whose participation added extra excitement to the occasion. The delighted king offered to confer the title of count on John Burden who politely declined, saying he wished to remain an Englishman, but adding tactfully he would greatly like to possess one of the king's paintings.

A year later the idyll was shattered. A savage fire in early December 1902 entirely gutted the new house. John Burden described the horror. 'On Sunday morning at 2 am old Joaquim was awoken at Palheiro by a crackling sound and by 6 am during a terrific wind the whole house was in ruins – just the kitchen left and the outer roof of the hall. The hoses were put on from the hydrants as soon as people came, attracted by the enormous glare – the flames licked halfway up the hill behind the house. Old Joaquim called Júlio and Virgínia and in entering from behind to try and open the hall door, he was overpowered by the smoke. Julio, hearing groans, broke open a side window and he and Virgínia pulled him out insensible. He was at once sent down to the hospital and is out of danger.'

With the help of two hoses threaded through the windows above the storeroom, a little of the silver plate was rescued. From under the verandahs the servants saved some of the pictures hanging on the walls and some curios. John Burden continued: 'Carpets, bedding, etc were all put away upstairs and were of course all lost. It was an awful fire and very sharp. I have come to the conclusion that it was a lightning strike as the top stack of three chimneys has one leg knocked away … I am insured for £5,000 and furniture for £800 and have asked Imperial to send out someone. I shall never rebuild such a house – it is too sad – but I must put up something as I

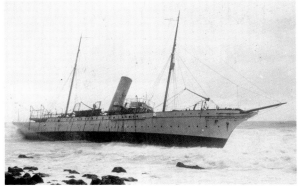

The Yatch Varuna wrecked on November 16, 1909, at Ponta do Pargo

look forward to rest at Palheiro for my now rapidly approaching old age.' Days later he again recorded his feelings. 'It is all very sad and those gutted walls have stared me in the face ever since – not a window left, nothing but the walls and the chimneystacks.' On 23 December he was thinking 'I would much rather only put up a small place' as his children were now grown up and departed.

Yet over the next year he changed his mind, and, perhaps encouraged by an understanding insurance company, completely rebuilt the house between 1903 and 1905. From the evidence of photographs

Leland Cossart, husband of Charles Ridpath's daughter Anne Mary

John Burden Blandy's monument in the British Cemetery in Funchal

a suitable flourish, carefully selected specimen trees were planted along its whole length.

In retrospect the decision to rebuild Palheiro was all the more remarkable as John Burden could simply have continued to live at Quinta Santa Luzia. In 1909, in a book on the gardens of Madeira, Florence du Cane had been enraptured: 'The palm must be given to the garden of Santa Luzia ... not only does it cover a much larger expanse of ground than any other [but] when owners take so much individual interest in almost every plant in the garden, as here everything seems to flourish and grow at its best, for flowers grow best for those who love them ... plants have been sent to them from all parts of the world, and the island owes many of its flowery treasures to this garden.'

John Burden's success in Madeira was a reflection of the commercial spirit of Victorian Englishmen. He took risks but demonstrated sustained business acumen in his numerous ventures, building up powerful positions in the coal-bunkering trade, shipping agencies, the supply of water and stores to ships, and a repair yard. He bought, built and maintained splendid houses with a dynastic eye, but put them to practical use as he entertained shipowners and illustrious visitors. Graham wrote: 'His influence was great locally and few projects were embarked on without those concerned consulting him for his wise advice.'

Under John Burden's direction Blandy's established what was soon to be a commanding position in the Madeira wine trade. Cossart Gordon & Co., it was true, were better known, especially in England which was their stronghold, but Blandy's had a worldwide business and stocks of old Madeiras which no other shipper could match.

His last years were spent in increasingly splendid style, fuelled by his second wife's taste for travel and society. They made regular visits to London and Paris and in summer to Vichy or Salzburg for the cures. But as he grew older his health began to suffer. He became prey to bronchitis which led to his death in 1912.

taken when the house was built a decade before, it looks as if the replacement was faithfully constructed to the original designs, even retaining the fragment of the 2nd Count's 1850s house still visible where an irregularly placed window and door survive at the back.

When he bought Palheiro John Burden would ride up to the estate where he had built a stable beneath the new *armazém* or warehouse. For the family it was a much slower journey by bullock. But by the time Palheiro burnt down the motor car had been invented and was about to transform the pace of travel. In Madeira John Burden was one of the first to own a private motor car, a two-seater Swift, first manufactured in 1904. A new motor road from the Cancela das Neves was begun in 1912 and finished two years later. To ensure guests would arrive with

4. War, Retrenchment and Hard Times

Always on the lookout for business, the London office of Blandy's was caught by a number of ill-starred contracts during the war. One of these was to supply 20,000 pairs of boots for the French army . . .

John Ernest Blandy in smart
pin-striped suit

When John Ernest succeeded his father on 5 December 1912, British power and British commerce were at their height. In England almost any leading family which had established such a fortune and amassed such property would have secured a baronetcy or a peerage. In distant Madeira, the Blandys showed no such ambitions. John Ernest, so far from handing over his business to subordinates and leading a life of leisure, like many of his contemporaries in England, committed his energies to the family firm.

He was an imposing figure, 6 feet 2 inches tall, who, in the words of his son Graham, 'always held himself well'. He had dark curly hair, a large moustache and a bronzed complexion, inherited from his mother Margarette Faber. At all times immaculately dressed, he wore spats even at dinner.

John Ernest had been born in 1866 in Durban, South Africa, returning aged four with his parents, John Burden and Margarette, brother Percy and sister Emily. He did not like his prep school near London, complaining that in summer the school was so short of water that the boys would squeeze their sponges to quench their thirst. His mother died when he was twelve and he and his siblings never took to stepmother Alice.

After leaving school John Ernest spent some time in France, becoming friendly with the Henriot family, who owned the famous champagne house of that name in Rheims. When Alexandre Henriot enlisted in the French army, John Ernest would accompany him on manoeuvres. This friendship was later to lead to the founding of Blandy Frères in Rheims, at 40, rue de l'Université, with Madame Louisa Henriot as agent for Blandy wines in France. Strenuous and partly successful attempts were made to promote Madeira as a fashionable drink.

John Ernest began in the Blandy wine business about 1885 at the firm's premises in Rua S. Francisco. As the atmosphere at Quinta Santa Luzia was awkward, with his stepmother bringing up a young family of her own, he leased the Quinta Nunes in Rua do Jasmineiro. Here he lived a bachelor life with friends from other leading English families: Harry Hinton, Johnny Welsh, Webster Gordon and the Cossarts. Poker was played for high stakes and John Ernest demurred until another

friend, the US Consul Jones, said: 'Ernest, you can play as well as any of them.' By the end of the first year he had a jam jar full of golden sovereigns.

Though the hotels had no dance bands, there were private dances at Quinta Santa Luzia and Palácio Torrebela, where Dermot Bolger's family used to live. Dermot was the grandson of Russel (or Russell) Manners Gordon and the Condessa de Torre Bela and was to become a good friend of Graham. He was convivial and a great supporter of English initiatives in Madeira, notably the British Country Club and the English Rooms bar. Bullock cars provided transport for married couples going out to dinner – the stately pace made it necessary to set out half or three-quarters of an hour in advance.

John Ernest was married in Baltimore on 28 December 1901. He first met his future bride Elinor when she accompanied her father Captain William H. Reeder on the New York sail training ship St Mary's to Madeira. The wedding took place privately as Elinor had just lost her mother and was in mourning. The New York Times reported the next day that the bride 'is an exceedingly handsome girl' and wore 'an exquisite gown of white chiffon, elaborately embroidered by hand … the ornaments were diamonds and pearls, and she carried a bouquet of white violets'. The newspaper report went on to enthuse misleadingly: 'The bridegroom is a nephew of Lord Kelvin of Scotland and a son of John Blandy, formerly also of Scotland, but now popularly known as the Prince of Madeira, from his ownership of the greater part of the island.'

Elinor grew to be an indomitable lady of great charm and style, indeed something of a grande dame in later years. Graham recalled, 'She was interested in fashion and clothes and always beautifully dressed. She was a great gardener and improved both Palheiro and Santa Luzia gardens. My father on the other hand was keenly interested in trees and planted many specimens, particularly conifers and cypresses, at Palheiro.'

In the early 1900s Alexandre Henriot produced an exotic proposal: 'If a concession was obtainable from a certain Russian prince, the production of wine in Turkestan would be highly profitable.' John Ernest was sent out in 1905. Russia was at war with Japan and British sympathies were with the Japanese. The

Launching of the Tug 'Lobo'

English were unwelcome in Russia so John Ernest was provided with a French passport.

They reached Baku to take the ferry across the Caspian Sea but found the captain spoke no French and had to converse in English. The next day the Chief of Police called to say that he had heard one of them was British. The penalty for such an offence was imprisonment in Siberia. Fortunately the police picked on Henriot and he was able to talk them out of a very serious situation. They proceed to Turkistan visiting Samarkand and Bokhara but there the proposition for wine from the Steppes of Russia rested.

In Madeira the wine business was prospering. The average shipments for the years 1909–13 were 6,900 pipes. This was shared between seven English firms and four Portuguese firms, with Blandy's shipping

The Duke of Kent, fourth son of George V of Britain, arrives at Funchal before the Second World War

13.6 per cent to Cossart Gordon's 29.5 per cent. France and Belgium headed the list of importers, taking 332 pipes followed by Germany with 123. A good deal of the Blandy shipments were made through the London firm of Herrfeldt & Campbell which shipped mostly to Russia. Shipments to Russia became payable after eighteen months rather than the usual twelve, leaving shippers dangerously exposed at the time of the 1917 Revolution. Prices were highly competitive, with Cossart Gordon offering wine at as little as £9 per pipe.

One of Blandy's most able and loyal employees, T. L. W. 'Tom' Mullins, had joined the company's wine department in 1914, tempted by a wage of £10 per month which capped the £9 10s offered by the rival firm of Rocha Machado. 'He became manager of the wine department under my father John Ernest,' Graham recalled. 'He was the acknowledged expert in Madeira wine and had spent all his life in the wine trade.'

At the outbreak of war in August 1914 there was a serious crisis as the shippers did not want to buy the *mosto* (grape pressings). Blandy's had the biggest stock – 2,000 pipes – and decided they must help their regular suppliers by offering to warehouse their *mosto* in their stores and casks free of charge.

Most of the wine shippers were soon in serious difficulties as a result of the war. Cossarts were awaiting payment for £23,000 worth of wine in France, Germany and Russia. Krohn Brothers were in still more serious trouble as their main markets were Germany and Russia. Elsewhere the demand for Madeira wine increased considerably and for Blandy's the main challenge was to find vessels that would ship to the UK, Sweden and Denmark.

In Madeira, wine growers suffered from an acute shortage of sulphur for the vineyards. This became severest in 1917 when virtually every bunch of grapes was mildewed and unusable. Blandy's purchases of wine up to August that year amounted to a mere 850 pipes, though in the circumstances this was a substantial amount and regarded as 'a lock-up'.

Always on the lookout for business, the London office of Blandy's was caught by a number of ill-starred contracts during the war. One of these was to supply 20,000 pairs of boots for the French army. They were ordered from the USA but proved to be entirely unacceptable. A substantial investment in a project to build concrete barges was also a complete disaster. A share in a Malaysian rubber company turned out to be more satisfactory and was retained until the 1950s. Another joint venture was a cocoa business on the west coast of Africa with the Lawrie Brothers. The firm also sent a small ship, probably a trawler, to Bear Island in the Arctic for furs which were sold in London. In Madeira the wine business was left increasingly in the hands of Tom Mullins.

Further wartime difficulties had developed with the virtual impossibility of importing coal from Britain. Coal was generally reserved for British and allied shipping, though Portugal benefited when it entered the war in 1916 on the Allied side. Hinton's had great difficulty in obtaining coal to operate their sugar factory. The Blandy wine stores also used coal. The inevitable solution, Graham explained, was to turn to wood. 'The pine forests were largely cut down, which accounts for the almost total absence of old pine trees today in the island, except for Palheiro.' John Ernest himself cut down trees for use as masts for sailing ships.

During the war Madeira was a coaling station for the 9th cruiser squadron which included *HMS Highflyer*, *HMS Argonaut* and *HMS Amphitrite*, first under Admiral Sir John de Robeck and then Sir Gordon Wilson Moore. Cory's or Wilson's held the Admiralty contract. *HMS Highflyer* had earlier taken part in the hunt for the German commerce raider *Kaiser Wilhelm der Grosse* which had been sighted at Rio de Oro, a Spanish anchorage on the Saharan coast. Finding the German ship taking on coal from three colliers, the *Highflyer* demanded she surrender. The German captain claimed the protection of neutral waters but his claim was denied and fighting broke out. The *Kaiser Wilhelm der Grosse* was sunk, the *Highflyer* losing one man, with six injured. Under Admiral Sir John de Robeck she was part of a squadron guarding West Africa against Admiral Maximilian von Spee.

The extent of the threat became clear on 3 December 1917 when a German submarine torpedoed the French gunboat *Surprise* off Funchal, as well as the cable ship *Dacia* and the French submarine depot ship *Kangaroo*. The U-boat then surfaced and bombarded the town. Blandy's coal lighters were alongside Surprise and one of them

The French cable ship SS Dacia *was sunk in Funchal harbour during a U-boat attack on December 3, 1917*

was sunk with the loss of several lives.

After the 1914–18 war the coal-bunker business of Madeira diminished and, although Blandy Brothers retained the lion's share of it, Cory's and Wilson's still hung on. It was not until 1944 that Blandy's finally purchased the shares of Cory's Madeira Coaling Co. Blandy's promptly sold the five Cory coal lighters to Bensaude & Co., in the Azores, who bought them to handle the large amount of war material arriving there.

By 1918 wine shippers were desperate to shift the large orders awaiting export – Cossart Gordon had more than 1,000 pipes destined for a thirsty Denmark. Blandy's had 515 pipes lying ready for Sweden but there was now a greater problem – a shortage of alcohol to fortify the wine. Part of the trouble was a quarrel between Hinton's and the *aguardenteiros*, the cane-brandy producers. It was evident that Harry Hinton would have to pay up, an event rather relished by the other English shippers. They had been stung by a ruling in the Portuguese National Assembly, after acrimonious debate, forbidding the use of wine brandy and requiring rectified cane alcohol in its place – the supply of which was controlled by Hinton's with their sugar factory.

At the end of the war John Ernest's stepmother Alice came back to Madeira and the Quinta Santa Luzia but soon announced her intention of living permanently in England. Her late husband, John Burden had stipulated in his will that Santa Luzia should be available as her home during her lifetime, but that if she wished to sell, it was to be offered to John Ernest for £10,000, then a considerable sum.

Machinery in the Blandy flour mill

The furniture at the *quinta* was left to Alice and also as much of the furniture as she wished at Palheiro.

'In the months of packing up the furniture, rumours reached my father that she was intending to sell Santa Luzia to Henrique Vieira de Castro,' recalls Graham. 'My father was by no means anxious to have the *quinta* but he did not wish to see the old family place sold to other hands … Incredibly enough Grandma Alice never discussed the matter with my father and time went on till the date when Escritura for sale was to be signed. My father then gave a power of attorney to Francisco Conceição Rodrigues, the firm's confidential clerk who was later to become Editor of the *Diário de Notícias*, to represent him at the Escritura and to Grandma Alice's discomfiture and embarrassment he exercised my father's option on the property, which was going to be sold outside for a much larger figure.'

Alice took with her much of the old furniture from Santa Luzia as well as pieces from Palheiro. These included the picture of a negro painted by King Dom Carlos of Portugal and given to John Burden who had delicately declined the title of Conde when the king came to lunch at Palheiro on 24th June 1901.

John Ernest had not been brought up to manage a large business and when the slump came in 1921 the firm found itself in difficulties. The capital requirements of the London business, especially the wine department, were substantial and there had been an unfortunate investment in national taxicabs

Before their amalgamation in 1900, the ships of the Union and Castle Lines competed fiercely on the England– South Africa run, the Castle Line usually having the advantage. After 1874 when the Great Eastern laid the cable to Madeira, passengers eagerly awaited the latest news which was available on arrival at Madeira. The ships of the two lines also provided transport for wine and produce for Covent Garden market, particularly French beans in the winter. In the 1890s and the early 1900s, eggs were shipped to South Africa in great quantities in baskets on deck. In addition, the ships took on large supplies of fresh provisions for the passengers and crew.

The Union ships were named patriotically after the peoples of Britain. Blandy ship accounts from 1868 onwards mention Celt, Anglian, Roman, Norseman, Briton, Cambrian, Saxon and Dane. The calls were initially made for coal and water which was taken out in wooden pipes (barrels). When Dane arrived on 18 June 1868 she took on four adult passengers and five children, all members or connections of the Blandy family, including the Reverend Hugh Nelson Ward, who was the son of Emma Hamilton's daughter by Nelson, and had married a Miss Blandy.

The first Castle Line ship to call was the Gothland which had sailed from Southampton in seven days, arriving on 14 February 1872.

The Fábrica dos Lavradores, Blandy's first flour mill early in the 20th century

which turned out to be a 100 per cent loss.

The Blandy venture into flour milling was also proving troublesome. In Madeira the degree of protection afforded by the government to the flour millers had been reduced, and foreign flour imports had increased, putting all the local mills into difficulties. The situation was aggravated by the violent fluctuations of wheat prices, which from high levels of £30 to £40 per ton came down to as little as something over £4 per ton for Danubian wheat in the late 1930s.

'Complaints about the price of bread and flour were constant,' wrote Graham, 'and there were frequently riots and disturbances principally directed against Blandy Brothers and Henrique Figueira da Silva, the only millers who continued in the struggle … popular feeling was stirred up against the millers, and the bakers took a leading part in these activities. The riots were very severe and Henrique Figueira de Silva's house, Quinta da Penha, had a bomb thrown at it. Conceição Rodrigues, the editor of the *Diário de Notícias*, regarded by many as the firm's evil genius, had to escape into the hills on one occasion and was smuggled on board a Castle boat on the way to England having shaven off his black beard and so being unrecognised. On another occasion

when walking along the streets of the town he was crowned with a familiar item of crockery!'

The firm then decided to make bread and macaroni itself. The position, according to Graham, 'was that the much-maligned millers were really making substantial losses, while the bakers, who had been leading the hue and cry against the millers, had been doing very nicely'. Plans were drawn up for the Padaria dos Lavradores buildings and plant which were completed in 1924–5 after the vast sum of £125,000 had been spent.

'It was built of brick imported in schooners from Portugal – said to be cheaper than masonry. A Mr A.K. Harris was consulting engineer and he designed everything on a big scale – evil tongues said that this was to increase his illicit earnings. It was established that he had received a commission from Babcock and Wilcox, the boiler makers, to which he was not entitled, but the firm did not take proceedings as it would have been useless.'

The mill was 'designed to bake enough bread for the whole of Funchal, and with its own power house, etc, it was a white elephant; instead of making money it started to lose it on a great scale for want of turnover'. The sales of bread after the initial opening were only about 20 per cent of the

John Ernest and Elinor Blandy with their son Graham in 1924

It was alarmingly apparent that a still more radical overhaul was needed, and in 1926 the partners decided to seek the advice of Sir Basil Mayhew, the head of their auditors, Barton Mayhew & Co., and of Sir Herbert Blain, a business doctor who had reorganised the London Underground and other concerns. These two gentlemen investigated the affairs of Blandy's in London and came out to Madeira and Las Palmas. Their recommendations were drastic and involved the partners in unpleasant decisions. This included the loss of many old friends who had jobs in one or other of the businesses.

capacity of the plant.

The position was serious and as a protective measure on 4 June 1925 the partnership was turned into a limited company (Sociedade por Quotas Limitada), Blandy Brothers & Co. Lda. The partners took up quotas in place of their former holdings, becoming directors. These were J.E. Blandy, chairman, C.M. Blandy, R.R. Faber and D.O. Davies.

In Madeira retrenchment began at the milling and bakery section. Richard Denis Blandy was the head, assisted by Malcolm Boileau who, despite his local experience, had no knowledge of the trade. Richard Denis, who had earlier been with the Indian police, left Madeira and his family finally settled in Australia.

Next they had to dispense with the services of W.R. Bardsley who was then joint manager with

I n 1904 John Burden Blandy and his partner Maurice Faber were drawn into a storm over proposals by a German syndicate to build sanatoria in Madeira. The heated correspondence, preserved in leatherbound volumes in the National Archives at Kew, involved the British Minister in Lisbon, Sir Martin Gosselin; the Foreign Secretary, the Marquess of Lansdowne; Consul J. Bowring Spence as well as the Portuguese Minister of Foreign Affairs, Senhor Wenceslau de Lima. The affair also provides an insight into the fierce commercial and imperial rivalry between Britain and Germany which led up to the First World War, complete with a sense of intrigue worthy of John Buchan's novel Greenmantle.

On 15 June 1903, Gosselin wrote to Lansdowne saying: 'The newspapers report that an endeavour is being made to found a company for the exclusive right to build sanatoria in Madeira for the treatment of tuberculosis, the State to receive one-third of the net receipts and in return to grant free entry for the materials needed and exemption from the property tax.' A week later Maurice Faber penned a letter to the British consul: 'Dear Spence, My idea of the whole thing is that a gambling concession must be included and that the sanatoria and other points are only a cloak. To me the suggestion of even getting a couple of million sterling for running sanatoria and a steamship line for the people to fill them is too preposterous. But given a gambling concession the whole thing becomes feasible.'

On 2 October 1903, William and Alfred Reid wrote indignantly to Gosselin:

'We have been established since 1850 when our father opened an hotel which was afterwards well known as the Royal Edinburgh Hotel. In 1873 he

Major Courtenay Shaw. Major Shaw was appointed sole general manager and W.R.Bardsley died a year or two later of cancer. E.W. Krohn, who was the joint manager with Simão Correia Neves of the new banking department, also had to go. E.W. Krohn's own wine business had collapsed with the disappearance of the Russian wine market and, although he had no previous banking experience, John Ernest had helped him by providing him with the job. Krohn then went with his family to Rustenberg in the Transvaal where he settled and became a farmer. His son Raleigh remained in Madeira in the employ of the Madeira Wine Association which however he left in the mid-1940s and joined an embroidery firm. He departed Madeira in 1953 for the Bahamas where he prospered, returning in the 1960s with his wife Heather and eventually settling in Porto Santo. E.W. Krohn who wore a pointed brown beard was nicknamed locally the Holy Father and consequently his father was called the Holy Ghost.

There were cuts too in the accounts department. These involved giving notice to a head bookkeeper and staff economies in the shipping coal departments where several older employees were pensioned off. Conceição Rodrigues was removed from the editorship of the *Diário*. Graham wrote, 'This man, clever and with a destructive pen, had often used the *Diário* for his own ends which resulted in prejudice to the firm. He confined his activities subsequently to being head of the Portuguese shipping department and to the firm's confidential matters. During the Madeira Revolution of 1931 he was implicated, imprisoned and deported and the opportunity was then taken of dispensing with his services and he retired on pension to Lisbon. The new editor was Professor Feliciano Soares who held the position for a year or two … He was not able to stand the strain and handed over in 1931 to his assistant, Dr Alberto de Araújo, in whose capable hands it continued for forty-three years. He took over on 1 April 1931, the day the Madeira Revolution started.'

In Las Palmas there were staff cuts at the central office, the motor department shop in Triana was closed, and unwanted premises such as the Bazar Victorias and an electricity undertaking sold. Blandy's coal and shipping interests were pooled with other firms.

In London the Wine Department was closed, dispensing with the services of two managers and their staff. Blandy's London office were not only the agents for the firm's Madeiras but also for other wines including Henriot champagne, hock, sherry, South Australian wine and Scottish and Irish whiskies. 'The capital involved in holding stocks and in debtors was considerable and the closure of the department helped the financial position very considerably,' said Graham. The firm left spacious and expensive premises at 106 Fenchurch Street for cheaper offices. Older employees were pensioned off.

opened and carried on the Santa Clara Hotel. In 1880 he also took over the Carmo Hotel, and in 1891 we, my brother and I, built and established the Reid's New Hotel. During all these years we have paid full duties for building materials, on all furniture etc imported, and now we learn … a concession has been granted … at the request of Prince Hohenlohe, to build sanatoria for rich and poor, and to provide luxuriously appointed hotels for rich only; and that all materials for building, all furniture, linen, fittings, however costly, are to be admitted free of duties.'

The next March Gosselin wrote to Lansdowne quoting the arguments for the sanatoria: 'Madeira had for so long been a place of resort for consumptive patients that the disease had got a stronghold of the native population, and it was highly desirable that some check should be put on the propagation of the disease … Prince Hohenlohe had stated he hoped to arrange that the steamers of one of the large German lines should call at Lisbon and Madeira, performing the voyage in twenty-four hours, about half the time now employed by the Portuguese steamers plying between the capital and the island.' Further alarm was sparked by the news that on 10 March a party of eighteen Germans had left Hamburg comprising 'medical men, hydraulic and electrical engineers, agricultural and farming experts and architects'.

On 3 June Gosselin received a letter signed by Blandy Brothers, Cossart Gordon, Leacock's and Reid Brothers, expressing concern at another proposed concession to the Germans relating 'to the exclusive right for the water supply. It is almost impossible for anyone not connected to the island to imagine the magnitude of this concession: the water rights in a climate, such as ours, are the most important feature in any property or industry, and enormous

With the reorganisation completed in 1927, it was decided to engage an expert at a high salary to try and solve the problem of the flour and baking business. 'Mr H. J. Ward of Southampton then appeared, made many economies at once and recommended that we put up the price of our flour from our mill and put the price of bread and macaroni down, so as to hurt our chief opponents, the bakers,' Graham recalled. 'This prejudiced the bakers considerably and they came to the erroneous conclusion that they too must have a mill to oppose us on equal terms. They built a mill, Moagem da Anadia, and equipped it with two cheap but inefficient Tattershall mills, but soon found they were running into heavy losses. It was clear that the only thing to be done was to amalgamate and they approached us for this process ... agreement was finally reached on the premises of some of the Companhia Insular de Moinhos partners who sold flour, macaroni and bread.'

Before the First World War Blandy's had been the agents of all the principal British shipowners, except Elder Dempster, who had established their own little office in Funchal. Blandy's also represented the Hamburg America Line and the Woermann Line. 'In those days there was free immigration into the United States and the Cunard Line used to operate liners between Italy and Spain and New York, calling at Madeira to pick up the Madeira emigrants,' said Graham. 'This useful business ceased with the US restricted immigration,

about 1919 I think, and the line was abandoned.'

In 1889 the building of the sea wall connecting the Loo Rock with the shore was completed. Beyond the Loo Rock a further 317 metres of docking area was added between 1934 and 1939. The final phase, adding a further 317 metres, was completed in 1961.

When the great hurricane of 15 December 1926 was approaching, the Captain of the Port ordered all craft into the shelter of the Pontinha. The owner of the yacht *Physalia*, built in Madeira by the Cabrestante, Humberto dos Passos Freitas, refused to obey. He was a flamboyant type, and his small yacht had been built with the idea of exploring the South Seas. Confident it would survive the storm, he remained on board with an Englishwoman. When the hurricane reached its height the *Physalia* was thrown up on the beach in front of the Palácio de S. Lourenço. Afonso Coelho, a Blandy harbour man, at great risk succeeded in boarding the yacht between two huge waves and wrenched open the cabin door to find it empty. The belief that Humberto might have survived persisted for a year until his ring was found on the sand with an inscription that tempted fate: 'only God can best me'.

Meanwhile Blandy's continued its substantial operations in the Canary Islands. 'When I first came to the firm of Las Palmas in 1925, the bunkering trade there was still brisk and we were in competition with Miller & Company, Wilson Sons & Co., and others,' wrote Graham. 'D O. Davies, one of

sums of money have been spent by British merchants and manufacturers in acquiring these rights, for their industrial and commercial pursuits ... The belief is indeed rapidly gaining ground that the real aim of the German syndicate is much more far reaching than the mere investment of capital, and everything points to its being meant to be used as the thin end of the wedge, with which British influence in Madeira will be destroyed and replaced by a predominant German one.'

Questions in Parliament provoked a furious response in Germany. An article in the Kolnischer Zeitung, on 18 July 1904, headed 'England as Dog in the Manger,' stated that '... criticism in the British House of Commons makes it the duty of German politicians to further this undertaking. We cannot possibly allow a German private undertaking, that is being carried out under the approval of a friendly power, to be undermined by English diplomacy

Due to the shortage of coin in Madeira, tokens were minted by companies needing to trade with local merchants

The staircase at Quinta Santa Luzia is made from mahogany salvaged from the clipper Red Jacket

etc.' In Madeira, business prospered greatly, helped by the fact that Wilson's depot at Ajuda was 'badly placed and unapproachable in bad weather. I came up from Las Palmas to Madeira in the summer of 1926 and this coincided with the British coal strike and we had enormous demands for coal made on us by the Union Castle and many other lines. Coal had to be imported from the USA (quite unheard of in those days) and I remember that when one large collier *Commercial Traveller* arrived after a long trip across the Atlantic, her cargo of American coal was already heating from internal combustion much to the detriment of our coal bags. These were made of tarred hemp sacking and tarred hemp rope, and cost many times more than the coal they contained.'

Supplies to the Union Castle were very large indeed. When the liners came in they were surrounded by a fleet of coal lighters and water barges. The latter were equipped with steam winches which were used to complement the ship's own winches for hoisting slings of coal bags on board. 'We were told that the speed of bunkering at Madeira compared favourably to that at Southampton where mechanical bunkering was the rule of the day,' said Graham. When the General Strike began in England on 3 May, halting supplies of coal, Madeira became a crucial source. On 18 May the *Edinburgh Castle* took 2,014 tons. The *Kenilworth Castle* took 1,999 tons a week later and the *Walmer Castle* 2,400 tons a fortnight after that. The Union Castle ships called weekly.

our partners, was the first to realise the advantages of joint handling arrangements with our neighbours in Las Palmas … This resulted in immense economies in office staff, crews of tugs and lighters, depots

… Certain Englishmen, about forty years ago, chose Madeira as a fresh-air resort. They built hotels and villas (quintas) and possessed themselves of the whole trade, especially of the wine trade and the coal depots. But they did not understand how to make anything out of this fruitful island.' These arguments, however, were undermined by the absurd claim that 'the hotels have gone to ruin, the villas are deserted, the wine trade lives on fraud, and Madeira, if things go on as they are, will lose its importance as a coaling station, at least for those lines whose steamers most frequently cast anchor there'.

Maurice Faber's gentle humour proved to be closer to the mark when he wrote on 31 December: 'Where is the sanatorium? It does not exist. The Germans have built at Sant Anna a splendid hotel thickly bedded in carpets and studded with mirrors, with American bar and billiard room, and now, this week, arrived three French cooks for it … is this a sanatorium? The Germans themselves acknowledge, when they are off their guard, that it is nothing of the kind, and they think the whole business a large joke, and it is.'

Despite the scare, the Blandys kept their coaling and water stations, and the Reids their hotels.

The strains of running such a large and diverse business empire were beginning to tell on John Ernest. When his son Graham joined the firm in 1927 he found his father 'a tired and disillusioned man' whose principal pleasure was the estate at Palheiro. 'In 1927 he developed diabetes and under pressure from his partners …decided to take things more easily, though like many men he thought he was indispensable.'

When his wife Elinor became seriously ill in the American Hospital at Neuilly, John Ernest was distraught. He took her to recuperate at Salzburg but put on a lot of weight. One day it was noticed he had a large lump on his elbow. Too late it was recognised as a clot which shifted suddenly, causing a stroke on 21 March 1930. The doctor, Graham recalled, 'was immediately summoned and gave him a heart injection after which my father talked a little and Dr Scott went off to a dinner party'. The next morning the severity of his illness was immediately apparent and he died a month later.

'My mother was heartbroken and it took her a long time to recover' wrote Graham. Her great joy was to take her daughters Hermione and Rosemary to Pontresina in Switzerland. Hermione became an expert climber and made the first ascent by direct route of the southern wall of Pomagagnon in the Italian Dolomites. She also made the first ascent by a woman of the north ridge of Piz Badile in the Bregaglia range, considered one of the great climbs. When the Second World War broke out Elinor was at Palheiro, where her sons had advised her to spend the summer in view of the tense international situation. Here she continued to come each summer during the war, spending the rest of the year at Quinta Santa Luzia.

'My father, while greatly respected by all, was considered rather aloof and unapproachable,' said Graham. 'Nevertheless in his own home he was a marvellous host and a remarkable raconteur. He wore an eyeglass, which when the point of the story was reached, he invariably let fall on to his starched shirt.' Dinners involved changing into evening dress with stiff shirts and collars after a bath, with four-course dinners consisting of soup, fish, meat and pudding followed by Madeira wine – his favourite was the São Martinho 1870. 'He enjoyed meeting illustrious people, who passed in large numbers in those days by the Union Castle, Royal Mail and Blue Star passenger liners, and often we had breakfast parties for them.'

John Ernest, like many of his generation, smoked Egyptian cigarettes (Abdulla No. 16). He enjoyed his pre-dinner drink, though 'he never touched whisky except in his afternoon tea when he was tired'. In his later years he became interested in coins, buying a large collection from Blandy's wine salesman in France, Monsieur Genin. Despite his shy and aloof manner, John Ernest was quietly both kind and generous. In 1925 the firm was unable to pay a dividend and Dudley Davies, a cousin and a director in Las Palmas, was in severe difficulty having just completed a new house, Greystones, at great expense. John Ernest promptly paid over half his director's fee of £1,500 to help with the education of Dudley's young children.

John Ernest and his son John Reeder, then 20, in the Azores in 1929

5. Riots and Revolution

Blandy's newest venture, banking was
proving an unexpected success

Graham Blandy with his
Rhodesian ridgeback Pondo at the
lookout point where the Palheiro
Golf club house now stands

Diaries, letters and business records help to reconstruct the lives of past Blandys but with Graham, who died in 1972, memories are still fresh. The ancient Blandy chairmen stare severely from their sepia portraits, their expressions stiffened by the long exposures of old camera film. Graham's life is more accessible and is given colour by those who remember him, not least his sons, Adam and John. Through him it is possible to imagine something of the character of his forebears. Foremost was his sense of duty to the company and to the British community. His researches into both the family and the firm form the backbone of large parts of this book. Writing came naturally to him. For many years he contributed reports to *The Times* of London and his booklet on the 150th anniversary of Blandy's in 1961 is a model of clarity and concision. Although not a contemplative man, he was widely read in history, which gave added interest to his meetings with visitors to the island such as Churchill and Anthony Eden.

Percy Graham was just twenty-five when he was thrust into the role of chairman on his father's death in April 1930. He had never liked the name Percy and to family and friends he was known as Graham – though in the many notes he wrote about the business he signed himself PGB.

Graham was born in December 1904, at Quinta Favila in Funchal, followed by Hermione, John and Rosemary. He was nicknamed Togo after the Japanese naval leader of the Russian-Japanese war, when Britain supported the Japanese. His father, John Ernest, kept a horse in the stable under the *mirante* or look-out tower. This also housed the ponies which Graham and Hermione exercised along the New Road, then still unpaved and more suitable for ponies.

On Sundays the children would be taken to the country and enjoyed kite-flying. They had an English nurse, Cissie Higgin, followed by a succession of governesses. In the summer they would go up to Palheiro, which John Burden lent to his son while he went to Salzburg or Vichy for a cure. 'We used to go up in a caravan, women and children in bullock cars and servants also, while my father rode up and the *arriero* (groom) brought up the ponies,' he wrote. Once at Palheiro they never left the estate except for picnics on the *serras*. On these excursions mother and younger children would travel by hammock, the older ones rode with their father.

In 1913 the family summered at Westgate-on-Sea, before Graham was left at prep school. Later he wrote: 'World War I broke out in August 1914, but I was able to come out to Madeira until the summer holidays of 1916, after which sea travel became too dangerous' thanks to German submarines. A number of his schoolboy letters and postcards survive. One reads 'Dear Dada, I have some proper bat oil now, the destroyer *Maori* has been sunk. Much love Graham' and another four-liner announces the sinking of the *Lusitania*.

Graham, who was 11 years old at the time of the Battle of Jutland in 1916, had a schoolboy passion for Royal Navy warships and filled a sketchbook with drawings of them

School holidays were now spent in considerable grandeur with Grandma Alice at Sidmouth, Worthing and 1 Wilton Crescent in London. She was by then living with a wealthy American called Louis Sterne, who was in his seventies. He had been an inventor and had founded the firm of L. Sterne & Co., refrigerating machinery manufacturers who supplied the ice-making plant at Palheiro. Sterne claimed that in his younger days he had been partly responsible for the transport of Cleopatra's Needle from Egypt to London's Embankment. During the war, when petrol was rationed, Mr Sterne had the luxury of an electric motor car.

It was not until February 1919 that Graham saw his mother and father again. By this time he was at Rugby and his parents had to exert great pressure on the school to secure him leave over a Saturday night. 'I found my father much aged: his partners Dick Faber had gone to London to manage the business and Walter Faber had been killed in action.'

Graham went on to Oxford where he rowed for Oriel College. He joined his father at the family firm in 1927 when drastic cuts were in full swing, though by John Ernest's death in 1930 things were improving again.

Blandy's newest venture, banking, was proving an unexpected success. The banking department had started in 1923 and was run by Simão Correia Neves. Prior to his appointment John Ernest had consulted the director of the Bank of Portugal, Francisco Meira, and received a telegram saying: 'You can count on Neves.'

Neves was with them till his retirement in 1958 at the age of seventy when Graham recalled: 'The banking department started with a tiny staff of half a dozen opposite the Portuguese shipping department. By 1927 they occupied the whole of the eastern end of the building. Growth was slow but steady, in spite of the American stock market crash of 1929 and its effects on all countries including Madeira.' A

Blandy's Bank in the 1930s – two streets down from the cathedral

Bags of flour seized by local people during the 1931 Revolution

series of local banks did close, Henrique Figueira da Silva (HFS) in 1930, followed by Banco da Madeira, Banco Sardinha and Reid Castro. The Banco Nacional Ultramarino and Blandy's banking department alone remained open, all the more an achievement in view of John Ernest's death in 1930.

'We were paying 8 per cent on current accounts, and charging customers higher rates on overdrafts,' wrote Graham. 'HFS were paying 12 per cent to depositors and were financing many firms which were bankrupt. In the final liquidation the creditors of HFS received a distribution of slightly over 30 per cent.'

Even so Graham recalled: 'Our enemies in Madeira did not expect that the firm would be able to maintain its leading position and to retain its important steam-ship agencies, as I was then a very young man and John was still at Oxford and had not started business.'

The Wall Street Crash nonetheless had a savage impact on the Madeira economy. American restrictions on the import of Madeiran embroideries increased unemployment and the flow of tourists declined sharply.

In January 1931, the government in Lisbon issued an edict re establishing a monopoly on flour imports – the so-called Hunger Decree which prompted public protests, followed on 6 February by a strike of the stevedores which brought the port to a standstill. People marched through the city streets shouting 'close it – close it', and for almost a week shops, industries, public offices and schools were shut. During a clash in Funchal's Pelourinho Square three people and a policeman died.

'The mill and the bakery were broken into and sacked and a great deal of damage of a superficial nature was done,' recalled Graham. 'The managers had to escape into the country to avoid being captured by the mob who were howling for their blood. The troops and police were quite unable to restrain the rioters and eventually joined them.' Though Blandy's had sold their shareholding the year before to the new company, Graham was

Loaves are brought out of the oven at the Blandy bakery

anxious for the security of Quinta Santa Luzia where the family were living.

'One morning while alone at the office which was closed during the riots except for a faithful continuo or two (like all other businesses) I received a report that the mob were on the way to sack it and the *Diário de Notícias*: I sent a messenger with a note to this effect to J.B. Browne, the British consul, who was at his home Villa Adelaide beyond Reid's and waited as patiently as I could for him to come. Nothing

Fireworks over Funchal welcome in 1935

eventually happened as the mob meanwhile turned their attention to looting the premises of some of the CIM partners who sold flour, macaroni and bread.'

The riots ended with the arrival from Lisbon of a Special Envoy, Silva Leal, with a Rifle Company and a Heavy Weapon Company under the command of Captain Almeida Cabaço. The Hunger Decree was suspended but a draconian witch hunt of Madeiran agitators led by the Special Envoy prompted the Madeira Revolution in early April 1931. The troops brought by Leal turned against him and arrested their captain who had been appointed civil governor.

Though in retrospect this may seem a minor, even slightly comic affair, at the time it posed a serious threat to life as well as property. Vivid details were provided on an almost daily basis by the firm's redoubtable manager Major Shaw. He reported on 6 April 1931: 'A military revolt has taken place …The Swedish Wine Co., Blandy's Madeira and ourselves are endeavouring to insure against riots, civil commotion, bombardment and fire … Although everything is outwardly calm it is freely rumoured that the de facto authorities have informed Lisbon … that they will not surrender in twenty-four hours or in twenty-four months. If this be true it is difficult to imagine the government in Lisbon can do nothing. If a revolt against their authority can succeed in Madeira it will be a signal for similar revolts in other islands.'

The port, he said, was full of shipping. No foreign steamers were being interfered with but ominously the *SS Guiné* which had arrived on Saturday morning,

Mildred and Graham Blandy at Palheiro in 1934 at the time of their marriage

Two days later, on 8 April 1931, a British cruiser, *HMS London*, arrived at Funchal, apparently on a mission as mediator between Lisbon and Madeira. Shaw reported: 'Anxiety is very great among the people as a whole and the revolutionaries are, I hear, extremely nervous and we were really much relieved to see the British cruiser.

PS I will try to get photographs but no cameras are allowed in the streets and I was only able to get the few I am sending by taking them from a building. I have interviewed one photographer and he definitely refuses to take the risk and is considering a retirement in the country.'

Most of Shaw's communications were sent via British steamers as he thought they might be stopped if sent in the ordinary way through the telegraph office. As owners of the daily newspaper, the *Diário*, Blandy's were in a doubly vulnerable position. The paper therefore adopted a stance of strict neutrality. 'In the edition of last Sunday a bare statement of the facts was given,' said Shaw. 'The *Diário* very properly expressed no opinion whatever. This needless to say has not pleased the new people who have made great but unsuccessful efforts to create a favourable press … We are adhering to our policy of reporting facts and no opinions.'

Three days later, on 11 April 1931, he wrote: 'The situation is extremely difficult for Blandy Brothers.

and was due to sail in the afternoon, was still there. Another disturbing aspect was that the takeover had been organised by deportees from Lisbon who had nothing to lose and everything to gain by making trouble.

'I joined in 1958. My father had sent me to London where I did a commercial management course. On my return I had to do National Service. When I finished Graham Blandy said, "Start tomorrow. We need someone in shipping and your English is good." I stayed forty-five years. Living on an island it was like visiting a different country every day. I'd have breakfasts with Russian champagne, British fry-ups and very good curries with the Indian crews on P&O ships. Union Castle called on Sundays, southbound for Cape Town, northbound ships called on Monday. They carried a lot of passengers. South Africans were not fond of flying. The ships brought tourists who would spend two weeks here. Then the flying boats started — we weren't the agents — but this finished suddenly with a dreadful accident in the Isle of Wight.

The Royal Mail had a line going to South America. The Blue Star Line also called in on the same route. We had the Brazilian Star, the Argentine Star and the Uruguay Star. The Booth Line from Liverpool called on the way to the West Indies and Brazil. We acted for the Elder Dempster Line serving Nigeria and the Ivory Coast bringing wood from Africa. Blandy's were agents for Norwegian-American, Swedish-American and the Bergen Line. In the 1960s cruising started with the Booth Line followed by Blue Star, Royal Mail, Union Castle and P&O. After the Suez Crisis in 1956 ships had to take the Cape route again.

The cruising boom also brought ships from Russia — the Baltic Steamship Co. from Leningrad and the Black Sea Shipping Co. from Odessa which lasted till the early 1990s. The Cunard Queens came with three funnels and then two — the Queen Mary and Queen Elizabeth and later the QE2.

Advice was given on the morning of the 9th to the Coasting Service verbally by the Captain of the Port that we could not send any steamer to Porto Santo ... or to the north of the island without his previous consent ... [He] explained he could not give written instructions as they were verbal instructions he himself had received from the military command.' A Blandy vessel the *Butio* had been sent by the revolutionaries to the nearby village of Santa Cruz on patrol work and the battery very nearly fired upon her when she dropped anchor. 'We have, of course, only the verbal assurance of the military command that they accept full responsibility for any damage done to the ship while acting under their orders. This action, of course, completely paralyses the Coasting Service.'

Meanwhile the revolutionaries had taken over the Bank of Portugal and started to issue decrees. 'I have just signed a cheque for 250 contos on the Bank of Portugal to see whether they are prepared to pay out the money,' Shaw reported.

The dictatorship in Lisbon then declared a blockade of the island. As a result the power supply was now under threat. 'I understand that there is only enough oil for keeping the town going for about a fortnight at the outside ... If the Portuguese government is capable of effectually blockading Madeira, it cannot be very long before the local

people, who are really not interested in the new government of deportees, begin to take notice ... Up to date the population has been completely apathetic. The popular demonstration last Saturday evening was almost entirely due to a natural instinct to see any fun. On Thursday there was a great parade and ... a multitude of spectators cheered the speeches and acclaimed the march past. Five minutes

Passengers from visiting liners are ferried to the town pier in launches

after the troops had gone there was hardly a soul left in the streets in town.'

The de facto authorities, Shaw said, were now anxious to prove that all foreigners and their property were safe. Though many private cars had

We had to clear ships through customs, both passengers and cargo manifests. We'd supply fresh stores, eggs and butter, water from our own barges and take off waste.

On New Year's Eve there would be a lot of ships in the bay for the fireworks. One year it was so rough they couldn't land passengers or cargo. They just watched the fireworks and steamed on. After India became independent the Americans sent big bulk carriers filled with wheat. To save money they used retired crews who would all come ashore as the ships were dry. It was a big job to round them up from the brothels and sober them up.

The Blandys were British consuls. I had to look after the crews of naval vessels returning from the Falklands War. They drank a lot. They were quite a handful and I didn't want to disturb Mr Blandy.

The Russians had very good captains. They never spoke about Communism. I'd take them ashore for a barbecue. They'd bring vodka and caviare which we ate with a spoon, fantastic crab and smoked salmon which we couldn't get.'

João Carlos Rodrigues, recalling his time in Blandy's shipping department

been requisitioned, foreigners were not affected. The government in Lisbon had sent troops to the Azores to suppress a parallel uprising, but were apparently relying on the blockade 'to bring Madeira to her senses. If they are strong enough to do this it will cause the loss of no life and the destruction of no property.'

A considerable number of visitors were now trapped on the island. 'The calling of the Cape boat tomorrow is doubtful,' Shaw wrote, 'but the homeward boat will be allowed to call in order to evacuate visitors. It may be that the local authorities will allow no mail to go on board but I believe that I have means of ensuring the posting of a few important letters.'

Meanwhile the *Butio* had been sent on patrol work and the crew were getting very nervous but it had since been handed back for a voyage to Porto Moniz, where there was a shortage of food.

Shaw's next message announced: 'We are pretty effectively cut off from the world and we cannot judge whether the patrolling of the streets of Lisbon and the mounting of machine guns at strategic points means simply a demonstration of force on the part of the government, or the result of insipient revolts. This suggested the government in Lisbon is in a tottery condition.'

On 14 April he reported: 'The electric current will be cut off during the day from tomorrow and will only be supplied to private houses between 7 pm and midnight. That will mean that all motors will be put out of action ... We are endeavouring to make special arrangements for continuing the publication of the *Diário* ... It is possible we may be able to fall back on our old steam engine for some work and a good many men will continue to be employed on the *Gavião*. But these are only purely temporary measures and the general activity of Funchal will die.'

Mildred Blandy in the Quinta do Palheiro garden in 1934

Many of the embroidery houses were being affected, putting out of work a very large number of women scattered all over the island. Fortunately Blandy's had sufficient work for some time provided there was money to pay the staff.

The revolutionary government now attempted to alleviate the problem by instructing the banks of the embroidery houses to draw foreign currency cheques on London, Paris or New York. 'You will readily understand that we shall be forced to refuse to do any such thing. No embroidery is being exported and Blandy's Bank are naturally not going to accept bills from embroidery houses on the direction of the Under Secretary for Finance. The British Ambassador has been advised,' Shaw said.

He continued: 'At the same time you will realise that, as we are probably the only bank with any substantial sums available abroad, we shall be in a position of having definitely to refuse to obey a decree nominally introduced for the benefit of Madeira.'

Hopes rose again with the news that the rebellion in the Azores had completely collapsed. Blandy's position remained extremely difficult. 'We have no right to express any opinion as to the suitability of any government that may be in power,' said Shaw. 'We have to endeavour to maintain a position of strict neutrality. This banking decree does not admit of any reasonable compromise ... If the worst comes to the worst I shall simply state that such procedure is contrary to all my instructions and that until I have the unanimous authority of all my directors, I cannot possibly agree.'

Further alarm was prompted by the reappearance on 22 April of the *Diário's* wayward editor, Conceição Rodrigues. 'His arrival at the present juncture is most unfortunate,' said Shaw. 'In the present situation of Madeira it would never do for Blandy's to get rid of one of their old and senior Portuguese employees who has been deported in the manner he was deported ... I have therefore allowed him to resume his work. If the Lisbon government beat the local movement I do not for one instant think FCR will be able to remain in Madeira. Even though

he has not recently taken any part in politics ... he is known to have strong political views and to have been an ardent politician in the past.'

Blandy's strict neutrality created its own problems. 'We are greatly criticised because ships and other agencies come in now and again for their normal commercial operations,' wrote Shaw. 'The Elder Dempster ship today dispatched petrol and cement. The people outside therefore accuse us of trying to keep the steamers away ... At the same time the local people believe that we are instrumental in creating difficulties for the Castle steamers when they arrive by trying to prevent them coming into port. Whatever we do we are liable to offend one or other party and we have had to fix a stereotyped message of instructions for the captains as follows: "Obey owners' instructions."'

What most alarmed Shaw were the financial implications. 'There is always a risk that ... a steamer calling at Madeira without the sanction of the Portuguese government may be fined. In such a case the master would naturally say that he had come into port on the instructions of the agents. This risk we dare not run. Also we cannot send instructions not to call as the local authorities would not forward the message.'

Next he heard that the Blandy vessel, *SS Butio*, 'was being prepared for a voyage to Casablanca and St Vincent, Cape Verde ... The consul ... had decided that it was time for him to make an official protest to the military government, pointing out that the ship represented British capital; that she was not licensed except for Madeira waters; that as soon as she left Madeira waters her insurance with Lloyd's of London automatically lapsed, and that by proceeding beyond Madeira waters British capital ran a grave risk of loss.'

With appropriate irony the rebellion collapsed on May Day. Shaw was exuberant. 'I am anxious to send you a few lines by *HMS London* ... We are all safe and sound. I need hardly say there has been complete paralysis of our business in all sections for the best part of three weeks ... A great number of our staff left Funchal and took their families to the hills and

Passenger liners at anchor in Funchal Bay, 1934

country. This particularly applies to the Coasting Service, the staff of which asked permission some two or three days ago to put their families in safety. There is a general return, however, to Funchal and I hope we may be working reasonably normally not later than Tuesday morning.'

The bank, he said, had kept open as long as possible. 'We closed on Tuesday at two o'clock and opened again on Wednesday morning for half an hour "to show willing". Apart from a few visitors to change cheques there was nothing doing towards the end.'

The main problem had been the bank's cash. 'The safe is an excellent one, but an uninterrupted period of two days – or even less – might have enabled an expert lock picker to open the safe and get away with the contents. Between the head office and the bank we had roughly £13,000. I had it all packed in a tin box and lodged for safekeeping on board the *HMS London*. Graham is arranging to bring this box back this morning.'

A new threat now emerged in Las Palmas, following the outbreak of the much more serious Spanish Revolution in April 1931. Graham Blandy, in his first business coup, was able to turn the situation to advantage. 'Very severe measures were applied against capitalists and owners of property,'

he recalled. 'At the same time, the Royal Mail group of companies under the chairmanship of Lord Kylsant got into extremely severe financial difficulties, resulting in the appointment of the well-known Scottish accountant Sir William McLintock as receiver.'

One of the Kylsant group was the Atlantic Coaling Co. Ltd which had a 45 per cent interest in the engineering company Grand Canary & Blandy's Engineering Co. Ltd. The other 55 per cent was owned by Blandy's Las Palmas firm. Graham was surprised to be asked by Sir William if Blandy's would buy the Atlantic Coaling Co.'s interest in the yard. When he put the matter up to his fellow directors, who were all of his father's generation, they were unwilling to consider the proposal, citing the shortage of capital, the business recession in the UK and the climate of insecurity in the Canary Islands. Deftly Graham persuaded them to make an offer of £5,000. This was considered ludicrously low but much to their surprise was accepted.

Following the brutal attack on Percy George Blandy and his subsequent death in 1902, he had been succeeded, as head of the Las Palmas firm, by John Burden's third son Charles Maurice. He was later joined by his first cousin, Dudley Oliveira Davies. During their time, the advantages of joint handling came to be appreciated and in 1930 the principal British coaling firms which had hitherto been competitors decided to amalgamate, and the Blandy coaling and shipping activities, including Lloyd's agency, were transferred. This resulted in immense economies. The joint venture was also a portent of the future. Apart from a permanent seat on the board of directors, Blandy Brothers took no part in management. Similarly the travel business of the amalgamation was independently conducted in the name of Viajes Blandy.

This step still left the Las Palmas firm with

business of its own. There was the banking department which had been established in the same way as the Madeira banking department, the motor department which held the Morris and Dodge agencies and the Grand Canary and Blandy's Engineering SA which operated two shipyards, the Blandy yard and the former Grand Canary yard.

In 1934 Graham married. His bride, Mildred Edmonds, had been born in South Africa of an English father, Walter, and an Irish mother, Elizabeth Marion Perry, known as May. Mildred's father had emigrated to South Africa when he was seventeen. The family were experiencing hard times, and he joined his brother-in-law who was farming in the Eastern Province. In the Boer War he served as a cornet in Hartigan's Horse. In 1930, when Graham was about to become head of the Blandy business, Mildred was invited by Eddie Dalziel (a cousin through his marriage to a member of the Faber family) to visit Madeira. She came out on the maiden voyage of the *Winchester Castle*, met Graham and married him four years later at the parish church of St Mary the Virgin in Merton (in which Lord Nelson used to worship). They were to have three children: Adam, born the next year, John in 1939 and Annabel in 1945.

In 1936 the Madeira firm celebrated its 125th anniversary and a grand outdoor lunch was held for the Governor and local officials and all the company

All-male banquet at Quinta do Palheiro in 1936 to celebrate the 125th anniversary of Blandy Brothers

George Bernard Shaw taking a dancing lesson while staying at Reid's early in 1925. Shaw, notorious for his forthright opinions, gave the dancing master Max Rinder a signed photograph inscribed 'To the only man who ever taught me anything'

employees in front of the old house at Palheiro on 24th June. The next year, almost by default, Blandy's made one of the most important acquisitions in its history. Though Reid's Hotel had closed during the First World War business had revived quickly. Among the first guests was Prince Arthur of Connaught, a grandson of Queen Victoria, followed the next year by the exiled Emperor Charles of Austria. In 1924 the Irish playwright George Bernard Shaw had come to stay, taking dancing lessons from the Reid's dancing instructor Max Rinder. When he left on board the *Edinburgh Castle* Shaw gave Rinder a signed photograph inscribed 'to the only man who ever taught me anything'. Amy Johnson, the pioneer aviator, came for a spring holiday in 1933. But the hotel was immensely expensive to run and the proprietors were continually forced to raise money, much of it borrowed from Blandy's, who invested in a new west wing. This was intended to provide a large number of comfortable modern bedrooms with superb sea views. Blandy's took control in 1937 but hardly had

The aviation pioneer Amy Johnson at Reid's in 1933. In 1930, less than a year after she gained her pilot's licence, she became the first woman to fly solo from Britain to Australia

the new wing opened when war forced Reid's Hotel to close in 1940.

The Second World War was in Graham's words 'the most critical time in the history of the firm, since all depended on the result'. Proud of being English, he had immediately tried to enlist but had been advised by the Foreign Office to stay in Madeira since his presence there could turn out to be useful to the

Lloyd George, the First World War British Prime Minister, emerges from Reid's during a visit in the 1920s

Allied cause. His children remember that he hung a map of Europe in the library, and excitedly moved flags to show the fast-retreating German army lines towards the end of the war years.

Following the outbreak of war, coal bunkering was brisk, particularly to Danish and Norwegian ships which had to make the longer voyage north round Scotland to reach their home ports. This ended with the German invasion of both countries. British and Allied warships were largely oil fuelled but coal was supplied to a number of armed merchant cruisers.

Switzerland had chartered a number of Greek ships to carry her wheat, coal and steel. When Greece was invaded in 1940 these ships – twelve or thirteen of them – arrived in Madeira consigned to Blandy's, staying for many months while arrangements were made for them to proceed to Italian ports to discharge their cargoes. Graham wrote: 'These ships burned a lot of coal keeping their auxiliary machinery going, and had to be bunkered periodically. Eventually we agreed, at the request of the Swiss Government, to stock their coal, specially imported for the requirements of their chartered ships at a handling charge per ton.'

One morning the remains of a convoy entered the port. The ships were *Volturno, Margot, Blair Athol, Polyktor* (Greek), *Anna Mazaraki* (Greek) and *Clunepark*. All were without their lifeboats except the Scottish ship *Blair Athol*. They had been escorted from Freetown by a British warship which had left them one evening near the Azores, advising them that another British warship would take over the escort the next morning. When dawn broke the German heavy cruiser, *Admiral Hipper*, was sighted. It quickly closed on the defenceless convoy and opened fire, sinking a number of ships at point-blank range. The crews of the remaining vessels rapidly jumped into the lifeboats, awaiting the imminent destruction of their ships. Suddenly a British warship appeared, and the German pocket battleship cruiser swiftly made off. The surviving crews reboarded their ships but were so shaken that none of them, except those on the *Blair Athol*, waited to haul up the empty lifeboats. These were abandoned and left to drift.

Funchal from the sea, 1944

The two or three lifeboats available in Funchal were supplied to the convoy and some local boats were turned into makeshift lifeboats by raising their gunwales and putting buoyancy tanks in them. The convoy was eventually collected by two corvettes and proceeded on its way, after being replenished with coal, water and stores.

Blandy's remained busy in Las Palmas, and Graham made two trips between the islands, first in November 1943 and then in December 1944, in the firm's coasting steamer Gavião. The journey was dangerous owing to German submarines. In Las Palmas he was faced with a serious problem. F. Morrison, who had taken over the firm when Charles Maurice Blandy died in 1940, had proved to have a drink problem and was charitably sent to England for a year to take a cure. It was of no avail and he had to be dismissed on Graham's second visit.

'In the circumstances the idea came to us of selling Grand Canary and Blandy's Engineering SA, which operated two shipping repair yards which now belonged 100 per cent to the firm,' wrote Graham. 'The firm had a most difficult time in the 1930s, but had started to flourish

during the war.' He and his colleagues took the view that this prosperity was likely to be short-lived, and that the employment of a large labour force in a foreign firm might be dangerous. This prompted an ingenious plan which he explained as follows: 'We also operated a banking department there but the capital of the Las Palmas company was only £50,000, and this had to do for the bank and for the motor department: the result was that the capital of £50,000 and more was locked up in the motor department – a highly improper and dangerous situation.'

Under the strict regulations of the Franco government, no new banks were allowed to open – the only possibility was to buy an existing one. Graham learnt that the powerful Banco Español de Crédito of Madrid wanted to open a bank in Las Palmas and an approach was therefore made to them on the basis that Blandy's would be prepared to sell for a goodwill sum of only £5,000, provided the Spanish bank found a purchaser at an agreeable price for the shares of Grand Canary and Blandy's Engineering Co. SA.

The Madrid bank found a purchaser in the shape of Juan March, an anglophile Spaniard of humble

1942 poster of the Blandy office with the tower of the cathedral in the background

Neatly ordered rows of office desks and filing cabinets in the Blandy offices shortly before they were rebuilt

mistake to have sold the Engineering Co., as it has continued to prosper. Its sale has greatly diminished the firm's standing in the Canary Islands. But about the bank I have no regrets at all, and the decision then taken was absolutely right.'

He added: 'The complicated negotiations with the Banco Español de Crédito and with Juan March's emissary, Don Emilio Suarez Fiol, were carried out in a magnificent way by Don Hammond, a most able negotiator.'

The business of the Las Palmas firm was now reduced to the motor department, which held the sole distributorship in the Canary Islands for Firestone tyres and the Morris and Dodge franchises, though at the end of the war there were no vehicles to sell. Don Hammond took the helm.

The Canary Islands at the end of 1944 were at an all-time low. Following the ravages of the Spanish Civil War of 1936–9, Spain had commonly been held to be pro-Nazi, in view of the massive help which General Franco had received from Germany. Consequently the Allies had done nothing to rebuild the shattered Spanish economy.

origin who, although almost illiterate, rose to become a millionaire and, incidentally, performed valuable services to Allied escape routes during the war. The sale of the bank and of the engineering company took place at the end of 1944 for the welcome price of around £200,000.

Reflecting on the transaction two decades later, Graham observed, 'Supported as I was by the unanimous advice of my counsellors, in view of the circumstances of that time, I now feel that it was a

The Lloyd's agency system, a global network of around 340 firms which provide surveying and adjusting services to the insurance market, was established in 1811, the year John Blandy set up business. Madeira was the thirty-fourth appointment made, one of the first four outside the UK, as minuted by the committee of Lloyd's on 27 November 1811. On 6 March 1878, Blandy Brothers took over, representing the Lloyd's agency at Las Palmas in 1896. A Madeira Centenary Luncheon given by the chairman of Lloyd's was held on 1 June 1978, attended by John Reeder Blandy and his son Richard, the sixth generation of the family in the business. Today Agencia de Navegacão Blandy Ltd. ranks twentieth in seniority amongst current Lloyd's agents and is one of only thirty-nine to have been appointed in the nineteenth century. Kristiansand are the oldest Lloyd's agent, appointed in December 1814.

The horseshoe staircase in the Blandy offices in 1949. This is still to be seen in the Rua de Alfandega. This staircase was also made from wood salvaged from the clipper Red Jacket

The London office also had a difficult time during the war. Dick Faber fell seriously ill with cancer of the lung, and though he continued to come to the office he became gradually weaker and finally died in 1943. 'Fire watching by the staff was the order of the day, and several incendiaries fell on the building and had to be dealt with,' wrote Graham. During the Blitz on 17 April 1941 a bomb fell outside and gutted St Olave's Church just opposite, and other sufferers in the neighbourhood were the Port of London Authority building and the Cornmarket. Mark Lane, where the firm had been so long, was almost totally destroyed. London House was marked with bomb splinters and had its windows broken but survived otherwise intact.

'V1s or flying bombs started about the time of the invasion of Normandy in June 1944 and it was not an unusual sight to see three or four of these machines from the windows of the office,' noted Graham. 'Then came the V2s or giant rockets, but London survived both of these attacks.'

After Dick Faber left the office, the operation was carried on by E.W. Tunbridge and J. Rawlings while N. Lane Matthews ran a subsidiary that did business with India. John Maurice Blandy, who was a junior member of the staff before the war, joined the London Scottish Regiment and was killed at the landing at Anzio on 4 February 1944. H.D. "Hopper" Read also joined up and was absent from the firm throughout the war.

In Madeira Blandy's did not cease all building activities during the war as would have been the case in London, and they were able to reconstruct their premises at Avenida Arriaga 11, known as *a Brasileira* (the Brazilian woman) as they had been the offices of the Brazilian Submarine Telegraph Co. when

Over the next twenty years, Don Hammond built up thriving businesses in both Las Palmas and Tenerife from almost nothing. 'As happens only too rarely, he was the right man in the right place at the right time,' said Graham. He was assisted by two able colleagues, Don Laureano de Armas and Andrew Dunlop. Don Laureano was a charming and able Spaniard who had been a great personal friend of Charles Maurice. Foreseeing the possible entry of Spain on the side of the Axis powers at the beginning of the war, Charles Maurice had appointed him in an honorary capacity to the board of the Las Palmas company, with full powers to take what action he thought fit should he, Charles Maurice, be interned by the enemy. Unhappily Don Laureano, who had married a Swiss woman, died in Switzerland in 1948. Andrew Dunlop, a Scottish chartered accountant, had been in charge of the Las Palmas office of the firm's auditors, Barton Mayhew & Co., during the war years. He left them in 1947 to become financial director and second in command to Don Hammond and served the firm loyally until he retired in 1970. He died in Las Palmas in 1978.

The Blandy coaster Gavião *passes the Norwegian ship* Enio *in 1948*

the first undersea cable to Brazil was laid in 1873. Blandy's had bought the building in the 1930s as it was between the wine store and Bentham's Tea Rooms, both of which belonged to the firm. Both the Brazileira and Bentham's were given a homogenous façade in 1940–1, in streamlined Modernist style. The east part (or Bentham's) was used by the British Consulate and Naval Control during the latter part of the Second World War.

One of the more curious cases Graham Blandy had to deal with as a Lloyd's agent concerned the local manager of the Fidelidade Insurance Company, Carlo Rocha. Before the war Rocha had stumbled as he came out of his house one morning and pierced his eye on an orange tree. Six months earlier he had taken out a personal injury policy and was claiming £10,000. Blandy's were asked by Lloyd's to investigate but as there was no suspicion of fraud Lloyd's duly paid up. After war broke out Mr Rocha's name re-emerged in a most unwelcome manner.

Blandy Brothers' business in Madeira was much reduced and rumours were circulating, wrote Graham, 'to the effect that not only was the firm in a bad way but that I myself was in difficulties and had had to borrow money. Mr Neves told me of these rumours but I dismissed them as being "just another Madeira story".'

He continued: 'In 1943 I was told that not only were these rumours current but that certain people had actually seen promissory notes signed by myself for £5,000. Photostatic copies of these were obtained and there appeared to be no doubt that my signature was genuine. In some cases I had signed as an individual and in others as director of Blandy Brothers with the appropriate rubber stamp.'

These promissory notes took the form of rather broad but narrow pieces of paper with the typing lengthways, in rather large characters, unlike those of Graham's typewriter or of any machine in the office. It was decided to make a request to the police for the arrest of Rocha, who was the holder of these 'promissory notes', for suspected fraud. The Chief of Police was at first disinclined to take action on the grounds that the prima facie evidence suggested that Rocha's story and the promissory notes might be genuine. But he was persuaded and Rocha was arrested only to be released. It was decided to apply to Lisbon for a detective to be sent to Madeira for the express purpose of unravelling the mystery. 'On his arrival we were still at a loss to explain the existence of these promissory notes, though we considered that my signature was probably genuine and that the wording had been typed above my signature afterwards,' said Graham.

The detective interviewed Rocha who stuck to his story. The police then had the idea of greatly enlarging the promissory notes and projecting them on to a screen by means of a magic lantern. 'This was done at the police station and it was evident that some of the notes had been typed on paper which had been used for carbon copies as the amplification threw up faint lines made by the roller of the typewriter, which were reproduced on the paper through the carbon copying paper. These lines were so faint as to be invisible without being enlarged. A search was made through our files of correspondence with the Fidelidade Company on labour insurance matters and of my own file dealing with the insurance of labour at Palheiro, and it was seen that the duplicates of "additionals" to Labour Insurance Policies consisted of a long sheet of paper on which the typewritten "additional" clause occupied quite a small space, leaving a fairly big space above my signature. It was then evident that Rocha had used the "additionals" (of which he often wanted several copies) for the purpose of faking promissory notes by cutting the paper in the right place and typing the promissory notes above my signature. During the course of years he must have acquired quite a stock of suitable bits of paper with my signature on!'

It was not thought that Rocha ever intended to present these promissory notes for payment. Graham concluded that 'as the £10,000 obtained from Lloyd's [for the loss of his eye] diminished, he no doubt used these promissory notes with my signature to hoodwink others and obtain money from them'.

The detective then saw Rocha and after several long sessions obtained a complete written confession from him. At the subsequent trial Rocha denied the truth of this confession on the grounds that it had been obtained under duress. A missing link was the typewriter on which the documents had been typed. No similar machine existed in the Fidelidade office. Rocha admitted that he had had a machine, but said he had sold it to someone who had gone to Lisbon. Interrogation of Rocha's servant brought forth the information that Rocha had been seen to go out at night with a spade and had been digging in his banana *fazenda* (plot). The detective proceeded to the spot and unearthed the typewriter which had been smashed, but enough remained of the keys to identify them as belonging to the machine used for typing the promissory notes. Rocha had also defrauded the Fidelidade Insurance Company of some thousands of pounds.

The trial took place in April 1946. Rocha was convicted and sentenced to fifteen years. Not long after, it emerged that his eye had been removed under anaesthetic by a compliant doctor.

After the Second World War Blandy's decided to open an office in Lisbon. Previously they had been represented by Senhor Arsénio C. Cunha and then

The workshop of the Blandy shipyard at the Arsenal, where the Porto Santa Maria Hotel now stands

While the office performed useful services for coal imports to Lisbon, there were severe difficulties in getting any worthwhile new business. In 1949 Tomás Santos fell seriously ill with alarming fainting fits. He had developed a disorder of the inner ear called Ménière's disease, and the firm arranged for him to be sent to the London Hospital under Sir Horace Evans, the King's physician. Tomás Santos recovered but to lighten his workload was redeployed to Madeira where he worked till his death in 1974.

Patriotically Graham wished to support the post-war British Export Drive and imagined that the capital he had nurtured so carefully during the war years would enable a Lisbon branch to trade profitably by the importing and selling of English manufactured machinery. In this, however, he was mistaken and it quickly became clear that Blandy's competitors in this line of business were immeasurably stronger.

The management of the Lisbon office was now entrusted to Lieutenant Colonel N.M.G. Leslie who had served for a time as military attaché at the British Embassy and appeared to have many valuable contacts. As Colonel Leslie had already started his own business, an agreement was made with him on the basis of a joint venture, which commenced operations in November 1950. This turned out to be a complete failure as Colonel Leslie, who had many social qualities, lacked the necessary business expertise for this difficult job. The joint venture was therefore terminated in 1952 and Colonel Leslie's place taken by Tom Mullins's son, Major Rupert Mullins, who had been manager of the Madeira firm from 1946 to 1951 and recently resigned to seek new opportunities. He took over the Lisbon office in September 1952 with Gastão Martins as manager. This combination proved successful and when Rupert Mullins moved to England in March 1964 the Lisbon office was running smoothly.

Banger's Pillar, a landmark on the Avenida do Mar that was demolished in 1939. Signalling flags for shipping were flown from the pillar

by his son Dr Paulo Cunha who became Portuguese Foreign Minister in 1950. Graham wrote: 'These gentlemen, great personal friends of ours, served the firm with great ability and success and dealt with important matters connected with the milling business, with the coal business and with certain aspects of the banking business.' Blandy's decided to give the job of running the office to Tomás Santos, who had been employed before the war by the Anglo-Portuguese Bank in London. He arrived in 1946. Finding offices near the commercial centre proved a problem but William Hinton & Sons, another longstanding Madeira firm, lent him a room.

6. A Sense of the Old Order

Reid's naturally had its share of
exotic and embarrassing guests

Graham Blandy's greatest challenge after the war was the reopening of Reid's Hotel. When the Churchills arrived in January 1950 Reid's had only been open for three weeks. The hotel minute books give a cryptic account of the difficulties involved in starting up again after nearly a decade. Special permission had to be obtained from the Civil Governor to employ a British assistant manager, Walter Jones. A certificate was required stating the hotel balconies were in good condition. Import duties on wines and spirits had increased from 20 per cent to 60 per cent.

In August the board was told the good news that Giovanni Patra, the chef in pre-war days, would be returning and was engaging his brigade. This was to consist of six Italian chefs including pastry, sauce and vegetable cooks. However Giola the pre-war head waiter had declined, fearing he might encounter difficulties if he wished to re-enter Britain. In his place a Portuguese head waiter was appointed who had worked in the hotel – a careful balance had to be struck between local staff.

A still bigger challenge was the construction of a lift shaft down to the sea where guests could swim. This involved blasting in solid rock and the completion date steadily slipped from October to December.

The aim was to open the hotel on 3 December but with three weeks to go the Italian chefs had still not appeared. The proposed room prices, though submitted to the tourism delegation six weeks before, had still not been approved. When he arrived the chef immediately wanted forty turkeys – the Blandys undertook to order these from the Azores.

Churchill's favourite way of relaxing on holiday was to paint. Mildred Blandy wrote: 'He goes to Câmara de Lobos, the very beautiful but smelly fishing village on the west, and he is painting the harbour there. He is also painting a view of the town from George Dalziel's garden.' As an alternative to the Blandy Buick, the Leacocks offered their Rolls-Royce specially provided with travelling bar in the boot.

As the weather was cold Churchill spent time on

Lady Prudence Jellicoe swallow diving at Reid's (The Sketch, April 1932)

his war memoirs. Bill Deakin had come to help with these while General Sir Henry Pownall, another collaborator, had arrived in Madeira in advance. Churchill would dictate to his secretaries until well past midnight. Mildred Blandy recorded: 'Tomorrow I am having a lunch party for Mr Churchill's two secretaries, Miss Sturdee and Miss Gilliatt. They are both charming girls and very keen to get around and see something of the island.' Jo Sturdee was later Countess of Onslow; Penny Gilliatt was daughter of the Queen's surgeon.

This was not Churchill's first visit to the island – he first stopped at Funchal while sailing out as a young war correspondent for the *Morning Post* to South Africa on the *Dunottar Castle*. His granddaughter Celia Sandys wrote: 'Disenchanted by sea travel, impatient less the fighting should be over before he arrived, and finding no news from the front when he went ashore, he took no pleasure in the visit.' By

Moonlight dinner on the restaurant terrace by Max Römer

the time he called in on his return voyage he had made his name and was eager to make the best of all the publicity which had made him a hero. The excitement had begun when an armoured train in which he was travelling was ambushed and he was captured and imprisoned in a POW camp in Pretoria. Churchill vividly described 'the noise of the projectiles striking the cars, the hiss as they passed in the air, the grunting and puffing of the engine, poor tortured thing, hammered by at least a dozen shells'. Escaping to Lourenço Marques with the help of an English mining engineer, he rejoined General Buller's army on its march to relieve the British at the Siege of Ladysmith and take Pretoria.

Churchill wrote two books on the Boer War and is sometimes mistakenly credited with a short story on Madeira, 'Mr Keegan's Elopement'. This is a confusion with his namesake, the successful American writer Winston Churchill whose novel *Richard Carvel*, published in 1899, the year Winston came ashore in Funchal, sold 2 million copies. The American was three years older and it was to avoid confusion that England's prime minister always wrote as Winston S. Churchill.

Churchill had intended to spend several weeks on the island but with his opponent out of the country, Britain's Labour prime minister Clement Attlee announced early in January that a general election would be held on 23 February. This was naked opportunism and Churchill was forced to change his plans. Rupert Mullins advised against trying to travel back by ship. The sea was very rough, as Funchal was still without a mole for large passenger liners, and it would have been very dangerous to try and get him on board. Instead Churchill decided to go back by Sunderland flying boat with Aquila Airways. He departed at six thirty on the morning of 12 January. The first officer, Christopher Blackburn, recalled: 'We

For centuries Madeira lacked a safe all-weather anchorage. Ships could anchor reasonably securely 500–600 yards offshore in 15–20 fathoms of water. Here they were protected by the mountains of the island from all northerly winds blowing in a wide arc of 135 degrees from west north-west to east north-east. Westerly and easterly winds affected ships at anchor but were not usually dangerous. Southerly winds were a mortal peril, especially if they came from due south. In a stiff south wind vessels had to slip their cables and claw off the shore. When a sudden storm, with high winds, hit hard and fast from the south, there was virtually no escape for ships anchored in the Funchal roadstead. This was as true for sailing ships in the nineteenth century as in the seventeenth. In October 1842, during a sudden storm, all five ships in the roads were wrecked, including the British brig Dart and the American ship Creole. Not until a great mole was pushed out into deep water in the mid-twentieth century did Funchal become a safe port.

Fred Capitani presides over Reid's Bar, 1950

made it and turned home.' The next day Churchill telegraphed his wife saying the nine-hour flight had been most comfortable but advised her to travel home by sea as planned.

Churchill returned in fighting form, giving the first speech of his campaign in a radio broadcast on 21 January when he attacked the damage done by five years of Labour government dedicated to 'equalising misery and organising scarcity'.

Before Churchill left Tom Mullins had presented him with a case of old Madeira, including one bottle of great age. He warned that it was very strong. Churchill replied: 'Don't worry, Mr Mullins, I have been drinking brandy since I was a six year old.'

Churchill certainly served Madeira at Chartwell. One of his advisers, Maurice Ashley, describes a visit to the house: 'Before dinner we had sherry, then champagne, brandy and port.' It was too much and the next evening he refused the port. 'Ah,' said the irrepressible Churchill, 'I have some excellent Madeira.' Afterwards whenever Ashley dined at Chartwell Churchill would say, 'Ashley likes Madeira.' Churchill, said Ashley, could not abide cocktails,

looked at the angry sea. Churchill was dead keen, we heard … He came aboard with a party of four, with plenty of champagne and cigars. We headed out into the swell. It must have been a good four feet and the flying boat was taking a real pasting. In the end we

Sea bathing from the hotel pier by Max Römer

preferring sherry or whiskies and sodas which he had at tea. 'I have taken more out of alcohol than alcohol has taken out of me,' he liked to say.

Clementine Churchill stayed a few more days in Madeira after Winston had left, catching a Castle boat back to Southampton. During the voyage she entertained in her cabin seven English children returning to school. Among them were John's daughter Auriol and Adam and John, Graham's sons.

A new chapter in the history of Reid's opened when Jean Burca arrived as the new manager in 1958. He sailed into Funchal Bay on 27 April on the Winchester Castle in torrential rain that blotted out any view of the island. Yet with the swift and sure eye of a César Ritz he summed up all that was good and bad about the hotel.

Graham Blandy, as company chairman, had come out on the Blandy launch to greet him, accompanied by his brother, John Reeder, with Jimmy Badham, the under-manager, and Carlos, the luggage porter. They drove to Reid's in a large eight-seater 1928 Chevrolet taxi where he was installed at the Villa Maria-Amelia across the road from the hotel. 'The memory of our arrival still haunts me: the walls of the villa were weeping with damp, and there was no means of heating the place,' he recalls. He was with his wife Lisbeth and his five-year-old son Marc whose elder brother Richard was at prep school in Surrey.

Reid's guests are shown how wicker baskets are made during a tour of Palheiro Gardens

The Burcas entered the hotel with the awe and apprehension one feels on entering a church. First impressions were not encouraging. High-ceilinged corridors were lined with sombre copper-studded Spanish chairs. The armchairs and sofas in the enormous lounge were in tired cretonne, though a welcoming fire blazed in the grate. The staff were reserved yet fawning. The guests, 'many of them over sixty, sat gravely in the various rooms, leafing through newspapers, taking tea or chatting in lowered tones as if they were in a London club'.

Jimmy Badham showed them twenty-five rooms and suites which had recently been redecorated and embellished with marble bathrooms. 'Apart from this novelty … the hotel had ninety rather ugly rooms, furnished with latticed wrought-iron bedsteads which had brass balls on the corners.' Mosquito nets hung from the ceilings. The bedside lamps, ceiling lights and standard lamps were without style. The few shared bathrooms reminded Burca of those in a sanatorium. 'The bidets sprayed jets of boiling water from beneath, scalding one's private parts,' he quipped.

Burca asked to see the chef. There was just a hint of reticence in Badham's manner. 'In principle, the

Jean Burca, manager of Reid's from 1958 to 1969

kitchen's his affair, I hardly ever go in there. But he's expecting you.' Burca ventured alone into the *sanctum sanctorum*, as he put it, to confront the Lord of the Domain, Marrot. He had been head chef at Shepheard's in Cairo. Burca knew it was important to be on the right side of such a person. 'I had heard that the food at Reid's was atrocious, and I had already devised a plan of campaign.'

Marrot was over fifty, well-built and with a moustache but reminded Burca of a French warrant officer he had had a contretemps with in Beirut in 1939. Marrot explained, 'It's almost impossible to get ingredients here. I should be most embarrassed if I had to discuss such things in front of my staff.'

Looking around with the staff standing awkwardly at attention, Burca saw that the kitchens were in an 'almost indescribable state of antique squalor' with grease glistening on the kitchen ranges and window panes. The restaurant seated 350 with floral arrangements lending an opulent air, but the first meal was not a success. The dishes, named in French, sounded mouth-watering but were inedible. The service, by contrast, was impeccable, with damask cloths and elegant china. Only the silver cried out for replacing.

The restaurant then was in three parts: the House of Lords, with windows opening on the bay; the House of Commons, overlooking the courtyard; and a narrow central square for passing trade. Tony Amaral, the pianist, who looked like Louis Armstrong, played classics of the 1920s, 1930s and 1940s. Gentlemen had to wear a tie, and cigarettes or cigars could be smoked but never pipes. Burca had two secretaries, one English and one Portuguese, and a Portuguese personal assistant who dealt with staff.

He explored the hidden quarters of the hotel, discovering a collection of Bavarian porcelain dating from the time Reid's had originally opened. He put the china in the best suites though it gradually disappeared. He found the equipment for clay pigeon shooting, popular in the 1920s when guests shot over the headland. There were roulette wheels and hundreds of chips left over from the old gaming

rooms. There was a huge collection of furniture – armchairs, sofas, lovers' seats, commodes – some of it rather fine.

A few days later the fog lifted and he discovered 'the magic of Madeira …the sea glinting silver and far in the distance the Desertas [three deserted islands 20 or so miles away], which we had not known existed'. They went down to the grounds where gardeners scuttled behind the bushes – one of them was watering the flowerbeds which puzzled him rather as it had been raining for a week. A

The Billiard Room at Reid's

multitude of wild cats fled as they approached.

As the manager's wife, Lisbeth, though unpaid, was constantly in attendance, arranging the large vases of flowers in the mornings, preparing bouquets for the suites. She was in touch with the housekeepers about guests' ailments and ran outings to the gardens at Palheiro, the wine lodges and the embroidery factories.

One of the enduring strengths of Reid's was the charm and sweetness of its staff. Some of the valets and chambermaids came from distant villages and slept in dormitory blocks, the women upstairs and the men below. Washers up and gardeners huddled in an abandoned house to sleep – though Burca found that none would easily agree to change. When one of the housekeepers fell ill the chambermaids took turns to look after her. The valets, most of whom had little banana plantations or sugar-cane fields which they tended at weekends, remained good-humoured despite their exhausting hours.

As hotel manager Burca would go out on one of the flat-bottomed motor launches which could take ninety people to the large liners anchored beyond the port. In rough seas the boat would rise and then sink six feet below the end of the ship's ladder. 'You had to persuade some holidaymakers to react to your very precise signal by taking a flying leap,' he recalled. Conscious that a younger generation preferred the Savoy, he organised festivities. 'About once a fortnight, besides the usual dinner dances for cruise passengers, we organised a dance on a theme; a Roman evening with sofas around low tables; an Egyptian night; masked balls and pyjama parties. Plenty of costumes were available, the staff responded to the party mood.'

Camacha dancers perform a Madeira folk dance during a gala evening at Reid's in 1959

The most memorable celebrations were on New Year's Eve and carnivals when it was impossible to control the crowds of up to 2,000 people who thronged the hotel. At Mardi Gras people came from the town in disguise 'whirling guests around in wild dances'. Once one of the older guests came to Burca to say that he had danced with a very pretty girl in a mask until three in the morning but as she left he had seen her going into the men's room. Among the familiar gatecrashers was Tweedy, a lady of well over sixty who 'looked like a little china doll and came to Madeira every year without a penny' but was taken in by one or other hotelier out of kindness. Disguised in mask and outlandish costume, she would nip from table to table knocking back glasses of wine and dancing with extraordinary brio.

One year Burca decided that he needed some new publicity material. By chance a famous travel photographer, Mario de Biasi, the father of Italian photojournalism, had been commissioned by the leading Italian magazine *Epoca* to illustrate a major feature on Reid's. Though the hotel was covered in scaffolding – a new wing was under construction – twelve pages of stunning photographs appeared. Burca ordered 500 copies and sent them to travel agents and newspapers everywhere. It was a huge success but a year later he received a letter from Alessandri Prison in Italy. 'A young man who said he was a student had seen the pictures of Reid's in *Epoca* and had robbed a bank to pay to come and stay here. Unfortunately he had been caught. He asked for nothing, but simply wanted me to know to what lengths his passion had driven him.' Burca understandably thought this was a hoax and wrote to the prison governor only to hear that 'yes this was the prisoner's sad story'. With the Blandys' permission he sent the young man 2,000 *escudos*, saying he hoped one day his dream would come true. 'I locked the correspondence in the hotel safe: but I wish now that I had milked the incident for all it was worth. However, you can't think of everything.'

The lives of a hotel manager and his wife were so intense that there was never enough time for the children. Their elder son Richard had been eight when they left him in England. They had few letters and school reports were evasive. Burca needed to go to Europe to interview for staff and talk to travel agents. He obtained Graham Blandy's permission to bring forward his vacation. When they visited Richard at prep school he was completely indifferent. 'He felt completely abandoned.' They took him back to London and made a fuss of him for a week till he finally seemed more of the boy they knew. Returning to Madeira they found that their younger son Marc had also been homesick and had run away from the Jesuit School at Monte, walking back to Reid's and taking shelter with the concierge. Marc was sent to a stricter school where corporal punishment was frequent but life took a turn for the better when General Batista, the Cuban

dictator deposed by Castro, arrived to stay at Reid's and remained for two years. Marc became close friends with Battista's youngest son, Carlos, and embarked on a new round of adventures running up and down the hotel corridors slipping notes under doors saying: 'Pay up or get out!'

Reid's naturally had its share of exotic and embarrassing guests. One was the Duchess of Leinster, once an American society beauty but then over seventy. She travelled with a companion, a young, pretty brunette. The two were inseparable – they even danced together in the bar, the duchess appearing in a transparent garb like a nightdress. People began to talk, but it was obvious she did not care. One night the Burcas were dining with the Blandys and Lisbeth, fired by Graham's 1863 Terrantez, recounted the escapades of the duchess, with verve and heightened colour. The captain of the liner sitting next to her intervened: 'I can just imagine. She is a remarkable woman, perhaps a little eccentric. My aunt, actually.'

Tricksters and conmen are another inevitable

Detail from Visit Madeira poster of 1930s

part of life in a grand hotel. Burca had a food and beverages manager selected for him by the manager of the Connaught in London. But this man borrowed money from other members of staff, stole the silver, falsely obtained goods on credit and told people his wife planned to import racehorses from Ireland. It was not wholly an idle threat for one day Graham Blandy told Burca that Madeira's Governor had received a letter from the Portuguese ambassador in Dublin, complaining that he had lent £300 to the manager of Reid's and had not had it back.

Cyril Lord, the carpet magnate, came for Christmas. The hotel was full and Burca relates that as the bar was very much the place for locals to be seen in, the reserved signs had a habit of disappearing off the tables after dinner. When the Lords arrived to take their table they found it occupied by a local dignitary whom the staff did not wish to disturb. An extra table was squeezed in. During the dancing

Cyril Lord shoved his chair back and started pulling faces. Finally the Portuguese got up and grabbed Lord ripping his jacket. Lord set furiously about his assailant, the two wives joined in and Tony Amaral launched into a frenzied samba to cover the confusion. The next day the local paper reported 'Leading Madeira citizen attacked by a lord at Reid's'.

The sense of the old order at Reid's was appropriate to the era. 'Everywhere empires were breaking up,' Burca wrote. 'Ships of the Compagnie Maritime Belge docked at Madeira carrying Belgian refugees from the Congo, and now it was Portugal's turn. There was trouble in Africa, and India took possession of Goa, Damão and Dio. The country people took no notice, but the better-off inhabitants of Madeira and Portugal were much distressed.'

One new arrival at Reid's in 1961 was not welcome. This was the notorious Dr Bodkin Adams. Between 1946–56 more than 160 of his patients

The Palacio São Lourenço, facing the Avenda do Mar in Funchal, was built in the 16th century

Oak barrels are rolled into the courtyard of the Wine Lodge

had died in suspicious circumstances. Of these 132 had left him money or other items in their will. He had been tried and acquitted for the murder of one patient in 1957. Subsequently he was convicted of prescription fraud, lying on cremation forms, and failing to keep a dangerous drugs record and struck off the Medical Register. In 1961, shortly before he arrived at Reid's, he had been reinstated. Adams had marched into Burca's office, 'a fat, bald, bull-like man who repelled me', brandishing a copy of the *Daily Mail* with a headline 'Dr Bodkin Adams seen dancing at Reid's'. Adams barked: 'It's caused great distress to my wife and myself. I shall be putting this matter in the hands of my lawyer.' It seemed that a journalist who had arrived on the same ship as Adams had come to a reception posing as a friend.

He had persuaded Reid's big friendly porter to show him the guest register and after that obtained a photograph. But Burca was able to point out that Bodkin's lady companion was not his wife, as declared in the register, and the affair died down.

In 1965 Burca read *Hotel*, the Arthur Hailey novel in which a shocking accident occurs in a hotel lift. He lent the book to Graham Blandy who two days later called him to say 'I got the message'. The lifts at Reid's, among much else, were antiquated, and the firm's usual architect Leonardo Castro Freire was called in. He had already done refurbishment at the hotel and in 1959 had designed the recently opened new Ritz Hotel in Lisbon. The opportunity was taken to build new pools on the terraces above the sea, replacing the summer pavilion.

also devoted to his American mother Elinor who he visited regularly at Santa Luzia.

Problems at the firm and with the home farm used to worry him greatly. Always a hard worker, Graham would leave the office early on Wednesdays to play tennis at the British Country Club, compensating in part for weekends when very often he would visit ships consigned to Blandy's. 'The office was open on Saturday mornings and Saturday afternoons were usually reserved for meetings with the farm manager at Palheiro,' says Adam. 'The farming activities were very diverse and included cattle, cereals, vegetables, oranges (he was very proud of his Washington navel oranges which he introduced to Madeira), lemons, chickens, pigs, guinea fowl etc. Some fifty to sixty people including five gardeners must have been employed at the time and much of the farm produce was sent down to the market and to ships calling at Funchal.'

When Graham did take time off to relax, he was great company, enjoying swimming, tennis, partying at Reid's and excursions to the wilder parts of the island; a favourite was to organise transport from Palheiro and a family picnic at Pico Arieiro. He also relished weeks spent *en famille* at the house in Santa Cruz and rarely missed his morning swim to the Lion Rock and back to the little pier.

The sea had a fascination for Graham and before the war he had a small motor launch, the *Sphinx*. On one occasion it broke down coming back from the Desertas and had to be rowed to the house at Santa Cruz. After the *Sphinx*, the firm's tug *Lobo* was sometimes commandeered in the summer for excursions to the fossil beds and Ponta de São Lourenço. The prize catches were barracudas and the occasional *enchova* or blue fish caught trolling with a hand-held hemp line before the days of nylon.

Graham was liberal in outlook and yet set great store on the established order of things. He believed

Graham and Mildred Blandy were very close. Their son Adam recalls: 'She never seemed to complain when he brought home business friends, ship's captains etc, very often at short notice. My early memories of him conjure up a fairly strict father, sometimes remote and always busy at the office or looking after people at home or at Reid's.' Life was a strict routine. 'We were all expected to have a bath and change for dinner. Dad always wore a dark green velvet smoking jacket and his favourite drink was a dry martini with ice, shaken not stirred. We sat in the dining room, were served by José Gois – later João Jardim who today approaches his nineties – and were told to keep our backs straight.' Graham was

in duty to the family, duty to the firm and duty towards all those who worked for him. Adam observes: 'As children we did not find him an easy man and at times were rather afraid of him and the very high standards he set himself and expected of us. He had great self-discipline and was always punctilious in his ways. He enjoyed smoking Philip Morris and rationed himself to thirteen a day from a silver case kept in his back trouser pocket.'

Graham often admitted to being too serious and said it was due to having too much responsibility as a young man – he had to take over the firm at the age of twenty-five when his father John Ernest died in 1930. Graham loved Palheiro, the garden and his walks around the estate, especially at weekends when there were no important ships in the harbour. Graham and Mildred entertained there frequently and there were tennis parties for friends and family, drinks and lunch parties for business contacts and local officials.

As agent for the Union Castle Graham would regularly sail to South Africa with Mildred after the war to spend time with her parents Walter and May Edmonds in Queenstown, visiting game reserves

The Cunard's Laconia anchored in Funchal in the 1940s

and returning with stories and slides of elephants, lion prides and countless buck. He was also very community minded and in the late 1960s became the first honorary British consul in Madeira after the last career consul Charles Arning retired. He remained consul until he died whereupon his brother John took over. Graham and John were well supported by Júlio Santos as friend and general manager and later by David Wilkie, a Scottish accountant who joined the firm in the 1950s as group financial director.

Another friend was their first cousin Walter Blandy, son of Charles Maurice. He spent his war years in the army, for which he was created an OBE, and then worked in Cardiff on shipping and coaling operations for Madeira and the Canaries. He moved back to Las Palmas in the 1960s. Walter's passions were horseracing, ships and beautiful women. Though he never married, he was immensely popular

View across the farmland of the Palheiro estate in the 1930s

The steamer Atlantis in Funchal Bay in the 1950s

and enjoyed entertaining in the house he built overlooking the port. He had a non-executive post in the Canary businesses and was outlived by his sister Joan.

The visitors' books of Santa Luzia and Palheiro are full of famous names, from the American writer John Dos Passos to the aviator Amy Johnson. Graham particularly enjoyed entertaining officers from visiting warships and used to summon any single girls at the office, including on one occasion Adam's future wife Christina, for drinks parties at Santa Luzia. The compliment was returned years later when a naval helicopter landed at Palheiro to take them out to visit a naval frigate in the bay.

Among other voluntary activities, Graham

supported the handsome folio volume illustrating Isabel de França's visit to the island. He also had the Bolton letters re-edited and historical accounts printed for sale at the English Church. Much of the correspondence was typed by his talented secretary Joan Fernandes when there was a lull in the shipping activity and not much was happening in the office. He delighted in corresponding with the American Blandys, including Admiral 'Spike' Blandy whom he and Mildred met in Washington.

In the late 1960s Graham's health suffered and he underwent a heart bypass operation in London. This was a partial success and he was not very well in early 1972. On 14 April he was taken by ambulance from Palheiro to the Clínica Santa Catarina. 'I was in the Canary Islands on business,' Adam recalls. 'Uncle John was at the airport when I returned to tell me that he had died in the morning of the 15th. My mother told me that he had been found dead by the nurses, the drip somehow having become disconnected during the night.'

Graham did not die a rich man. Palheiro was a huge drain on his reserves. The land that later became the golf course was just maritimus pine that was largely sold for firewood. Yet within two decades all this dead land was to be transformed into valuable assets.

The Royal Mail steamer Almanzora in Funchal Bay

7. Soldier, Builder and Mountain Climber

John Reeder Blandy and his older sister
Hermione explored the length, breadth and
heights of the island

John Reeder at
Quinta da Achada

John Reeder Blandy was born in Madeira on 20 November 1909, the third child of John Ernest and Elinor. John came between his two sisters, Hermione and Rosemary, and Graham was his older brother. The family residences were Santa Luzia and Palheiro. There was a governess and the early lessons were all taken at home.

When he was eight, at the end of the First World War, he was sent, like Graham, to Streete Court School at Westgate-on-Sea, Kent. He always talked of having enjoyed this period of his life, despite not being able to return to Madeira to see his parents at every school holiday. Sometimes he returned home only once in the year. John loved the sea journey, including the arrival in Madeira. He recalled that, until the ship rounded the Garajau headland, there were few lights to be seen. After Streete Court he went to Rugby School, where he excelled at rifle shooting, tennis and rugby. He then went up to St John's, Oxford, and shot for the university at Bisley and later for the national team, winning a pair of Holland & Holland shotguns. On holiday in Madeira he would spend his time riding at Palheiro and walking in the hills.

At the age of twenty-two he fell in love. He married Cynthia Marguerite Lees on 21 July 1932 in London and their daughter Auriol was born on 1 May 1933. But the marriage was not a success and they separated in 1936 and were divorced in 1939. The divorce – not easy in those days – marked John's life.

When the Second World War broke out, it seemed a chance for a new beginning. As a fine shot, he felt he had the skills required for the army and immediately signed up. On the day he enrolled he met the writer Laurens Van der Post and they became lifelong friends. Their friendship was partly cemented after they were both given First World War uniforms that required considerably more cleaning and polishing than the newer versions. He was put in the Intelligence Corps but to his disappointment his first posting was to the Azores, part of neutral Portugal, where he found himself with an old Madeiran friend Horace Zino. The Allies considered the Azores of high strategic importance and he was given the posting because he spoke Portuguese. The result was that, rather than an exciting war which had been his objective, he was stuck in a backwater.

John had inherited the Quinta Santa Luzia from his father. His mother continued to live there until her death and during the war years he lent a smaller house on the property, Quinta das Malvas, to his sister Rosemary who had married Eugene Vermes, a Jewish Hungarian who could no longer live in occupied Europe. In 1941 John successfully applied for a transfer and was sent to the Intelligence Corps in Singapore. Here he came across two old friends, Laurens Van der Post and Charles Fisher, another old friend. John Reeder's son Michael recalls: 'My father enjoyed his war years and I remember him telling the story of flying "Over the Hump" with Laurens.' The Hump was the name given by Allied pilots

The schoolboy John Reeder at Reid's, 1920s

In the swim: Young Blandys and friends in the 1920s dry off by the old swimming pool at Palheiro, now a croquet lawn in front of the Casa Velha Hotel.
From left: Dermot Bolger, Rosemary Blandy, her brothers Graham and John, sister Hermione and unidentified friends

during the Second World War to the eastern end of the Himalayas, over which they flew to supply the Chinese Government of Chiang Kai-shek and units of the United States Army Air Force based there. While in Calcutta he took a trekking holiday into Sikkim in September 1942 with his friend Basil Goodfellow (who served in Special Forces) to make an attempt on an unclimbed peak, Lama Anden, and wrote a diary of his travels.

He was back in London for VE Day (8 May 1945) and liked to recall how 'all of London turned out' and the gas lamps in St James's were lit once more as the blackout ended.

He left the army at the end of the war as major and joined Blandy Brothers in London. On a visit to Madeira he met Sylvie, the daughter of Raymond and Elia Monier-Vinard. Raymond was a brilliant neurologist who had studied in Paris under one of the great pioneers in the field, the Pole Joseph Babinski who worked at the vast Hôpital de la Pitie. Raymond had a glorious record in the First World

War. Entering the Ambroise Paré hospital in 1920 he was characterised as 'a person of exceptional distinction, very independent-minded'. A colleague in the Resistance, Auguste Tournay, wrote: 'Whenever with Monier-Vinard, so alive and vibrant, I found once again the companionship of our youth which began in that unforgettable year when we first became Babinski's spiritual children.' Raymond had

Quinta da Achada when the Monier-Vinards were living there in the 1930s

died in Paris, shortly before the liberation, having worked at the hospital throughout the war as well as aiding the Resistance as a doctor. After the war Elia and Sylvie had decided to move to Elia's family home – the Quinta da Achada in Madeira.

Whilst John had known the Monier-Vinard family before, his new bride Sylvie was sixteen years his junior. They were married quietly in Paris on 28 August 1946. Michael says: 'There was a deep, loving and lifelong bond between them.'

They lived their first married years in London at their flat at 1 Sloane Gardens while John worked from the City office of Blandy Brothers. Sylvie gave birth at the London Hospital to Richard on 14 June 1947, and to Edward on 1 July 1949. Edward had a difficult time after his birth and very nearly died. Indeed, his parents had all but given up hope when he began to recover.

They moved to live in Madeira in 1950 and Quinta das Malvas became their home while John entered the firm to work with his brother Graham. John's main interests became Reid's Hotel and the Madeira Wine Company, while he happily shared with Graham the responsibility for other company business. He and Graham negotiated the sale of Blandy's Bank in the early 60's to the Espírito Santo family who owned one of the leading Lisbon Banks. John and Leonardo de Castro Freire, a renowned Lisbon architect planned the building of the new Blandy offices in town and the garden wing and pools at Reid's. John oversaw all of these in meticulous detail – the building work was carried out without recourse to bank loans. They referred to the group as 'the firm', running it as partners.

John and Sylvie's third son Michael was born on 12 May 1952. At this time John decided to build a house at Santo da Serra on land bought from the Gouveia family immediately after the war. Quinta Madre d'Agua, or the Santo house, as it is known in the family, was finished in 1953, designed by an architect friend, Peter Bicknell, who lived in Cambridge.

In April 1958, Sylvie's mother Elia died and Quinta da Achada became vacant. John and Sylvie

seized the opportunity to move into a large house with beautiful grounds. The death of John's mother Elinor Blandy in March 1961 was followed by the birth of a daughter, Rosemary, on 3 November. That same year new Blandy offices designed by John and Leonardo de Castro Freire were opened, coinciding with the firm's 150th anniversary. John had now caught the building bug and rebuilt Santa Luzia. Once again, his friend Leonardo de

John Reeder in the Swiss Alps in 1936

Castro Freire did the architectural work, with John closely supervising on site. As he put it, his idea (which was not shared by his brother Graham or sister Hermione) was to turn Santa Luzia into a manageable house for modern living. He installed bathrooms for every bedroom, car access off the Rua Santa Luzia (previously the only vehicular access was via the long drive built by John Burden Blandy at the beginning of the century) and generally reduced the size of the house by taking off one and a half floors.

The works at Reid's were spread over many years

Quinta Madre d'Agua at Santo da Serra, designed by the English architect Peter Bicknell in the 1950s

'I remember returning to Madeira by Union Castle liner for one of my holidays from school,' Michael recalls. 'We were met as usual by our parents and Edward and I were taken to Reid's to see the last night of works before the garden wing opened. Carpets were still being carried in for the corridors, cleaners were everywhere, staff were carrying furniture, but as had happened before and very many times since, everything was ready to receive guests the following day and the family dined in the new Grill Room that evening for the first time.'

John and Sylvie entertained regularly at home and lunch and dinner parties at the Achada happened as often as twice a week or more. John did two spells as honorary British consul for which he was made an OBE in 1963. His brother Graham also did his term as honorary British consul and both were fortunate

and in general John was responsible for many of these, liaising with the architects and general managers of the time. The main building had been constructed in the classical way with rooms leading off either side of the corridors. But it was felt that if Reid's was to hold its position in the market all rooms should be sea facing, which involved moving the corridors to the back of the building; at the same time all rooms were given a private bathroom. The next investment was to install air conditioning throughout the hotel. Then the main bar was built.

But the largest project of this period was the addition of the garden wing and pools. This was to vastly increase the public areas as well. Jean Burca as general manager was keen to ensure that Reid's maintain its reputation and it was unacceptable not to be able to offer guests pool swimming. The old and charming lunch pavilion was sacrificed – it had become impractical as staff had to carry food the equivalent of seven floors from the main kitchen. Leonardo de Castro Freire's architectural skills were again challenged and it was a combination of his careful design and the ability of Lady Ellis and her team from Lisbon, who was hired to oversee the interior decoration, that enabled the old building to work so harmoniously with the new garden wing.

The new Blandy office facing the Avenida do Mar which was completed in 1961

to be able to rely on the support of Tom Lee, the shipping manager at Blandy's, who acted as pro-consul.

John had wanted to step down at sixty but this was the very year when his brother Graham was due to retire, so he stayed on to take over the chairmanship for five years, passing it on to his nephew Adam when he reached sixty-five. John always maintained his greatest contribution to the business in those years was to recruit the Welshman John Lewis, who had started his accountancy career in Oporto as the group's finance director. He replaced the formidable Scotsman David Wilkie, who had died while still

Unmistakable Englishmen: Major Courtenay Shaw, Blandy's general manager, the visiting British Ambassador, and John Reeder Blandy

working for the firm. Lewis, a convivial man at ease with all sorts of people, was very sharp commercially and assumed a leading role in helping the family directors resolve trading problems. He became a trusted friend of John's and a support to Adam and Richard after John's retirement and later to Michael and the team in the Canary Islands. Michael recalls that at one difficult moment Lewis advised him: 'There is no more money coming from shareholders, so the company must be managed with this in mind.

Edward Blandy, who died in 1989 aged 39

If you want your salaries paid, keep it very tight.'

John was a good amateur photographer and was invited by Laurens Van der Post to take photographs for his book, *Journey into Russia*, published in 1964, a commission he felt too busy to take up. He was also a weekend painter in oils, but the Santo garden, which he laid out himself, was his special pride. From an early age he had been a keen walker. He and his older sister Hermione – the sibling he was closest to – explored the length, breadth and heights of the island. In later years his daily constitutional, straight up the steep hill behind the Malvas house, was a routine he gave up only when his legs could no longer cope in the 1990s.

In 1978 the family suffered a grievous loss when Sylvie was diagnosed with terminal cancer in December. She died just one month later, on 21 January 1979. Her death was the more tragic as Edward had just become engaged to Georgie Bickford.

Edward and Georgie decided to proceed with their wedding on 21 April 1979. An old friend of John's and of the family, Bridget Civval, who was by now widowed, came to the wedding. Both were lonely and they married within six months, in October 1979.

In 1983 Edward and Georgie arrived in Madeira and John offered to move out of the Achada, which Edward had inherited from Sylvie. John and Bridget returned to live at Malvas which was smaller and more manageable.

Edward had been educated in England, at prep school in Kent and then at Marlborough College. On leaving Marlborough in 1967, he took a gap year working on archaeological digs in Iraq. Edward was the photographer and loved his time there until he contracted sand fly fever and had to return to Europe on health grounds. He had not enjoyed good health as a child and throughout his life suffered from a severe stutter. He graduated from the University of East Anglia as a mature student and, before moving to Madeira worked for the Economist Bookshop, ran his own champagne sales company – buying vintage champagne at auctions and selling it on to private clients – as well as doing accountancy with Binder Hamlyn.

Then in April 1989 there was another terrible loss. Edward too succumbed to cancer after an eighteen-month battle. Georgie was left with a two-year-old son Hugh and a large house. Edward's time with Blandy's was short but he is still remembered at the *Diário de Noticias* for the changes he introduced when production went from movable type to an offset printer, which was acquired and installed under his direction. He also had responsibility for travel and shipping departments.

Georgie continued to live at the Achada after Edward's death. In 1993, wishing to provide Hugh with a good education, she returned to the UK, settling in Dorset. She kept the Achada going till 1999 when, after much heart searching, she decided to develop it into a five-star country-house hotel. She did this with local partners after first offering Blandy's the opportunity to invest. The *quinta* came back to life as the Estalagem Jardins do Lago, which has enjoyed good occupancy since opening. Georgie retained her links to the Achada through a share of the hotel company as well as building a new house in a fine location at the south-east corner of the property.

8. Youth in Charge Again

Adam's entry into Blandy Brothers brought a breath of fresh air into offices that had only recently abandoned stools and upright desks

Young man and the sea: Adam Blandy comes back from a fishing trip on Geisha, his first boat

Successive Blandys have endured a baptism of fire on taking over the family firm. Adam Blandy was due to succeed his uncle John as chairman when he set off to the Canaries in April 1974 for the twice-a-year business conference at Las Palmas. He sailed in his 32-foot motor yacht, the *Cigana*, built the year before in Weymouth. With him were the harbour pilot Valério Andrade and a colleague João Manuel Gonçalves.

Sailing back on the evening of the 24th, they had stopped briefly for a swim at the Salvage Islands (Ilhas Selvagens). This archipelago, 160 nautical miles south-east of Madeira and 90 from Tenerife, comprises a cluster of rocky islets that shelters a spectacular number of seabirds.

When they berthed at Funchal at six the following evening they were met with electrifying news. Twenty-four hours earlier Portugal's long established dictatorship had been overthrown by a group of army captains determined to end the country's gruelling colonial wars. Though known as the Carnation Revolution, it brought a very real threat of extreme Socialism, or even Communism, and with it confiscation of businesses and property.

Portugal's President Tomás and its Prime Minister, Marcelo Caetano, had been temporarily 'exiled' to Madeira and held prisoner at the Palacio de São Lourenço, just across the street from the Blandy office. Within weeks rather than months both family business and properties all looked under threat. Adam's uncle, John Reeder, feared the worst and had suitcases prepared so that the family could leave with their clothes if eviction suddenly threatened.

Born in 1935, Adam had been brought up in Madeira during the war years. Two brothers, José the butler and Ernesto the cook, and two maids, Maria and Gabriella, looked after the family. Adam's parents, Graham and Mildred, lived at Santa Luzia in the winter, moving in summer up to Palheiro, which was then a working farm, with some fifty labourers. 'There were cattle, cereals, vegetables, orchards, forestry and gardens and always plenty going on,' Adam recalls. ' I would go to the sawmill (powered by a water turbine) or watch the woodsmen cutting wood with a long-bladed saw with two handles. We had a resident bull, Friesian cows and oxen. There was also a small dairy, sheep, chickens and pigs, a blacksmith, several "eiras" in the fields where wheat was threshed with the help of a team of oxen. Curiosities included peacocks, guinea fowl and bantam cocks. The farmworkers made catapults for me and I rode on a pony to Montana where I caught a bus running on *gazogenio*, or anthracite, to school in Funchal.' He paints an idyllic picture. 'In summer Jimmy Welsh, the Leacock girls and Anthony Miles came up to play. The swimming pool below Casa Velha was filled with drinking water and copper sulphate blocks were laid on the bottom to keep the water clear and the mosquitoes at bay.'

When war ended in 1945 Adam was sent promptly to St Peter's prep school at Filleigh, near Barnstaple in North Devon, for a term before the school was moved back to Seaford in Sussex. Though he had suffered from polio he quickly took to school sports, swimming (winning the school groyne-to-groyne race), and .22 rifle shooting. At Stowe, where he played in the school squash team, Adam did well enough in his French, German and Spanish A levels to get a place at Oriel College, Oxford. But the freedom of Oxford in the days when there were only two exams, at the end of the first and last terms, proved too intoxicating. When he retook his 'prelims' and omitted to turn over the question paper, a talk with his father prompted the decision to leave university and start serious preparation for the family business. Long years of training as a chartered accountant in the City of London were to ensue. This was a pattern repeated with John Reeder's children – not the charmed life of Oxbridge but the relentless grind of learning to deal with figures.

First Adam was given a brief taste of the family business with a month in the office at Las Palmas. Then it was seven years' accountancy beginning as an articled clerk with Barton Mayhew. Life in the capital was spartan after the comforts of Madeira: a North London boarding house for a year, then a basement flat in Notting Hill – though £500 from

and lived like an ordinary farm worker. It was just as well I got a job on *The Times* and returned to London. If I had stayed in Madeira it would have been disastrous. Adam is a very forbearing character but his patience would have been severely strained and we would have quarrelled.'

Before coming out as a newly qualified chartered accountant aged twenty-seven in 1963, Adam spent some months in Blandy's London office in London Wall where the local directors were Jim Rawlings and Jack Merrett, in charge of shipping, and Donald Browne, handling finance. The businesses included a travel agency, an issuing house (Seton Trust), a hire-purchase company and the Vulcan Fumigator company with plans for manufacturing under licence and distributing in India! None of these ventures were to last after the local directors retired.

In Madeira Salazar was in power running a right-wing dictatorship and Angola and Mozambique were still Portuguese. The Blandy directors were Graham, John and David Wilkie. They were later to be replaced by Adam, Richard, John Lewis and Martin Miles. Martin, who was married to Adam and John's sister Annabel, worked with the firm in Madeira from 1972 till 1976, when he moved back to England with his young family. He was responsible for marketing and worked in the travel, shipping and wine businesses. Annabel was to die from a brain tumour at their home in West Sussex in December 2000.

It was a happy firm, Adam recalls; the main business was shipping, which included calls by Union Castle, P&O, Blue Star, Royal Mail, Yeoward, Bergen steamship, Insulana, and Nacional and cruise vessels mainly from the UK but some from the States; there was also cargo handling, including building materials and grain for the island and the export of bananas. Then there were the casual callers and naval visits. In addition, Blandy's held the important and influential Lloyd's insurance agency.

'We and Leacock's were dominant in the business life of Madeira,' says Adam. 'At the same time Blandy's was highly respected for fair dealing and did not compete with local traders and businesses; of course many of the locals small businesses

depended on the firm for trade. One local weekly paper embarked on attacks on the firm and family. Graham and John were much distressed but opted not to retaliate through our own newspaper, the *Diário de Notícias*, headed by Dr Alberto de Araújo. He was one of the two Madeira deputies to the Parliament in Lisbon and a loyal friend of the family.

Much nervous energy was devoted to shipping, which arrived at any time of day or night, often with little warning. The harbour extension had not been completed so most ships anchored in the bay and were served by launches including the agency launch *Mosquito*. 'My father visited most of the passenger vessels and encouraged me to do the same,' Adam recalls. 'He made a point of looking after and entertaining captains, shipowners and visiting VIPs. This served the business well and allowed his brother John to concentrate on Reid's and the wine.'

The firm's properties and negotiations with local authorities were entrusted to Odorio Homen de Gouveia. His son, Luciano, was later to join the firm and Palheiro Estate. The shipping business was profitable, employing some fifty staff including a burgeoning travel agency headed by Bill Flux. Tom Lee was in charge of foreign shipping, Hugo Leitão Portuguese ships and Bill Clarke accounts. Later the shipping department was headed by Duarte Reis and João Carlos Rodrigues.

'We had a near monopoly of agencies handling 80 per cent of all callers; we also supplied water and stores,' says Adam. 'The firm enjoyed further protection through the archaic "*alvará*" system or business licence regulations. Any new agency had to have a government-issued licence before they could trade. This was typical of the Salazar regime and bureaucracy, making it difficult for newcomers to start up.'

Adam lived first at Malvas, a house on the Quinta Santa Luzia estate, rented to him by his Uncle John. He drove an MG which he could park by the office doorstep. Later Adam's father built two houses near the football ground in Funchal, one for him and the other for his sister Annabel. 'The firm worked on Saturday mornings until 1 pm and to compensate for weekend work shipping staff often left the office on Wednesdays at 4 pm to play in a regular tennis foursome at the British Country Club (now Quinta Magnolia). I was quick to join and continue the tradition … Life in Madeira in the 1960s was good.'

There was then just one restaurant in town, the Combatentes, which still flourishes overlooking the public gardens by the Blandy offices. Social life for expats and Anglo-Madeira families centred on the British Country Club for tennis, squash, snooker and afternoon teas. The English Rooms offered a library, snooker table and bar. Reid's, the Savoy and Miramar hotels all had a dance band playing after dinner while the English Church held an annual fundraising fete. The nine-hole golf course at Santo da Serra, which opened in the mid-1930s, was somehow maintained with about twenty-five to thirty members.

The Madeira airport opened in 1964 and as the passenger liner calls from Union Castle and other traditional shipping companies decreased, flights and cruise vessels replaced them. Blandy's started a travel agency independent of the shipping department. Package tour firms, led by Vingresor from Sweden, began flights to Madeira. Blandy's secured the agency and soon also represented Thomas Cook and a host of other operators.

In the 1970s, Russian passenger vessels called regularly at Madeira. Blandy's were nominated agents for Aminter, the umbrella association for Russian shipping companies. The passengers were European – mostly German and English. 'During the Cold War it was obvious that the Russians used the vessels to gain intelligence,' Adam recalls. 'We always had to wait before seeing the captain either on or near the bridge – quite unlike ships of other flags. This was presumably while they concealed sensitive equipment. On the whole the captains were a fine lot and I sometimes managed to ask innocently why they never came with Russian passengers.

Russian ships in Funchal. Left: Taras Schevchenko and right: the Leonid Brezhnev

Sometimes, but not always, there was a thuggish-looking KGB officer on board, presumably there to keep party discipline and ensure none of the crew asked for asylum.'

As honorary British consul Adam's father, Graham, would give parties for the officers of visiting Royal Navy ships. At one of these Adam met Christina Bengtsson, from Gothenburg, who was working as a guide for Vingresor. They were married in the chapel at Palheiro in August 1970 by the English chaplain, Canon Dixon. It was a family wedding which included Christina's parents, Olof and Sigrid, and her brothers, Carl Johan and Per Olof and his wife Marie Louise, who had earlier arrived from Sweden. Christina and Adam were to have four children, Louisa, Jessica, Emily and Christopher.

In 1972 the firm started to grow orchids at Palheiro with the Guinness group as partners after a certain Peter Hynes had met Graham during a visit to Madeira. Plant Development supplied meristem plants and growing knowhow while Blandy's provided the climate, land and local management. It was the dream of one of the Guinness directors who envisaged supplying Europe with orchids from growing centres in Madeira, the Channel Islands and West Africa. Blandy's later bought out the Guinness share after they decided to rationalise their activities under Ernest Saunders and concentrate on drink.

After the 1974 Revolution the family inevitably felt acute fears for the future of their businesses and property. Though Blandy's had never owned vineyards they had a large portfolio of property in town, including long sections of shorefront acquired for the coaling and watering businesses and their coastal vessels. Dextrously they avoided expropriations through initiating their own development projects and launching into joint ventures – the next great chapter in the firm's activities.

From the late 1960s much of Adam's energies had been concentrated on building up an electronics assembly business which at the time of the 1974 Revolution was employing some 500 people. The initiative had begun when Victor Foll, the chairman of Muirhead's, had come out to Madeira to explore the possibility of manufacturing synchro stators – a delicate and complex form of winding gear – and asked if it could be done on the island as he had problems in England with manufacture.

Muirhead's were a leading electronics firm that had pioneered the manufacture of scientific instruments for wireless telegraphy. Victor Foll, who took over as managing director in 1928, was a brilliant inventor in his own right. The Second World War had given the company a new lease of life as it was able to turn out instruments for aircraft and ships. One speciality was the synchro used for transmitting data. Synchros were wound with very fine wire about the thickness of a human hair.

Maria Augusta, known as Alda, one of the girls who worked in the factory, explains: 'Workers in Madeira were very skilled with their fingers. We

At Blandy's Electronics Division Madeira women skilled in embroidery work at assembling circuit boards

joined very young. We were told by the engineer that we shouldn't talk about the work outside the factory. Some of the work was on UK defence equipment. It was confidential. There was a Nato stamp on technical drawings. All this was new to the island. The possibility of this kind of employment, as opposed to the traditional embroidery houses, was very exciting. Some of the girls started aged fourteen. I was nineteen.'

The girls did not know the destination of the parts they were making, though they believed they were aircraft and missile components. In the excitement some were thought to be intended for the American rocket to the moon, others for submarines. The work with some twelve girls was originally carried out in first-floor premises in Avenida Arriaga above the British Consulate. Later, as demand increased, the operation transferred to large factory premises in the Rua Fernão de Ornelas where additional assembly contracts were obtained, notably medical equipment for Portex, cable harnesses for Aeronautical General Instruments and relays for Oliver Pell and others.

As the girls became more skilled, Muirhead's sent out more equipment so they could do more finished items. One of the managers, Teotónio Rodrigues, recalls: 'The electronics were a great success. The staff took pride in their work. There was a big social centre. There was stability and full employment. There was no great pressure on salaries. There was discipline. There was respect.'

He continues: 'With the Revolution everything changed. For a while things carried on normally. Then cells were created within the 600 female staff. Then began the "outside influences". As happened everywhere there were demands for higher salaries, better conditions. Union representatives were nominated. Monthly meetings were held. Production declined. Workers' cells were formed. The new girls were easily manipulated.'

At the same time the companies which bought the synchros began to take fright over uncertainties. One day Adam went to the factory to announce that Portex had cancelled its contract, involving the loss of over 200 jobs. 'This was followed by a great commotion. The younger girls were threatening to destroy equipment. We had to keep a watch on the entrances to ensure extremists did not get in.'

Adam suddenly found himself held hostage with the production manager in the factory by the workers. 'We were sprung by the Governor, Brigadier Azeredo, who sent a platoon of soldiers,' he says. 'They smuggled us out past a demonstration in the street outside.'

When Alda asked what they were demonstrating about, the answer was 'we just wanted to be involved'. 'There had never been a strike in Madeira,' she says. 'We didn't know what strike meant.' Later came a worse calamity. There were fewer people working by this time as the Muirhead contract alone continued. 'We had left in mid-afternoon on Friday 12 October 1979. A few hours later the factory was burning. An oven had been left on. They used ovens to bake the completed stators. There were also glues and varnishes around. The Muirhead works were destroyed except for the canteen. There was real fear that work would end. Then Adam called everyone together a week later – 250 in one room. He told them they would restart in other premises. I said we would continue. Muirhead supported us. We were all very relieved a week later when two aeroplanes chartered by Muirhead's brought out new equipment which was stored in the canteen. In ten days we were producing again. People came from England to help get it going.'

Teotónio recalls: 'I still meet people who say "it was the best time" – the laughter, the ambience and the friendships. Talking was allowed as we worked. You had to keep up your production rate or you were in trouble. We had Christmas parties. Then the market changed. With the digital revolution there was less demand but there were other contracts. We did cable harnesses for Aeronautical General Instruments and windings for synchro stators.'

These were years of spiralling inflation with bank interest rates of 30 to 40 per cent. As parts of the electronics business closed, substantial sums had to be found to pay staff who were laid off. Clearly it was not possible to finance this with bank borrowings. The alternatives were simple – either to use group reserves from outside Portugal or to sell assets. Fortunately, and despite the hard times, Blandy's were able to sell a key property to a Madeiran emigrant, Senhor José Goncalves, who had just returned to the island from Venezuela having made a large fortune. Soon after, Blandy's won a legal action in London for compensation against Portex, one of the companies which had cancelled contracts in the aftermath of the Revolution.

Michael Blandy later observed: 'Perhaps it was because our business was diverse and Madeira-based that we escaped nationalisation. Yes, there were strikes and the family became low profile. It was a very difficult time.'

During the Revolution problems with the *Diário de Notícias* were acute. The paper had been run by Dr Alberto de Araújo, a staunch supporter of the old regime. 'Within a short time there were street demonstrations and later cars bombs planted by the nascent Flama right-wing independence movement,' Adam recalls. 'Some weeks after the Revolution, I received a delegation of would-be politicos who urged me to change the *Diário* editor or risk serious consequences.'

He continues: 'Dr Alberto decided to resign when he realised his position was untenable. In his place we appointed a progressive-minded Lisbon

John Reeder, top centre, and Graham, right front, with their families on the Bella Sombra tree at Santa Luzia in 1969

university graduate and priest, Padre Paquete de Oliveira, who was living in Madeira and whom I knew from the newly formed Madeira Lions Club. He turned out to have strong leftish sympathies but was friendly to Blandy's and did his best to support us. In May 1975 he resigned, probably threatened by right-wing elements in Madeira. Then we appointed the deputy editor Sílvio Silva as interim director and he managed to keep the peace at the *Diário* for a number of years.'

During this time, Madeira's future president, Dr Alberto João Jardim, came to the *Diário* office. He was then editor of the *Jornal da Madeira*, and one of the subjects for discussion with Adam and the journalists was salaries. Supported by Dr Jardim, in the heady years after the Revolution, they all voted themselves a very substantial increase. 'I calculated quietly that the *Diário* would start making losses but being completely outnumbered I kept quiet,' says Adam.

John Lewis, who had been group financial director for many years, had to have a heart operation before his retirement date and was replaced by John Ritson who by this time was group finance director for the Canary Island businesses and who agreed to move to Madeira.

Though business began to improve in the early 1980s and tourism increased dramatically, the possibility of expropriations remained. 'Palheiro had been threatened several times, notably for a missile launching site on the flat land around the folly,' says Adam. 'At the same time the farming operation and the garden upkeep were becoming ever more difficult.' Following his mother's death in the summer of 1984, he and Christina decided to move immediately to Palheiro to secure the future of the estate. From Adam's perspective, his cousins Richard and Edward – sons of his uncle John Reeder – were firmly established in Madeira while their younger brother Michael was making an impressive fist of operations in the Canaries.

Christina with José Fernandes, the head gardener at Palheiro, in the sunken garden

9. Boom Times, Big Decisions

Richard was fascinated by politics and had
a very diplomatic way of handling tricky
political situations

Richard Blandy was
chairman from 1986 to 2001.
He died in 2002

Richard Blandy took over Blandy's when the island's prolonged economic boom was gathering pace. Tourism was growing exponentially; property developing was racing along the coast. Blandy's as owners of Reid's, Madeira's most famous hotel, were a prestigious company on the island. But with prosperity had come change, challenging the firm's commanding position as air travel took over from shipping, and mass tourism brought bigger hotels which offered economies of scale even if they could not match the elegance of Reid's. The traditional Madeira wine business was threatened by the massive growth of new wines and drinks distributed by powerful international distributors. Handsome, genial and speaking fluent Portuguese, Richard was faced with a commercial world moving far more quickly than ever before.

Born in London on 14 June 1947, Richard was the eldest son of John Reeder and Sylvie Blandy. At the age of eight he followed family tradition and went off to boarding school at St Ronan's, Hawkhurst, Kent. To get to school he, and later his brothers too, sailed to England by ship, usually on one of the Union Castle liners.

Richard then went on to Gordonstoun, and made the most of what the school had to offer. Rugby was his game. He also became a member of the school mountain rescue service as well as being head of his house in his last year.

'He soon learnt what it was to shoulder responsibility,' his younger brother Michael recalls. 'This is what Gordonstoun teaches. I am here today only because he saved my life. Richard, Edward and I were sharing a cabin with Malcolm Flux, travelling home from England on the *Lakonia*, a Greek ship which caught fire 150 miles north-east of Madeira on 23 December 1963. I remember being shaken – "Michael, wake up, get up, we must move fast and there is no time to get dressed."'

Richard, aged sixteen, at his father's request, wrote a description of the drama while it was still fresh in his memory. It remains in the family archive, neatly handwritten on lined paper with a fountain pen in blue ink. On the evening of 22 December, the night before the ship was due to arrive in Madeira, a tramps' ball was in full swing when disaster struck.

'It was about eleven o'clock when the first alarm was given. Edward and I were watching a very good film, *Call Me Bwana*, starring Bob Hope, when a bell went. At first we thought it was part of the film and did nothing. The cinema was enclosed on the promenade deck, in the middle of the boat …We could smell burning but there was little or no smoke … we went to the stern stairs … to fetch Michael and Malcolm out of the cabin. The crew were already dragging fire-hoses along towards the fire ….when we got to the cabin we found Michael and Malcolm sound asleep. Waking them up was quite a hard job, and without waiting to get dressed, we put on lifebelts and went towards the stern … there was quite a lot of smoke but not enough to be called dense. We were going to make our way up to the promenade deck and then to our lifeboats when we were told to go down to the dining room, which was at the stern. Slowly all the passengers

LIFE

Exclusive Pictures of the Lakonia Disaster

FIRE AT SEA

FLAMES LICK AT AFTERDECKS OF THE DISABLED LINER

JANUARY 3 · 1964 · 25¢

congregated there. We found Mrs Stevens (Richard Burca's grandmother) and eventually Richard joined us.

'The fire is said to have started in the barber shop, or in the fusebox below it. This was perhaps one of the worst places where it could have started because the bridge was almost immediately above it, about three decks higher up. It destroyed the bridge and the radio station very soon after it started, and the smoke and flames prevented the forward lifeboats from being launched at all easily, if at

Richard and his father at Zermatt in the Swiss Alps in the 1960s

all ... The crew had not had a fire-drill so far this voyage and I believe that it was the delay due to their inexperience and the lack of any form of drill that enabled the fire to get a good hold and then spread with such disastrous results.

'After about five minutes in the dining room we were told to go up to the promenade deck, and slowly people began to file up. There was no panic ... when we arrived up there we found that none of the boats had been lowered ... By this time I had managed to get Michael and Malcolm some blankets to go over their pyjamas. We all went as far forward as we could and got into a lifeboat. There were two officers there, one a very junior purser, the other a bit more senior but also a purser. The lifeboat filled very quickly, so that we were the first to be lowered, and as the ship was still moving we soon dropped astern. Many people became wet at this point as the outlets for water etc in the ship's sides were still open. The rudder had been smashed while the lifeboat was still on its davits, as it had swung about and hit another lifeboat ... There was food in a sealed locker which we opened while searching for flares, it consisted of biscuits, various tinned things and some water ... the flares were in a locker which

was locked by padlock and nobody had the key to it ... at first we did no rowing as we were not in any danger. The fire had taken hold very strongly and we could see flames shooting up into the sky. Several lifeboats passed us, and we did nothing until someone realised that we had drifted back with the current, and the Lakonia had turned a bit, and we were in danger of being overwhelmed by the burning *Lakonia* ... by general consent we all started rowing in one direction ... having rowed for one and a half hours we had managed to pass astern and get on the other side of the *Lakonia* and eventually drifted further and further away. Both Edward and myself had to row. Michael and Malcolm sat on

The Lakonia caught fire in December 1963 on her way to Madeira. Richard Blandy and his two brothers were among those on board

the bottom of the boat keeping out of the way, and keeping warm at the same time'.

After about two and a half hours they could see the lights of an approaching rescue ship, the Montcalm. The sea was choppy and there was also a swell, so that it was impossible to use the rope ladder. Instead a rope was handed down with a loop at the end which they passed underneath their arms and were then hauled up.

Once on deck they were taken inside and given hot drinks and sandwiches. Richard found a bunk for Michael and Malcolm in one of the cabins and they immediately went to sleep. He went outside for some fresh air and suddenly a man was thrust into his arms. 'That is how I started to look after survivors who had been injured, giving them first aid and people who needed it artificial respiration ... other people had to be hauled out of the sea having been in the water for about five hours.'

As soon as it was light the motor lifeboat was launched followed by the other lifeboat which had to be rowed. 'The two lifeboats were out all day until about half past three, when there were no survivors left in the water,' wrote Richard. 'During the day there were always at least two planes in the sky: USAF and RAF and also a TAP plane that appeared. The airforce planes dropped rubber rafts near to survivors who were quite far from the rescue ships. They also dropped flares to mark their position.'

The Montcalm, Richard noted, had had quite a journey. 'She had been the last ship to get out of the ice up by the Great Lakes in Canada, had then run aground and had lost two of her anchors trying to get afloat again, and then of course she ran into us. She was a single-screw cargo boat with a crew of thirty-six in all, and the skipper was only twenty-nine years old ... all her crew were magnificent, giving up their clothes, food and cabins to the survivors. While Michael and Malcolm slept, Edward served as a messenger and did jobs in the galley.'

'Both my parents spent an extremely anxious day and a half until news came through that we had all been rescued,' Michael recalls. 'The worry was the greater as Blandy's were the ship's agent in Funchal. The Montcalm, a cargo carrier, decided not to divert to Madeira, but rather take us and other survivors to Casablanca. We were looked after by the Lloyd's agent there, Frank Barber and his family. After obtaining new temporary passports we returned to Madeira, via Lisbon, arriving on the island well after Christmas on 30 December.'

After Gordonstoun Richard took a gap year, doing Voluntary Service Overseas. Originally destined for Tanganyika (today's Tanzania), he was switched to Pakistan at the last minute because of trouble in Tanganyika and ended up at the Cadet School of Rawalpindi. Five days after his arrival, war broke out with India and he was soon leading the cadets in

Richard Blandy meets King Carl Gustav and Queen Silvia of Sweden

trench digging, instead of serving as assistant English teacher as intended. He loved his time in Pakistan and was able to take time off and travel to the foothills of the Himalayas and explore the Khyber Pass.

Richard did not enrol at university but returned to Scotland to study accountancy and became an articled clerk with Chiene & Tait, sharing a flat with two medical friends, Richard Logan and Iain

Aged 50, Richard took a sabbatical to Nepal with his sister Rosie. Here he sits in the school they sponsored and helped to build

McQueen. He was keen to join the family business and went to work for Blandy Brothers in Lisbon under Gastão Martins. Here he met Rosemarie Lindley whom he married in the seaside resort of Cascais on 12 April 1971. Richard loved Lisbon and was a regular visitor to Rosemarie's parents' house in Cascais, as well as to her stepfather's house in Tomar, and the family house at Barca, north of Oporto.

Blandy Brothers Lisbon held the representation for a Swiss pharmaceutical company Robapharm. As well as distributing machinery of various kinds, the firm had set up a small bottling and distribution business of wines and spirits. Imported spirits were very expensive in Portugal and the company soon had a flourishing line in Queen Elizabeth gin and Tower of London gin, made from concentrates.

Richard settled into office life easily, speaking nearly fluent Portuguese, with a wife whose mother tongue is Portuguese. He became responsible for Reid's, Madeira Wine Association, Madeira Engineering (MEC – the ship repair yard) and the Lisbon office. Adam was chairman.

'Daddy loved a joke and he loved using humour to prove a more serious point,' Richard's daughter Katrina recalls. 'I remember one occasion when the *Diário* was under fire from Dr Alberto João Jardim, the president of the regional government of Madeira, and who at that time was continually issuing *notas oficiosas* (official communiqués which had to be printed by all the press), railing against the group and the family. My father and mother had been invited to a carnival party hosted by a close member of Dr Alberto João Jardim's family. Daddy went in a suit with lots of pieces of paper pinned to him. When asked what he was, he replied "I'm a nota oficiosa", which elicited much laughter. But the message was received and Dr Alberto João Jardim subsequently stopped that line of attack.'

Richard was always fascinated by and well informed about politics and had a very diplomatic way of handling the tricky political situations he found himself in. In a conversation with his son Andrew during lunch one day, he remarked that he had rejected the idea of becoming a politician but the way in which he ran the business, the ethos and principles he stood by, was his contribution to the society in which he lived. The ethos of being 'of service' to the community was strong in every aspect of Richard's life.

Richard took over the chairmanship of the group from Adam in January 1986. With him at the helm, Blandy's embarked on the joint ventures which rapidly proved to be one of their enduring successes. Richard had recruited Bill Risso-Gill, an Anglo-Portuguese who was and continues to be a person of enormous energy. With Balfour Beatty, the contractors and developers, Blandy's built Reid's Gardens on the site of the old Vila Victoria, which had at one time been an annexe of Reid's and was owned by the firm. Reid's Gardens consisted of a block of forty-four apartments and town houses just east of Reid's Hotel, overlooking the bay. 'By building Reid's Gardens, it was our aim to control the environs of Reid's,' says Michael. However, it wasn't all success because before Reid's Gardens was sold out the economy was struck by the first Gulf War and sales dried up. 'With real-estate development you win or lose on the timing and the state of the economy, but we did well enough to undertake a second development with Balfour Beatty, seventy-two apartments at Ilhéus, built for the Madeira housing market which sold out reasonably well.'

Richard on board the Royal yacht Britannia

of scale. The hotel with its 201 rooms looks big, its silhouette softened by a cascading series of Shangri-la roofs and balconies peaked at the corners in the oriental manner. It is built on a Y-plan, giving every room a sea view – with a select few on the point having sea views both east and west. The main restaurants and bar open on to two levels of terraces with tables and umbrellas to eat al fresco as well as lawns planted with splendid flowering frangipani trees from Madagascar. There is an indoor-outdoor pool at the top of the cliff as well as a much larger pool below with a pier and steps providing easy access to the sea. The lift shaft is freestanding – a tall square column with observation balcony at the top to tempt guests down.

Bill and Richard worked well together and it was at this time that the joint venture with the Symington family, famous for their port wines, was concluded. In the 1980s the Madeira Wine Company was 85 per cent Blandy owned but, despite enormous effort, the difficulty was always to hit sales targets. Bill and Richard realised that the company needed to have better access to the markets. The decision was taken to look for a partner with experience and capacity in this field. Blandy's were a diverse group, not specialising in anything, rather like the old empire trading groups but on a small scale. Contact was made with the Symington family in Oporto who came in initially as equal partners with the option to take majority control. This they duly did but the company is run very much on a joint-venture basis.

Bill and Richard also recruited David Vallat, who was later to become group finance director, replacing John Ritson who returned to work in London before retiring. David was cerebral, Oxford educated and a chartered accountant and used to say of over-wordy reports: 'A long report shows the writer hasn't thought about what he wants to say.' His own reports were concise and usually confined to a single side of A4 paper. He remained with the group until illness forced him into retirement too.

The agreement to set up Porto Bay was born and concluded under Richard's chairmanship. He and

Michael continues: 'I put together some further real-estate developments with Ocean, our Porto Bay partners, working with David Caldeira, on the São Francisco and São Lourenço properties. The old *Diário* building, next to Blandy's office, was also redeveloped. The aim, always, was to activate dormant assets and create investment funds for the firm's core businesses.'

The São Lourenço property, formerly part of the Madeira Wine installations, was developed as a small shopping mall with offices above. A substantial amount of underground car parking was also created, taking advantage of a great shortage of town-centre parking at the time.

Bill Risso-Gill also put together another joint venture which was to build the Cliff Bay Hotel. Cliff Bay, standing dramatically on the promontory west of Reid's, is a deliberate attempt to capitalise on Reid's greatest qualities while providing economies

Michael worked closely on the deal which was an interesting three-way negotiation between Blandy's and Ocean who in turn dealt with Thomas Cook. 'My brother Richard took the role of group chairman very seriously and was on top of every detail,' says Michael. 'People look to the chairman for the ultimate decisions. I enjoyed working with Richard enormously even though we didn't always agree. But disagreements were reserved for the boardroom and outside that 'people would not know of our differences. I worked for him as chairman and learnt an enormous amount from him. He had flair, enormous patience and a huge capacity for detail. He was always fair and like me never wanted yes men on the board. He seemed to absorb stress but this probably did his health no good.'

Richard's enduring legacy to the family business was to create a new vision of the future. But he also pushed himself hard, perhaps too hard. 'He was his own worst enemy,' says Michael. 'Notes were taken of everything and carefully filed. He had a memory for every detail but he was equally a great listener and wanted the business run truly professionally. He particularly enjoyed his involvement with Reid's and Madeira wine and would enjoy presenting our wines at tastings here and abroad.'

Richard had a long spell as honorary British consul, which he enjoyed though it was time-consuming and the entertaining made considerable demands on his family. He kept a scrapbook relating to this period and the high point of his tenure was to welcome The Duke of Edinburgh and Princess Alexandra when they visited Madeira in March 1985 aboard the *Royal Yacht Britannia*. Richard was awarded the MBE for his support of British interests after he stepped down as consul.

Shortly after his fiftieth birthday he went to Nepal with his sister Rosie. His son Andrew also joined them and he was away for nearly two and a half months. But it wasn't just the trip that he loved, it was getting to know Andrew better which made it special.

In April 2001, Michael invited Richard for Easter lunch. 'Richard was very quiet and didn't have a drink. He said he was seeing a doctor in London the following week. I still remember the call: "Michael, it's bad news – cancer of the pancreas – the prognosis is not good but I am going to fight this. I will not be returning to work and I will send you my office keys. Good luck." He continued to take an interest in the office and business affairs but concentrated on beating the cancer and was therefore unable to do any further executive work.

Richard embarked on a course of chemotherapy in London, and would fly to Madeira as often as possible where he spent many hours on the verandah at Santa Luzia. The chemo slowed him down enormously and this would irritate him but he persevered with everything he could. He set himself goals – Rosie's wedding in July 2001, Christmas and then Katrina became engaged and was to be married to Richard Mayson in July 2002. He was determined to be at his daughter's wedding and he got there – he walked her down the aisle and the start of her new life. He was weak but managed to say a few words at the reception and stayed for the whole party.

He never gave up but the cancer beat him and he died in London on 9 August 2002.

Richard´s many friends at his funeral in Madeira heard Anthony Miles, who had worked closely with Richard as chairman of Madeira Wine, pay tribute to his courage and steadfastness.

10. New Investments and New Ways

At its peak Blandy's were selling 6,000 new vehicles a year in the Canaries, split equally between Las Palmas and Tenerife

Michael Blandy started working for the firm in Tenerife in 1977. He succeeded his brother Richard as chairman in 2001

As with every Blandy before him, Michael had never been put under pressure to join the family business. His early recollections include his two grandmothers – 'Grandmama', Elinor Blandy who lived at Santa Luzia, and 'Dan', Elia Monier-Vinard who would always speak to his mother in French. 'Occasionally, when my parents went off to England, by ship in those days, I would be sent to stay at the Achada,' he recalls. 'On one occasion they were due to return on the *Edinburgh Castle*, but the ship was twenty-four hours late due to a huge storm and when it finally came into the Bay of Funchal it was too rough for passengers to disembark.' So he and his older brother Edward were left waiting while their parents sailed on to the Canaries and came back on the next northbound Union Castle ship a few days later. That, says Michael, shows the level of isolation of Madeira even in the 1950s when air transport within Europe and to America was already commonplace. Flights from Porto Santo airport began in 1958 but there was

always the torment of taking the ferry to catch the plane and therefore whilst the liners continued the family travelled by ship to the UK until the Madeira airport opened in 1964.

When Grandmother Dan died in April 1958 Michael's parents decided to move to the Achada which his mother, as an only child, had inherited outright. The house stands in a commanding position surveying Funchal Bay across the rooftops of the town. The main front, restrained but well proportioned, is given charm by an arched loggia at the top. Inside the living rooms have dark polished floors and handsome chimneypieces as well as an imposing sideboard said to have been brought to the island by General Beresford. At the end of the house is a verandah inset with a remarkable picture of Barcelona formed of painted tiles dating from the seventeenth century and acquired by Raymond Monier-Vinard. He had been shooting in the Pyrenees in 1922 near Aramon, Gard. There was a spell of bad weather during the shoot and the party sheltered

The gardens of the Quinta da Achada where Michael Blandy grew up with his brothers, Richard and Edward

in a farmer's shed where he found some lovely tiles lining the floor. He asked the farmer if they were for sale and was told, very firmly, no. After the day's shooting, Raymond went to the local pharmacist in Aramon, introducing himself and asking him that if the farm should ever come up for sale, would he kindly advise him. Some fifteen years later there was a telephone call – the farm was to be sold at auction in two days' time. Elia, his wife, was dispatched south with instructions: 'preferably buy the tiles only; alternatively buy the farm'. She returned to Paris with the tiles purchased – she had managed to persuade the auctioneer to sell them separately. Sadly, Raymond never saw the tiles up. They were stored in the Paris house in Rue Vital throughout the war, and he was killed shortly before the liberation of the capital. Elia and Sylvie moved to the Achada in October 1945; the Paris house was packed up and later sold and the tiles were put up on the verandah in 1946.

Spanish tiles at the Achada portraying the city of Barcelona

The Achada stands in extensive gardens shaded by magnificent trees and is one of Madeira's finest *quintas*. In the 1960s it received and became home to a remarkable denizen, a twenty-year-old tortoise brought to the island by John and Sylvie's friend, Raleigh Krohn and his wife Heather.

'The relationship I had with my father was quite

Columbus the tortoise was left for safekeeping in the Achada gardens by Raleigh and Heather Krohn

strained at the end of my schooling years at St Ronan's and Gordonstoun,' says Michael. 'Whose fault it was I am not sure but I was certainly not the favourite son for a while. I didn't go to university so there was no question of taking a gap year.' He therefore enrolled for a management course with what was then the British Motor Corporation but this didn't work out. He then got a job in Newcastle in the summer of 1971, an introduction that came from Jack Merrett of Blandy's London office. 'This is where life turned for me – I loved the business life, working in shipping for Mathwins. They obviously liked me and encouraged me to take the shipbroking exams. The UK was suffering from a series of coal strikes, and although the business was mainly coal exporting, mainly to Germany, during the strike we actually became coal importers ... coals to Newcastle, or at least to the minor ports south and north of Newcastle which didn't have union labour.'

His father felt he needed wider training and encouraged him to study accountancy. 'Reluctantly I went to Edinburgh but quickly found I enjoyed the work and had a great social life.'

Throughout this time Michael expressed his interest in working for the family business. The opportunity finally came and he started with Blandy Brothers Tenerife in January 1977. He was chief accountant reporting to Charles Brown, the Tenerife managing director.

The Canaries, unlike mainland Spain, were duty free and therefore cars could be imported from anywhere in the world. The duty-free status had begun in General Franco's time with the aim of generating foreign exchange for the country.

'The business had taken off in 1973–4 when we obtained the Toyota franchise, importing directly from Japan,' says Michael. 'Charles Brown and my cousin Cristobal Bravo had been to Japan and had met with various manufacturers. Honda had been the first choice but we didn't get the franchise. Instead we went for Toyota. This turned out to be a blessing as they offered a complete range of commercial vehicles, 4x4s and passenger vehicles. In Tenerife, in those days, there were a lot of pick-up trucks, mostly Peugeots, but the Toyotas were decidedly superior. The workhorse of the farmer was the Land Rover made by Santana in Spain. We were able to offer the more reliable Toyota Land Cruiser. The build quality was better and the price too – providing a huge competitive advantage. Japanese engineers came out and noted everything in minute detail. They even made a "Tenerife" specification car to cope better with the island's steep hills.'

One of the big issues with the Toyota franchise was the exchange rate on the yen. Orders had to be placed six months ahead of delivery and Blandy's were committed to paying in Japanese currency. This was a high risk as the yen fluctuated enormously over the years but there were opportunities as well. These were times when margins went up to 30 or 35 per cent. 'It only happened because the exchange rate went in our favour,' says Michael. 'Persuading the banks to open the Letters of Credit was a nightmare – we needed very substantial facilities and offered only the vehicles as security. Furthermore 85 per cent of the sales were on credit and this was before the existence of finance houses for retail purchases. We therefore had to create an internal credit department, discounting the bills of exchange received in payment from our customers who often elected to buy over as much as three years. We invested in better premises and smarter showrooms and the business continued very well

until the late 1990s when we lost the importing rights but continued with the dealership in Santa Cruz de Tenerife.'

Blandy's had another important motor business on the neighbouring island, in Las Palmas de Gran Canaria. 'When I arrived in 1977 the business consisted of what was left of British Leyland – Morris Marina, the Allegro, the Mini, Austin Princess and Rover 3500. The build quality of these, and even the Jaguars, was never good, and sales suffered. We just didn't have the product to compete in the market.'

Michael continues: 'Those who could afford them bought cars manufactured outside Spain but as a strategy we decided not to apply for a Japanese franchise for Las Palmas. The exchange risks seemed too big. The Las Palmas business was in trouble until 1982 when Blandy's secured the Opel franchise in Las Palmas from the newly formed GM España. My cousin Cristobal Bravo and I worked very hard to get this. We were not the exclusive dealers for Opel in Las Palmas but managed to secure 70 per cent of Opel sales. The Opel business was complemented by the remnants of UK franchises including the new models offered by Land Rover and Jaguar. As a result both companies traded very strongly and profits boomed.'

At its peak Blandy's were selling 6,000 new vehicles a year in the Canaries, split equally between Las Palmas and Tenerife. A thriving after-sales business was developed too. But Michael felt the good years could not go on for ever and recommended selling out in 1988. Even after a very favourable valuation, the board would not agree to sell. Here was the classic business challenge, which Blandy's have repeatedly faced – when to sell a high-performing asset that is regarded by the board as a golden goose.

The 1990s were less favourable for the business in the Canaries. 'Land Rover insisted on pricing in sterling and this worked heavily against us when sterling revalued,' says Michael. 'The Jaguar dealership was disposed of and the core business in Las Palmas became Volvo and General Motors.

Neither Volvo nor Opel had a good range of commercial vehicles, which was important for a balanced business.'

More serious troubles began in the late 1990s when Toyota terminated the importing franchise for Tenerife. 'Our management team had missed a trick,' says Michael. 'It coincided with a huge excess stock, created by a strong revaluation of the yen which pushed up the price of Japanese cars. Sales became sluggish. The Tenerife company had to file for protection from creditors (the equivalent of Chapter 11 in the USA) but, following a tricky period and extremely able management by Bill Risso-Gill, we re-emerged to build a very successful dealer business reporting to the Las Palmas importer.'

According to Michael, the motor trade changed for ever in the 1990s; Blandy's motor business division just wasn't big enough for the new market. At last the board agreed it was time to dispose of the Canary Island interests. 'The question was how to achieve this,' says Michael, who was by now group chairman. 'Las Palmas was sold to the management in 2004, which included my cousin Cristobal Bravo. The next challenge was to secure an exit from the Tenerife business and we managed to sell to the Las Palmas Toyota importer in 2005. He was ambitious and powerful. The negotiations were prolonged and we had the difficult task of maintaining the business to avoid pressure to bring down the price. We were fortunate to have an extremely good and loyal manager, José Antonio Rodriguez, who saw through this very difficult period.' José Antonio also purchased the remainder of Blandy's machinery division in the Canaries, which sold JCBs and Toyota forklifts.

Blandy's had another investment in the Canaries: a sister company which was managed independently from the motor business. It owned the remnants of shipping and travel agencies of the former Blandy Shipping of the Canaries. Additionally, it owned a distribution company (Johnnie Walker whisky and others) as well as the tugs and stevedoring business in Las Palmas harbour. Blandy's controlled 25 per cent and the other shareholders included Cory

Brothers and Hull Blyth. Whilst the company had senior local management the board was London-based which was not very satisfactory. Eventually it was agreed to sell out and the business was bought by the Spanish consortium Boluda.

Michael met his wife Val in 1978, while playing tennis at the British Club in Puerto de La Cruz. Val, originally from Yorkshire, had arrived in Tenerife from Athens and was working at the British Yeoward School as PE teacher and looking after juniors. The romance, which had started on the tennis court, continued after 1980 with Michael commuting between Gran Canaria and Tenerife. They married in 1985 and Val taught for a short period at the American school in Gran Canaria. Their children, Caroline and John, were born in Las Palmas in 1986 and 1988 respectively.

Michael moved to Madeira in May 1990 to take over from Bill Risso-Gill. His new portfolio was alarmingly large, consisting of the Canaries with Peter Wicksteed reporting to him, Reid's, the completion and sale of the Reid's Gardens apartments, the *Diário* (excluding editorial responsibility which was overseen by Richard), the travel and shipping departments, Madequipre (which was the remainder of the electronics business started by Adam), the construction of the Cliff Bay Hotel with partners, Madeira Wine and property management. 'Despite the fact that Bill did much of the work on the negotiations for the new ventures, not surprisingly, I found all this tough,' he says. 'I knew the motor business backwards but I was a new boy again in all other areas. We had good strong management in parts of the business but weaknesses elsewhere.'

Reid's was closed for six months in 1990 for essential engineering works. All this was planned and supervised by Bill Risso-Gill and his team. A new boiler house and laundry was built and at the same time the bar, the link to the elegant Les Faunes restaurant and the sixth-floor suites were all refurbished as well as the pools. 'Reid's had been an extremely successful business when led by Richard and my father before him,' says Michael. 'My task was to continue this. It turned out to be a great deal more difficult than was anticipated. Reid's was a deluxe hotel, operating on an island which was moving downmarket. Whilst there had always been regular investment, the closure programme of 1990 meant the company was carrying a lot of debt at a time before the fall of interest rates to those that have come to be considered more normal in the twenty-first century. Then came the first Gulf War and a direct fall-off in business.'

The issue was sales. Everybody worked very hard, the company made profits, but it wasn't achieving the occupancy levels or the margins desired. Many regular guests had been former names at Lloyd's of London and seen their fortunes eroded. The hotel wasn't attracting new guests and needed further investment too.

The board decided to change the top team at Reid's in 1993. Kurt Schmid replaced Peter Späth and a new non-executive director was appointed, Colin Bather, who had worked for Orient Express hotels at the time they had bought the Cipriani. 'He understood historic hotels and their refurbishment and was a guiding light,' says Michael.

Kurt worked tirelessly, building business from Germany, Switzerland and elsewhere. At one board meeting following the usual tour of the recently refurbished parts of the hotel, Michael extended the visit to include all the areas badly in need of investment. 'The truth was that the hotel needed serious money to be invested in the property and this clashed with the requirement to service the debt and to pay regular dividends,' he says.

Managing Reid's required a sharp sense of humour especially when faced with the complaints. Kurt Schmid turned to Michael's wife Val one evening saying, 'I received a fourteen-page letter of complaint about the tea at Reid's today … fourteen pages, can you imagine.' Val replied drily: 'Perhaps it's a good thing they didn't have dinner!'

'It happened at this time we were faced with 25 per cent of the group's shareholders looking for an exit,' says Michael. 'This is perfectly natural and happens in family businesses which survive for

several generations. The remaining shareholders couldn't afford to buy them out and one alternative was to make the group smaller. The sellers appointed an independent negotiator and this greatly eased the discussions. The group was valued, and a deal was struck whereby a capital reduction would be made, allowing the departing shareholders to be paid within an agreed timescale.'

Obvious candidates for disposal were the two country-house hotels in England, Bishopstrow House and Charingworth Manor, and the investment in the marble companies operating in mainland Portugal, all of which were under-performing, but further assets had to be sold.

The focus turned to Reid's, the group's trophy asset. Reid's was carrying the debt of the refurbishment carried out in 1990 when £10 million had been invested in the hotel. A series of contacts were made with potential purchasers, including a very interested party from Libya, but this was turned down. The negotiations with Orient Express were prolonged but the chairman, Jim Sherwood, liked the hotel and eventually the deal was done, several months after the agreed target date. 'I was never the originator of the idea to sell Reid's,' says Michael. 'I felt we could get a better price. But Richard persuaded all the board. He had the vision for the group to move on and he pushed through the sale personally. And there is no doubt today that it was the correct decision.'

The sale of Reid's financed the share capital reduction and left a substantial sum for further investment. 'If a family business is going to continue to thrive through many generations, you can never remain static,' says Michael. 'We had to change the group from what was a successful old-fashioned trading company and give it a new life. No reinvestment plan existed but a wish to continue in Madeira was confirmed and we wanted to be in the hotel business.'

At this point the firm's share in the Cliff Bay Hotel proved rewarding. 'We had also committed to the regional government of Madeira to develop what today is the site of the Porto Santa Maria

Hotel,' says Michael. 'For years this had been the location for Madeira Engineering (MEC), a company which had been sold and a deal had been struck in 1991 whereby the government would build new installations for MEC in the duty free zone at Caniçal and we would commit to developing the site. As happens so often, the government delayed on its part of the bargain - to our advantage as it happened as over time the area had improved and therefore made a hotel investment less risky.'

Blandy's now formed a new partnership with Ocean Islands Ltd, a company controlled by Antonio Trindade, David Caldeira and Jimmy Welsh. Ocean, with the Bianchi family, had been founding partners of the Cliff Bay Hotel. Ocean also owned the already

highly successful Eden Mar resort further along the coast and the idea was conceived of pooling experience and resources. Porto Bay was born.

Tony Trindade agreed to give up his political ambitions and to dedicate himself to hotels. 'My family was in the hotel business though my own academic background was law,' he says. 'Two years after I started to practise my father asked me to join him. This was in 1973. We had a small hotel chain which I had to run for six months till a general manager was found. It became my life. I was running hotels. In 1986 we decided on new partners, the Dorisol Group. Our partner was David Caldeira, a chemical engineer. Father's hotels were three-star. We had a boutique hotel, Quinta Favila, run by my

Michael Blandy, top right, and extended family on the spreading roots of the same Bella Sombra tree at Quinta Santa Luzia where an earlier generation had gathered 40 years previously (see page 117)

parents. There were twenty-five rooms, mini golf, and a tea garden. Unfortunately it was demolished. The English made up 80 per cent of the guests, the others were mainly Swiss or German. We also had the Quinta Hollway. I lived there in the late 1950s and early 1960s. Madeira had just 4,000 beds then.'

The two groups – Blandy's and Ocean – were to be equal partners in the Porto Bay Group. They then invited Thomas Cook to take 25 per cent in the new company, as well as guaranteeing a percentage occupancy of all the group hotel rooms. Some minority partners who had been shareholders at Cliff Bay also joined. Porto Bay was finally created on 24 August 2000 with Cliff Bay, Porto Santa Maria and Eden Mar as well as the land on which the future Porto Mare and Residence would be built. Blandy's and Ocean owned 34 per cent each.

Later in 2005 when Thomas Cook was needing to raise cash, both Blandy's and Ocean bought back the Thomas Cook shares on the basis of an agreed valuation and today both have 45 per cent. 'A 45 per cent share of a very successful company is much better than a majority in a company which is struggling,' says Michael. 'The success of Porto Bay stems from having the right product – the right location – good service – very strong sales and marketing. Tony Trindade is passionate about the business and it is his enthusiasm which has underpinned the growth of the company.'

Cliff Bay was never intended to compete with Reid's. Porto Santa Maria was designed as a four-star hotel with the objective of being better than the competition so that guests' expectations would be exceeded. The same thinking was applied to Porto Mare and the Residence which together with the Hotel Eden Mar make up the Vila Porto Mare complex of some 450 rooms. Porto Mare and the Residence was a 45 million Euro investment and the three hotels look out over a large subtropical garden, with lush green grass and plentiful palm trees and a host of exotic plants and shrubs. There are two outdoor pools with pavilion bar and one indoor-outdoor pool, as well as the full panoply of luxury spa with sauna, steam baths, gym, aerobics studio,

putting green, petanque tennis and squash courts, billiards and table tennis. The complex has six bars, four restaurants dedicated to different cuisines – Portuguese, Italian and Mediterranean (here Greek and Moroccan). 'We can't and won't allow the product to get old or date,' says Michael.

Porto Bay has also expanded to the Algarve and Brazil, with hotels in Rio de Janeiro, Buzios and São Paulo. Ownership is shared with partners but the management is by Porto Bay. The view of the team was that Brazil seemed to offer a great opportunity though some business risk in geographical terms. There is a saying that money which goes to South America never comes back but the economics seem sound, with Brazil being a net food exporter, a net energy exporter and with its own industrial base. The current Socialist president has created a stable economy.

Madeira's principal daily newspaper, the *Diário de Notícias*, acquired in 1896, continues in Blandy's control. In the turbulent times following the 1974 Revolution Blandy's considered disposal. 'The paper was loss making and causing a huge headache but we were able to negotiate a quirky tax rebate,' says Michael. 'Adam hardly believed it given that relations were rocky even then with the president of the regional government, Dr. Jardim.'

José Câmara, who has managed the newspaper for twenty years, explains: 'We have an almost daily battle with the president who constantly denounces the paper. There have been repeated court cases which the *Diário* has won.' Michael is not intimidated. 'When I arrived in Madeira in 1990 the rumour circulated that I was a member of the labour party! Rather a pity as my only connection with politics had been to be a member of the Young Conservatives! On a small island mutual respect is important and I have always personally admired what Dr. Jardim has done for Madeira, but too many years of power seem to have made him autocratic and wary of criticism and his model for government is now outdated.'

In the 1990s Blandy's sold 40 per cent of the *Diário* to the multimedia Lusomundo Group following the company policy of working with strong know-how partners. 'The tension with the regional government increased further when the government-financed *Jornal da Madeira* was turned into a free paper at the beginning of 2008 and also dumped advertising prices,' says Michael. The *Jornal* is owned by the Madeira Government and has absorbed some 42 million Euros of public funds during the period 1993-2009. 'Ideally we should have a level playing-field, typical of a free market economy. Healthy competition is good for business but presently we are having to compete with a state funded newspaper which is not good for Madeira nor our business. We submitted a complaint to the competition authorities of Portugal stating that no private company has the resources to fight a state financed competitor on the free market. Apart from affecting the profitability of the *Diário*, the action of the regional government has directly threatened the jobs of more than 120 staff. The complaint alleged that the support given for the *Jornal* infringed not only Portugal's constitution, but EU legislation in respect of state aid and competition rules. We have met with the Commission in Brussels who were extremely helpful both in explaining how best to present our case, but also pointing out the pitfalls we might encounter, including the delaying tactics that could be employed by a government reticent to collaborate.'

In mid-2009 the president of the regional government committed to disposing of the *Jornal* after the general elections held at the end of September that year. 'At that time it seemed senseless spending a lot of money in taking this issue to the EU if the *Jornal* is to be privatised in the short term and he is to leave office as he has indicated in 2011. A year on, the *Jornal* continues in government ownership and if anything relations have deteriorated further and it seems that Dr Jardim is positioning himself to stand yet another term. We are therefore being forced to consider the legal alternatives available', says Michael

Michael continues 'I believe that when the history books are written, many people will be sympathetic to the view expressed by the then President of Portugal, Dr Jorge Sampaio, when in a speech given at the Journalists Club of Portugal in Lisbon, on September 19, 2005, he said of the *Diário* " The service which they give to the democratic community of this country is immense" going on to thank the Blandy family for their support of the paper "which is not easy" in the circumstances'.

The story of Blandy's ownership of the *Diário* and related difficulties with the government will run on for a while yet and in Michael Blandy's view, 'may only be resolved when Dr Jardim steps down'.

Cliff Bay Hotel looking down to the sea

11. Palheiro Moves into the Twenty-first Century

The course lived up to its scenic promise — each hole is set dramatically amidst contours well sheltered from wind but with glimpses of azure sea

The golf course laid out
by the American designer
Cabell Robinson with the
sea 1500 feet below

When Adam and Christina Blandy moved to Palheiro in the summer of 1984, few people could see a future for large country houses or estates in private hands. Though a near-Communist government had been replaced by the right-of-centre government which has continued in power, the pace of development was gathering furious momentum, both house building and new roads. Soon another beautiful country house, the Quinta da Palmeira belonging to the Welsh family, was to come under serious and prolonged threat, only finally resolved by the building of a tunnel for a new expressway immediately below the house.

Adam initially tried to put the Palheiro farm on a more commercial footing but, for all the need for local produce, it did not succeed. This was the moment when membership of the European Union had suddenly opened up the way to a massive surge in tourist-led projects financed by substantial subsidies. Madeira was particularly favoured in relation to roads and infrastructures. And so the idea of building a golf course at Palheiro took root. An approach was made to the American Cabell Robinson, whose designs at Sotogrande and Las Brisas in the 1960s had opened a new era in grand scenic golf courses for the international circuit. Robinson had worked with Trent Jones, the doyen of golf-course designers in America, and was also the only leading member of the American Society of Golf Course Architects residing in Europe.

Robinson is a man with forthright views, particularly on golf players who turn to golf-course design. In his opinion, the golfers-turned-architects tend to work from a lexicon of remarkable holes they have played. They try to translate these to the courses they design, even though the topography or climate make them inappropriate. 'I believe there are sites where God himself would find it impossible to build a decent course. I'd say I've turned down 25 to 30 per cent of the sites I've inspected,' he told the magazine *Golf Europe*. 'It is no coincidence that golf has its origins in Scotland and Holland where there is grass, sandy soil and rain in abundance. The best courses are those that have been draped on to a natural landscape: Turnberry, Ballybunion, the old course at Sotogrande – they were all built on great pieces of land.'

The initial idea at Palheiro was for a nine-hole golf course using forested land to the south of the house but this quickly changed to eighteen holes using more open farmland to the east. The one problem lay with the considerable number of stately trees scattered across the site. At one point Robinson turned to Adam and said stonily: 'You have to decide whether you want a golf course or a park.' Adam conceded.

The project was presented to Madeira's president Dr Alberto João Jardim and his colleagues. With their support, official funds were provided to build a new reservoir to ensure a plentiful supply of water for the greens, tees and fairways all through the year. 'This was probably the happiest period of my life' says Adam, thrilled at the sight of the

View of the Folly from the Second Tee

The garden front of Casa Velha after restoration as a country house hotel

giant earth movers which began to shape out the drives in spring 1991. The new clubhouse and course opened two years later, on 3 October 1993, with John Stocker in charge. The course lived up to its scenic promise – each hole is set dramatically amidst contours well sheltered from wind but with glimpses of azure sea and the great Bay of Funchal.

In 1994 the former Portuguese president Mario Soares visited the gardens at Palheiro. Observing the dilapidated Casa Velha, he drew attention to the existence of funds to restore the *patrimonio*. The decision was taken to apply for subsidies and in April 1997 the old hunting lodge reopened to accommodate visitors.

Casa Velha was Madeira's first country-house hotel, situated 1,500 feet above sea level and looking on to one of the loveliest gardens on the island. The drive runs through woodland to emerge in a clearing shaded by the magnificent trees which are the hallmarks of the Palheiro gardens. The grass circle in front of the gates contains a huge multi trunked Metrosideros or Christmas Day tree from New Zealand.

As soon as you step out of the car an atmosphere of friendly informality pervades the scene. A pebbled path is bordered by flowering shrubs and flanked to the left by a bedroom block with rooms opening on to a long verandah like a plantation house in the West Indies. From the front door there is a view straight through into the garden. The staircase sets a grander note, with matching flights on either side rising to first-floor bedrooms. Doors open on to an *enfilade* running across the house and linking the library with the drawing room and dining room. Steps lead down to a terrace with tables and chairs. The large lawn in spring is a carpet of tiny purple oxalis flowers. To the right is another verandahed wing with bedrooms. Beyond, the garden steps down to two further terraces, one inset with a large pool stocked with goldfish and koi carp. The formality of terraces and lawns is softened by spreading trees which shade the paths. At the bottom is another immense Metrosideros and a new tea pavilion offering snacks to golfers and visitors.

Casa Velha with Christina in charge is decorated in fresh pretty colours. The dining room has a plantation feel thanks to polished wood floors and mahogany furniture. It has been cleverly extended by a conservatory retaining the original outside windows which now provide indoor views from one room to the next.

Meantime plots of land were sold beside and

Verandahed guest wing at the Casa Velha hotel with the Palheiro chapel in the background

Bedroom in one of the corner pavilions at Casa Velha

below the golf course for a series of very grand houses built mainly in the modern style. This led to the idea of building a complete village-resort set on the steep hillside below the golf course, providing houses with breathtaking views out to sea. Michael Brown, an English architect working in the Algarve, was invited to visit the site. 'It's an impossible site really, on the side of a mountain or a volcano,' he says. 'They were looking around for an architect. I jumped on an aeroplane and got the job through sheer force of presence. They wanted a Spanish hill village. I'm very keen on Spain. I did some quick sketches and off it went like a rocket. I'm passionate about it, love it – these villages go tumbling down the hillside. They're all haphazard roofs, houses painted in different colours.'

Michael Brown had a team working on the project for eight years. 'We did very detailed drawings of every element because of the slope. If you had 2,000 years to play with, you'd build one house at a time. Here we had to design it all at once with all the road gradients.'

Small flourishes make a difference. The roofs are tweaked, an idea suggested by Portuguese colonial architecture which, says

Brown, has a strong Chinese element. 'It's what I was longing to do, a hill village. I just started with a sketch on an A3 sheet and handed it round with colour pencils and said to everyone colour it in. It has hardly changed since. The colours are taken from eighteenth- and nineteenth-century Portuguese architecture. We had drawings of the whole village painted in different colour combinations.'

He continues: 'The Blandy's were wonderful clients. Initially I dealt mainly with Adam's daughter Jessica. She took me round. I did the early design stuff with her. She was crazy about Spanish hill villages too. The site is very steep. There is only room for one principal road or it would be impossible to build. So we have branches off it, where possible these are horizontal so the houses can be built in a line.'

Inside, the houses are given an added sense of space by vaulted ceilings. 'I always do these,' says Brown. 'If you take out a flat ceiling you save money. They have no purpose beneath a shallow pitched roof. Without them you have an incredible feeling of space in even quite a small room. Low ceilings feel cramped.'

Michael Brown started his practice in 1967 doing houses in London, mainly mews developments. 'I've always done houses,' he says. 'I love doing them.

Here in Madeira the first thing you do is to

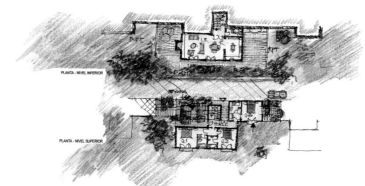

Sketch by the architect Michael Brown for Palheiro Village houses

introduce large windows. There was no room therefore for radiators so we have underfloor heating. People on holiday want to be outside. They want terraces, barbecues and pools. Here there is no room for pools; instead we have an 18-metre pool shared by the residents and a few plunge pools.'

Roger Still, who was brought in to take on project management, had previously worked with Bovis for twenty-two years which was then part of the P&O Group. 'There's nothing like this in Madeira,' he says. 'The team is from the Algarve, with years of experience. The aim was to do a sensitive development around the golf course. There are thirty plots for large villas ranging from 2,000 to 6,000

square metres. The village descends down to the old airport road and covers 6 hectares. In the Algarve we wouldn't build on a slope as steep as this. Here land is very precious. The foundations are expensive, but as each unit looks over the one below, it has an uninterrupted view which adds value.'

The marketing launch in 2006 attracted a surge of buyers from the UK and Ireland. However, the savage recession of 2008 had an impact and a number walked away from their deposits. With the completion of construction in 2009, the property rental activity took off and a fresh marketing campaign resulted in sales to a wider international audience.

In tough times, Blandy's strengths – a strong asset base and consistent emphasis on quality – should enable Palheiro to take advantage of the expected improvement in the economy.

The houses of Palheiro Village are set on a steep hillside overlooking the sea. The concave roofs were suggested by Portuguese colonial architecture

The Palheiro Gardens.

Palheiro is a garden for all seasons, ablaze with ravishing colour throughout the year. Far from being a tropical garden, with little distinction between winter and summer, it is one in which successive waves of bulbs, shrubs and flowering trees come into bloom, month by month.
Even regular visitors to Madeira rarely have the opportunity to experience its glories in full. Palheiro is a garden planted and shaped by its owners, and even more by their wives, aided by generations of Madeiran gardeners blessed not only with a Himalayan stamina but the greenest fingers in the planet. It is a garden you have to explore, alert to every flower from the tiny clover-like oxalis to the exotic red pin-cushion flowers of Metrosideros excelsa from New Zealand's North Island. Unlike the great formal gardens of France, there is no one grand coup d'oeil where the whole extent and splendour of the layout unfolds before you. Yet like all great gardens Palheiro has bones: vistas and walks, avenues and groves, expanses of lawns and garden rooms. But as Christina Blandy says: 'It is impossible to be too formal in this climate where growth is so rapid.'

The 1st Count of Carvalhal chose Palheiro as it was one of the few places in the island which offered an expanse of relatively flat land suitable for laying out pleasure grounds on an ambitious scale. Early visitors compared his quinta to an English park. He planted large numbers of trees, notably the great avenue of planes leading east from his house, now the Casa Velha. He introduced the first double camellias with a profusion of white and red flowers as well as banks of camellias intended as windbreaks. He also appears to have been the beneficiary of exotics sent back from Brazil – where the Portuguese court had

Colourful planting in the box-edged beds of the Jardim da Senhora

Magnolias and azaleas flowering in Spring

emigrated in 1807 only returning in 1821.
From this early period also date the delightful
baroque chapel (already a little English with its three
Palladian windows) and a folly or belvedere, now on
the golf course, with a view out to sea. When John
Burden Blandy acquired Palheiro in 1885 he built a
new house designed by George Somers Clarke, the
architect of the new Reid's Hotel and Shepheard's
Hotel in Cairo. Below he laid out a formal garden in
French style with large squares of grass quartered by
paths, with pebbles formed into diamond patterns.
The pebbles were sized in traditional fashion by
sifting them through bamboo poles. Immediately
beneath the house were two large hothouses of
which only the footprint remains. The walks were
shaded by pergolas made of trunks of wild acacia
which have been replaced every fifteen years or so.
Beyond the formal garden, across a ravine, is an
almost druidical ring of tall plane trees forming a
circle fifty paces across. Of the original fifteen or
sixteen trees just eight remain today.
Water is the mainspring of any garden. At Palheiro
mountain springs are collected by levadas and

fed into two large reservoirs at the top of the
property. The passage of water through the garden
is celebrated by a rustic grotto which feeds into a
bubbling brill and then into a series of lozenge-
shaped pools edged with tritonias. The lower garden
to the east has two beautiful still canals with water
lilies flanked by lawns.
Palheiro's claim to fame lies no less in the size
and splendour of its trees – forest species like
oak, beech, chestnut and cedar grow beside
exotics like eucalyptus and araucaria pines. The
monarch of the garden is a splendid specimen of
Araucaria angustifolia, the candelabra tree from
Brazil, run close by the Hymenosporum flavum,
the Australian jasmine tree. Other noble trees are a
huge Californian redwood, Sequoia sempervirens,
a magnificent 38-metre-tall Araucaria excelsa from
Norfolk Island and a huge Araucaria bidwillii with
pineapple-shaped cones.
Daffodils appear in January when the camellias
have already been flowering for three months. The
rare Saint Helena ebony bush flowers for most of
the year. The blooms of dozens of magnolias glow
luminously against brilliant-blue February skies
– as well as their cousin Michelia doltsopa from the
Himalayas. Cascading purple heterocentron basks on
walls, while white wistaria enfolds the trellises.
In April the blue Paulownia tomentosa flowers with
the purple wistaria. The handkerchief tree, Davidia
involucrata, and the tulip tree, Liriodendron tulifera,
follow in May. High summer is marked by the globe
flowers of hundreds of blue and white agapanthus
lining the drives and paths together with the
flowering Eucalyptus ficifolia and the Lagerströmia
indica, followed by banks of hydrangeas. In
September large drifts of pink belladonna lilies
spring from the ground. The first Sasanqua camellias
appear in October. Mildred Blandy, who grew up in
South Africa, regularly sailed home on the Union
Castle Line bringing back a magnificent series of
proteas which grow in profusion on a bank just
below the main house. Among these are the King
Protea, shaped like a giant pink artichoke.
In his time the Count made an entrance at the top

The Palheiro house seen from the sunken garden that was created in the late 1940s

of the property with elaborate iron gates bearing his initials. This is today the point of arrival for visitors who in spring descend a drive bordered by camellias and a mass of mimosa, succeeded in summer by long lush banks of agapanthus.

This massed planting is one of the thrills of Palheiro – an abundance most gardeners can only dream of. Another wonderful bank of agapanthus runs down from the chapel. Most spectacular of all is the grove of daturas or brugmansia as they are now called. In Madeira's benign climate these grow to the size of apple or pear trees. In late summer they look like Christmas decorations, with tier after tier of trumpet-shaped flowers in shades of white, yellow, orange and amber.

Christina Blandy says her motto is 'edges and hedges'. They give the gardens form and satisfying order, some as straight as plumb lines, others snaking through lush borders and banks of shrubs.

A similar sense of symmetry is evident in the series of garden rooms. While Mildred was away in South Africa in the late 1940s, Graham laid out a sunken garden below the house. When she returned he led her blindfolded into the new garden planted with brightly coloured flowers, including gazanias and lampranthus. Here freesias, ixias and nerines seed themselves freely. In the surrounding rockeries are agaves, aloes and dieramas.

At the bottom of the garden are a number of different banksias, the Australian cousins to the proteas with barrel-like clusters of flowers, a rich source of nectar. Nearby is the rare camellia, C. Granthamiana from Hong Kong, and equally rare Sauraja subspinosa, a Burmese tree with pale pink flowers marked with red and followed by a crop of luscious berries.

Another room in the Jardim da Senhora or lower garden is formed of neatly clipped topiary which

Another view of the sunken garden with giant camphor tree in the background

One of the lily ponds in the lower Jardim da Senhora, the oldest part of the garden

Box topiary in the shape of peahens with fantails

looks like clusters of peahens with fantails. The latest addition is a rose garden created in 2007 by Christina Blandy around stone rings salvaged from Banger's Pillar, a 1798 landmark on the Funchal waterfront demolished despite strong town opposition in 1939. This is planted with old-fashioned roses which are trained up the arches.

Look out for the grass tree from Australia with its thick fire-resistant trunk. From the delicate scent of the freesias in February to the overpowering fragrance of the daturas on a September evening, Palheiro is a garden which never fails to entrance at every step.

12. Champions of Madeira Wine

Have some Madeira, m'dear,
It's really much nicer than beer.
I don't care for sherry, one cannot drink stout,
And port is a wine I can well do without.
It's simply a case of chacun à son gout.
Have some Madeira, m'dear!

Workers line up
for a ration of
Madeira wine

Like other family enterprises, Blandy's most renowned business, the making of Madeira wine, has become a joint venture. This time it was in 1989 with the Symington family, leading port shippers in the Douro, who own three of the most famous names in port – Dow's, Graham's and Warre's. Symington's strengths complement Blandy's, and still more important, they have a sales and marketing department with the potential of greatly boosting Blandy's sales.

James Symington, who worked with Richard Blandy to achieve the merger, explains: 'I always say that Madeira is like a Ferrari. Everyone knows the name but very few have sampled it.' For ten years an impressive marketing exercise has been underway using not only the Blandy name but the other well-known historic labels owned by the Madeira Wine Company – Cossart Gordon, Leacock's and Miles. The Blandy wines have smart new labels selling the four main grape varieties – the dry Sercial which makes an excellent aperitif, the fuller Verdelho which is closer to a medium sherry, the Bual which combines an intense sweetness with an acid tang and is delicious chilled, and finally the very rich Malmsey, a rival for any leading dessert wine. There are five-, ten- and fifteen-year-old blended wines as well as much older vintages. For the popular market three-year-old wines are sold under the names of

famous English royal dukes. The sweetest is naturally named after the Duke of Clarence who famously drowned in a butt of Malmsey wine. The medium sweet is the Duke of Cumberland, Rainwater is a medium-dry pale Madeira, while the Duke of Sussex is the driest, a light delicate wine.

Apart from taste, it is of course colour which distinguishes Madeira from all other wines. Around the world table wines are red, white and rosé, occasionally golden like Sauternes and Tokay or with the greenish tinge of vinho verde. Madeira wine will grace any dining table with a completely different palette of shades of brown or amber, ranging from Karelian birch through oak, cedar and walnut to darkest teak or mahogany. In softly burning candle flame this adds a new dimension to the enjoyment of wine.

The traditional image of Madeira was of a wine which often circulated rather anonymously in a decanter at formal dinners after the meal was over and the table had been cleared. Symington's, working with the Blandys, have progressively changed the perception of Madeira, putting an emphasis on quality and individuality, and gently pushing Madeira not just as an after-dinner wine, or wine for special occasions, but as both an aperitif and a pudding wine – an alternative to Sauternes and the rapidly increasing number of dessert wines

They erect wooden pillars at regular distances, to support a lattice work of bamboos, which slopes down from both sides of the walk, till it is only three feet high, in which elevation it extends over the whole vineyard. The vines are, in this manner, supported from the ground, and the people have room to root out the weeds, which spring up between them. In the season of the vintage which begins early in September, they creep under this lattice work, cut off the grapes, and lay them into baskets. This method of keeping the ground clean and moist, and of ripening the grapes in the shade, contributes to give the Madeira wines that excellent body and flavour, for which they are so remarkable.'

N.C. Pitta, Account of the Island of Madeira, 1812

A famous pipe of old Madeira had lain under the sea in the hull of a ship wrecked at the mouth of the Scheldt in 1779. The wine was brought to the surface in 1814, and when Louis XVIII heard of the discovery he ordered his ambassador in Antwerp to acquire 'the precious treasure'. A portion of the pipe passed into the cellar of the Baron de Raguse, and at the time of the sale of the effects of the late Duchesse de Raguse in 1858 the remaining bottles were sold. This wine had lain under the sea in wood… The pipe had been protected by submarine incrustations, so when Louis XVIII bottled the wine there was no ullage from evaporation. Being unable to breathe the wine would not have developed as much as wine kept in wood on the surface for thirty-six years. However it must have been very fine, for Baron de Rothschild chose to pay 'their weight in gold' for the forty-four bottles remaining in 1858.

on offer from both Europe and the New World.

Traditionally many Madeira bottles were not labelled but instead were stencilled with large white letters usually proclaiming the grape variety, the shipping house and the vintage. Given the propensity for labels to detach or disintegrate in damp cellars after twenty or more years, this was a sensible precaution with a long-lasting wine. But labels of course are crucial in selling wine on shelves and Blandy labels today are distinctively coloured

with smart lettering, whilst the vintage wines are still sold in stencilled bottles with a back label to comply with current legislation.

For their port, Symington's have a worldwide distribution network which Blandy's could never aspire to with the much smaller quantities produced – currently some 300,000 bottles a year. Sales at this volume could never generate sufficient sums for an advertising campaign on any scale and Symington's have relied instead on attracting interest from wine writers, wine magazines and the wine trade, by putting an emphasis on the grapes and the age of the wine and seeking to increase quality across the whole range. When the Symingtons first came to Madeira they were rather surprised to find that the five-day week continued even during the harvest. True, the harvest is unusually long in Madeira, extending over more than a month, but this meant that grapes picked on a Friday were often not pressed till the Monday, by which time fermentation might already have begun.

To simplify marketing, Symington's dispensed with some

Giant vats stand proud at the Blandy Wine Lodge

'I started with Blandy's in 1990 and was invited by the Symington family to take part in the harvest that year in the Douro. The production was one of the biggest in terms of quantity and the quality of grapes was amazing. We slept just two hours a night. After this the Symingtons said, 'Perhaps you should become a winemaker.' I was always connected with wine and my family opened the path for me after many harvests spent at our Quinta at São João on the north of Madeira.

When the Blandy Family asked the Symington Family to join in 1989, the Symingtons introduced a more traditional style of winemaking and brought new technologies which helped improved the process.

Madeira wines are distinguished not only by the grapes but by the process of fortification. I add the neutral and flavourless vinic alcohol to stop fermentation according to the type of wine that I am producing.

In November I spend time tasting all the wines in cask. I spend eight days tasting maybe eighty-five different wines. I start at 10 am. I take a break of fifteen minutes. I taste up to twelve wines each time and I do it alone. When I taste I need to be alone, without interruptions, the mobile phone switched off. The most important thing in tasting is to be honest with yourself. If there is any commercial pressure, I know from experience it will produce problems in the future.

What do I look for? The first thing is the wine must not have defects and as this is a blind tasting I try to judge the age of the wine and its potential.

of the older names which had gathered under the umbrella of the Madeira Wine Company – such as Shortridge – and concentrated on Blandy's, while continuing with Cossart Gordon, Leacock's and Miles which each had distinctive and loyal markets in terms of character and price as well as the countries where they traditionally sold.

'In Madeira any wine that was twenty years old or more could be sold as vintage,' says Dominic Symington. 'Our principle was that all vintage wines should be of superb quality. In addition a range of five-, 10- and 15-year-old wines were introduced. With this came a new range of single-year wines in 50-centilitre bottles aimed at people interested in vintages or wishing to buy wines to celebrate particular dates or anniversaries.'

A new wine, Alvada, was introduced aimed specifically at a younger market with a black bottle and shocking pink label. This was a blend of Malmsey and Bual 'seductive like chocolate', says Dominic – which could be drunk as both a stand-alone drink in a bar and a dessert wine. In London Conran partnered it with sticky toffee pudding.

The UK remains Blandy's strongest market but there are other distinctive markets that are being carefully husbanded. In Scandinavia, Leacock's is the main brand. In Sweden, where there was a state monopoly on alcohol, Madeira was for long

Francisco Albuquerque, three times 'Fortified wine-maker of the year'

the country's largest-selling wine – partly because very little table wine was drunk until some time after the Second World War. Madeira remains the wine drunk after funerals in Scandinavia. This is interesting in itself in countries where schnapps is

If I discover something very good I make a note that it has the potential to be either a vintage or a colheita wine and when it should be bottled. I rate the wines from nought to five. To me the tasting is key. Beside me, I also have an analytical report from the lab and if both are excellent I recommend a bottling date. Otherwise, if both are very good, I identify them as wines for blending. Memory is all important as I need to ensure that our blended wines maintain their characteristics.

I also send samples to the Madeira Wine Institute for certification as they have to issue a permit before bottling can proceed. The alcohol content needs to be 17–22 per cent in volume.

When considering Vintage Wine, the regulations are different in Madeira from those governing Port. For a wine to be classified as Vintage, it must be a minimum of twenty years in wood. As I believe that a Vintage Madeira hasn't reached its full potential until it has spent at least 25 years in cask, I do not think about bottling any Vintage until it has reached this time in cask.

Vintage Madeira can be stored vertically in a standing bottle. If placed horizontally the wine destroys the cork in ten years. You can keep an open bottle of Madeira for five years if you store it in the dark, away from ultraviolet light. Sometimes a small deposit will form but it does not damage the wine.'

Francisco Albuquerque, Blandy's winemaker

the traditional drink, but a small glass of Madeira on such an occasion is at once elegant and dignified as well as an icebreaker. While Madeira of the more inexpensive kind has long been much in demand for cooking in Germany as well as France, it is now being used increasingly for cooking in Japan, the most discriminating and sophisticated market of all.

Blandy's are also fortunate in having one of the world's leading winemakers heading their team. Francisco Albuquerque has the so far unique distinction of winning the title of Fortified Wine Maker of the Year three years running from 2006 to 2008.

Madeira has a distinct and beautiful wine landscape thanks to a system of terraced cultivation as remarkable as the hillsides of the paddy fields in Asia. With this goes a tradition of growing vines on pergolas. The terraces often rise hundreds of metres up the hillside and are the result of a system by which a tenant gained from making improvements to his landlord's property. They are used not only for vines but for bananas (which only grow on land up to 400 metres above sea level) and for vegetables and cereals. Now, with higher employment and increasing prosperity, many of the terraces, especially ones at higher level, are steadily being left uncultivated.

Equally, encouraged by EU regulations, the traditional method of growing vines on pergolas is being replaced by the more familiar pattern of planting in parallel lines. From a scenic point of view this is a matter of concern. The Madeira pergolas are the more appealing

Vines growing in the traditional manner on a trellis

'**P**rofessor Saintsbury wrote that he had drunk 1780 Madeira when it was nearly ninety years old "and in perfection – a thing to say grace for and remember". I can believe it. I tasted a Verdelho of 1779, at the Savile Club, in 1934, as Stephen Gaselee's guest, and his generosity was such that he gave to me, to Eustace Hoare and to a few other wine lovers among his friends, some of this wonderful wine. It was a truly magnificent wine dating back to the pre-estufa period … On 17 October 1934, the thirty-fourth anniversary of our wedding day and a few days before leaving London for our first post-prohibition American tour, my wife and I entertained three very dear friends, Ian Campbell, Francis Berry and Maurice Healy, and gave them two "Gaselee" Madeiras, the Verdelho 1770 and a Terrantez 1850; both were beautiful, but the 1779 was certainly the finer wine of the two … Curtis Moffat, when he lived in Fitzroy Square, had some delightful 1790 Madeira which came from Alnwick Castle. Dr George Williamson, when he lived at Guildford, used to give his guests a wonderful Bual 1840. Stephen Gaselee, at Ashburn Place, had an extraordinary range of old Madeiras and rarely gave his guests the same wine twice; his 1821 Sercial was among the very best. Francis Berry had bought from the Castle Milk Sale two Sercials, the one being called 1846 and the other 1849; they were irregular; they had probably been bottled too early or not kept properly. But at St James's Street Berry Brothers had a Bual 1820 – not for sale but for fun – which was still fresh and delightful in June 1932 … Curtis Moffat used to give us at Fitzroy Square an 1860 Madeira, ex Welbeck Abbey, which was very fine, and Ian Campbell used to have at Elm Grove, Ockham, a very delightful, '70 Sercial.'

André L. Simon, *Vintagewise: A Postscript to Saintsbury's Notes on a Cellar Book*, 1945

Terraces on the north coast
in September almost invisible
beneath the vines

These casks are known as "The Lions", because it took men with enormous strength to move them. Each cask bears the name of a cooper

autumn the growth is so thick the pergolas become as matted as a thatched roof, entirely cloaking the terraces in their rampant exuberance.

Vizetelly, writing in 1870, explained the origins of these terraces. 'In many parts the vines are planted in soil piled up in terraces supported by stone walls. This system was originally adopted as a precaution against the periodical rains which wash the soil away down the precipitous mountain slopes. Today whenever it is possible to accumulate soil and raise a wall this is certain to be done by the occupier of the land, even though the land is unlikely to be commensurate with the time and toil expended. But then, according to the system of tenure universal in this island, a landlord is unable to eject a tenant without first of all compensating him for all the so-called improvements – which, by the way, do not include actual buildings erected – that the tenant has made upon his patch of land. These *bemfeitorias* or improvements are valued by government officials, who invariably lean to the side of the tenant and

as their character changes sharply from season to season. In winter, when the vines have shed their leaves, the pattern of rectangular posts and beams contrasts strongly with the gnarled twisted shape of the trunks of the vines. In spring, a wealth of wild flowers bloom both under the pergolas and along the roads bordering the vineyards, lending brilliant colour to the landscape. In early summer new leaves add bright fresh tints, while in high summer and

'Let us begin with Sercial, which, in my view, is the most precious and exquisite of all grapes, not least because of its expense and rarity, and because it takes so long to meet perfection. The grapes seldom reach a perfect ripeness, always maintain a slight tartness and, being grown on the coast are scorched by the sea air and southern sun. No less than ten years are needed for this liquid to acquire the flavour aroma and hint of burnt-toffee which characterises it. Sercial is followed closely by Malmsey, a sweet beverage that many prefer to Sercial and consider equal in superiority and value. The comparison is valid, given that the best Malmsey grapes make only about 200 pipes a year. This fabulous nectar, with its mellifluous flavour, has the pungent aroma of a posy of sweet-smelling flowers. This precious beverage is ready to drink after eight years, but is even better left longer, but even at only a year old it is agreeable, giving off its perfume and full flavour of the grape.'

Paulo Perestrelo da Camara Breve, *Noticia Sobre a Madeira*, 1841

One of numerous small vineyards
on the craggy north coast which
supply grapes to Blandy's

estimate them at a high value. The consequence is that the more soil a tenant heaps up and the more walls he raises on his small plot of ground, the more certain is he of never being turned off it, for in time these erections, to which the peasant and his family devote all their leisure ... often exceed the value of the land itself.'

As the pergolas fall out of use and disappear the landscape is the loser. While this might seem the inevitable march of improved cultivation, the traditional pergola has its merits. When farmers cultivate their vines using a pergola they grow crops beneath, most commonly potatoes and other vegetables. These provide the soil with natural nitrates.

Today all Madeira wine exporters are struggling in the recession. 'Sales have fallen 15 per cent in volume terms and that hurts,' says Michael Blandy. The very strong Euro against a weak sterling and US dollar in recent years has added to the difficulties of the sector. The markets simply do not accept the increases that should be put through to compensate the currency movements and at the end of the day we have to be commercial and respond. Furthermore, costs of production are always under pressure and of course there is the anti-alcohol lobby to fight, especially as Madeira wine is fortified.'

Nonetheless, with Symington's help, Blandy's have now established themselves as the leading brand of Madeira. 'We still need to find a way of becoming more efficient,' says Michael. 'The sector remains crucial to the economy of the island. Unfortunately this brings government intervention by people who don't always do what's best for the industry as a whole.'

Though both production and sales of Madeira are far below those of port and sherry, Madeira has enduring strengths which look set, once again, to appeal to increasing numbers of connoisseurs and lovers of fine wine around the world. It has shed its clubby image to appeal to the many, often younger, drinkers who enjoy a digestif but do not want to drink something as strong as Cognac or Calvados, or necessarily to open a whole bottle of Sauternes. With Madeira it is possible to keep several bottles on the go, conveniently stored upright in a cupboard.

Madeira's strength is that it combines an instantly appealing acidity or tang with sweetness – and this is true of all four main varieties: Sercial, Verdelho, Bual and Malmsey. Traditionally Madeira was served at room temperature but, with changing tastes, the interesting question is whether it improves by being chilled. 'I suggest the drier Madeiras are served at 16 degrees, the sweeter ones at 17 to 18,' says Dominic Symington. Opinions will always vary but the difference in flavour between Madeira served chilled, and at room temperature, is quite remarkable.

'A Funchal wine merchant, Pantaleão Fernandes ... observed that the wine improved when stored in hot places, principally in the heat of the sun, heated a warehouse of young wines by stoves, day and night, and got exciting results ... a little later, another Funchal wine merchant also placed young wines in a warehouse where heat was circulated by pipes of hot air and called it a hothouse. He observed that the wine lost its young flavour and could be shipped early without changing.'

Count Canavial Funchal, 1900

'André Simon in A Wine Primer (1946) says that Madeira was understood in America as it was never understood elsewhere. The Americans discovered that it needed more air to breathe than other fine wines to enable it to live and expand. They kept their Madeira in demijohns, not in cool cellars but in their lofts, under the roof where it would have plenty of air, and would feel the alternatives of summer heat and winter frosts. When the wine was ripe it was siphoned from the demijohn and passed through cheese cloth into decanters where it was given yet more air, before it passed to the "red-brick" noses and palates of the tribunal of old connoisseurs for judgement.'

Noel Cossart, Madeira: The Island Vineyard, 1984

Some of the most percipient comment on Madeira wine has come from the wine writer Richard Mayson, the husband of Richard Blandy's daughter Katrina. His father-in-law, he recalls, 'used to say that a Bual was marvellous with curry – like chutney'.

He explains: 'At its best Madeira is one of the most thrilling and ethereal of wines. A wonderful bottle blows your senses away - no other wine has this resilience. The older wines are now close to extinction. There's a niche market for them and the fan base is increasing.'

He believes the future lies in quality. Really good Madeira, he says, needs five to ten years' ageing. 'You don't get thrills till a wine is eight to ten years old. You can see the link between an inexpensive ruby and a great vintage port. By contrast a young Madeira has very little relation to an older one. Madeira which has not been aged in cask doesn't have true character. There are no shortcuts.'

Today many wine drinkers take a keen interest

Casks of Madeira maturing in the warm lofts of the Blandy Wine Lodge, with more wine stored in demijohns

British merchants began to fortify Madeira wine in the mid-eighteenth century. In 1756 a Mr Burgess wrote from London to Michael Nowlan, an associate of John Leacock: '... some Gentlemen here that are knowing in the Wine Trade assure me that if a couple of gallons of fine clear Brandy was put into each pipe of our best Wines twill improve them greatly'. He also noted that 'Madeiras drunk here in gentlemen's houses are fine pale amber colour nothing tending to a reddish'. Francis Newton also wrote to his partner in London, George Spence, on 27 October 1853: 'I really impute the complaints I have had of wines to my not putting a bucket or two of brandy in each pipe as other houses do.' French brandy was used initially but soon superseded by brandy produced locally in stills imported from France. In 1911 a bill was passed outlawing stills and granting a monopoly to the Hinton still which produced brandy from sugar cane and continued to do so until 1974.

'I know no wine of its class that can beat Madeira when at its best ... In fact, I think Madeira and Burgundy carry combined intensity and complexity of vinous delights further than any other wines. There is possibly something of the unlawful about their rapture.'

George Saintsbury, Notes on a Cellar Book, 1924

in vintages – people like a year to latch on to. With Madeira the problem was that the wine had to be twenty years old before it could be considered vintage. Sherry has the same handicap of never being sold under a single year and thus lacking an element which appeals to so many wine enthusiasts. A decade ago a new category of Madeira was introduced – Colheita – which provides younger wines of a particular year in bottle. 'People love to pinpoint wines and Colheita brings a date. It can be bottled in very small quantities – from just one cask,' says Mayson. Colheita offers the wine enthusiast the chance to enjoy a wine with a distinct personality and allows the producer to choose the optimum moment to bottle and market a wine which has character but might or might not go on to become a great vintage. With a sophisticated following in Japan as well as in America, Britain and Scandinavia, the scene is set for a steady flow of Madeiras to come on the market.

The newly installed wine library. Madeira, unlike port and other wines, is stored upright

George Washington's Madeira Wine.

When George Washington, first president of the United States, looked out over the mighty Potomac River from his family estate at Mount Vernon, one of his first concerns was the safety and wellbeing of goods and victuals he had ordered from Europe. And the most important cargo of all was Madeira, the wine that was used to toast the Declaration of Independence in 1776.

Washington's well-organised correspondence and order books abound with references to pipes of Madeira (a pipe was equivalent to 600 bottles). His greatest fear was that the shippers would unload it not at Mount Vernon or nearby Alexandria but on the far side of the river where part of the cargo was invariably pilfered or diluted with water or inferior wine.

Washington ordered prodigious quantities of wine for his own consumption at Mount Vernon, where he entertained on a grand scale. As early as 1760 he received a letter from Hill, Lamar & Hill in Madeira concerning 'a pipe of wine which altho' very dear we hope will prove satisfactory after standing a summer to show its quality in which as well as the colour we have endeavoured carefully to please you'. The shippers explain: 'The demand for new wines having been pretty brisk & the expectation of a West India Convoy touching here make the Portuguese stand out for such extravagant prices as the English Factory have hitherto been obliged to pay.' The same merchants wrote again to Washington on 28 February 1762 about a pipe of pale wine. 'It is 40 shillings per pipe cheaper than the particular wines of last year & promises to be much better than any we saw of the former vintage.' From Mount Vernon, on 23 February 1768, Washington wrote to his agents: 'Gentlemen. By Captain Dent bound to the Madeira's (a careful honest Man) and, who will return with his Vessel to this River again, I should be obliged to you for sending me a Butt (of about One hundred and fifty Gall'ns) of your choicest Madeira Wine.' He also requested a few 'cuttings of the Madeira Grape (that kind I mean of which the Wine is made) but if … there be any sort of Impropriety I beg that no notice may be taken of it.'

When war broke out with England Washington continued to consume large quantities of fine Madeiras, ensuring a copious supply wherever his campaigns took him. His 'Account of Expenses While Commander-in-Chief of the Continental Army 1775–1783' shows he bought 108 bottles of Madeira on 11 October 1775 and 109 bottles on 22 October. For 27 June 1776 there is a voucher from Samuel Fraunces, tavern-keeper in New York, for one dozen bottles of Madeira wine.

A glass of Madeira in hand, Washington takes leave of his officers at Francis's Tavern in New York in 1783

On 13 May 1780 he wrote from his headquarters at Morris Town, to the Continental Congress Admiralty Board, delighted with the arrival of 'two pipes of Madeira which came safe'. From his headquarters in Bergen County in New Jersey on 15 September 1780 he acknowledges an order for the delivery of a pipe of Madeira.

The next consignment mentioned was for his own personal use, to be delivered to Mr Lund Washington on the Potomac River 10 miles below Alexandria and hard by the Mount Vernon estate. This was for 'two pipes of old Madeira wine'. Once again Washington entreats 'that they may be committed to safe hands, to prevent wasteage or adulteration'.

On 14 September 1783 Washington wrote in fury from Princeton to Lewis Pintard: 'I have since received a Letter, Invoice, and Bill of Lading for the two ... Pipes of Wine from Mr Searle together with a Box of Citron, and two Baskets of Figs; but instead of their being sent to my House on Potomack River agreeably to my *express* request, and according to the Tenor of the Bills of Lading, I have received advice of their being Landed at Baltimore in Maryland; Sixty odd Miles distant by Land, and more than 300 by Water; how to Account for this I am at a loss, for it is not only contrary to my Order and expectation, but it is so contrary also to my wishes that I had infinitely rather they should be in Madeira; not on Acct. of the expence of transporting them from place to place, inland, nor on acct. of what is really pilfered; but because the quantity drawn is generally made good with something else, and the quality of the Wine, very often, totally ruined by it.' Washington further explains the threat of adulteration in a letter two years later. 'As I have been very unlucky hitherto, in the transportation of

Washington enjoying a glass of Madeira with friends at Mount Vernon

Wine (in the common Craft of the Country) from one port, or one from one river to another; I had rather the old Madeira ordered ... for my use should remain with you (as I am not in immediate want) until a conveyance may offer directly to Alexandria.' Four years later, in 1789, he was corresponding with Gouverneur Morris, the author of large sections of the constitution of the United States, about plated ware with the idea of obtaining 'handsome and useful Coolers for wine *at* and *after* dinner'. For his prodigious entertaining at Mount Vernon he was in need of '*eight* double ones (for madeira and claret the wines usually drank at dinner)'. Each of the apertures was to be sufficient to contain a pint decanter, with 'an allowance in the depth of it for ice at bottom so as to raise the neck of the decanter above the cooler'.

In 1795, four years before his death, there is a note of another order for two pipes of the best Madeira for the president, to be picked up by the Ganges sailing from Philadelphia to Madeira on its way to the East Indies, thus giving the wine the benefit of the long hot voyage.

13. The Adventure Continues

The latest venture is the creation of a new
brand of hotels — Inspira — intended to form
an oasis of quiet in the heart of big cities

Newly planted vineyards at
Quinta Santa Luzia

Two hundred years is a commanding run for any family firm. Mere survival is impressive enough, even more so when most parts of the business are in good health. Blandy's were well prepared to weather the worldwide crash of 2008. As 2011 approaches the group continues to invest, launching into new ventures both at home and overseas. 'My term as chairman has been very tough,' says Michael Blandy. 'I took over from Richard in difficult circumstances. Business has not been easy and some decisions taken have proved to have been wrong. My mission is to complete the work started with Richard – to restructure the group and hand it to the next generation in a way that they can take it forward.'

Michael is concerned to avoid any impression that all the work is his: 'I was part of Adam's team – then Richard's – and today I lead the team. We were fortunate to have recruited Philip Wiles before David Vallat became ill and Phil was able to fill the top financial position naturally. At Porto Bay the leader is very much Tony Trindade. At Madeira Wine our partners, the Symingtons, take a strong and personal interest in all aspects of the business. And finally José Câmara who I have known most of my life and with whom I have worked since I joined the Madeira team in 1990. We have good people coming through as middle managers, including Adam's son, Christopher Blandy. And I am fortunate to have received enormous support and friendship from Adam whose counsel is worth listening to.'

The latest venture is the creation of a new brand

Blandy directors, from left, José Câmara, Daniel Frey, Philip Wiles, Michael Blandy. Chris Blandy, Bill Risso-Gill and Adam Blandy

of hotels – Inspira. Daniel Frey came to Madeira as general manager of the Cliff Bay Hotel. In 2001 he married Michael's sister Rosemary and they went to live in Geneva where Daniel worked for Kempinski. However, they decided they wanted to return to Portugal, and with Daniel initially working as a consultant the Inspira concept was born. Daniel then joined the group and the strategy has since been developed in conjunction with partners Investoc, led by Filipe Osorio de Castro.

With Daniel as CEO, the first Inspira Hotel opened in Lisbon in 2010. The aim is to create a chain of three- and four-star hotels which will form an oasis of quiet in the heart of big cities. 'The hotel becomes much more than just a place to sleep – where guests can recharge their batteries while also enjoying first-class facilities for meetings and events,' says Michael.

Interior design is contemporary and adventurous, using environmentally low-impact materials. It's all to be eco-friendly and carbon conscious, based on sustainable principles, with simple, fresh food from fairtrade sources. Inspira's second hotel, in an eighteenth-century palacete located in historic Oporto above the River Douro, is due to open in 2012.

The greater part of Blandy's extensive seafront property in Funchal and elsewhere in Madeira has now been developed or sold. 'We are not property speculators, our interest lies in buying sites to build hotels,' says Michael. Before the 2008 crash Blandy's had built up substantial funds on deposit, putting the group in a strong position to invest when prices were advantageous. 'Most other big hotel groups don't own the hotels they run,' says Michael. 'Sometimes they use pension funds or other investors to hold the real estate, while they concentrate on the operations. We continually review how best to improve shareholders' interests and we may one day change our investment criteria, for example arranging a sale and leaseback of the hotels or refinancing the business in another way.' Even so, in Madeira, mainland Portugal and Brazil, the Porto Bay hotels look set to be a major growth sector in the near future.

The stairwell in John Blandy's town house with the Blandy lion on the ceiling and the motto Ex Urna Resurgam ('I arise out of the ashes')

Meanwhile Blandy's Wine Lodge continues to be one of the most popular attractions of Funchal. The main courtyard is surrounded by wooden galleries like an old coaching inn, with white walls and grey stone surrounds to the windows. Visitors can simply enter the courtyard and visit the shop or take a tour which introduces them to the whole process of Madeira winemaking. Around the world wine is matured in cellars. In Madeira it is first stored in lofts as the heat improves the wines. The interior is a labyrinth where you ascend from one level to another, with dozens of barrels laid out in parallel ranges, sometimes with small top-up barrels resting on larger barrels below. The floors are supported on massive beams and columns. Other stores are filled with vast vats standing upright, some containing 20,000 litres of wine and more. Every barrel is labelled with the name of the grape and the year, with the seal of the Madeira Wine Institute certifying the contents. In Bordeaux, wine is stored in new barrels which are replaced after just four years. Here barrels are cherished for their age which brings stability. There is not a barrel that is less than seventy years old and four coopers are permanently employed repairing and rebuilding them. They are sealed and made watertight by placing a sliver of banana leaf between each plank.

The tour takes visitors past rooms where shelves bow under the weight of ancient leatherbound ledgers which record the shipments of wine. They're written in beautiful copperplate handwriting – detailing shipments to islands in the West Indies, to England and to all the main ports on America's eastern seaboard as well as to India. Tours end with a tasting – in a room with murals of vineyards and winemaking painted by the German artist Max Römer in about 1940. He lived in Madeira for nearly forty years. Another wall is lined with Madeira wine labels – not only of Blandy, Cossart Gordon, Leacock and Miles but other once-noted shippers. Tastings are also held in the Vintage Room (Sala Frasqueira) where bottles fill the shelves from floor to ceiling as in a great library. They are the more visible as Madeira bottles, unlike other wines, are stored standing up, so the labels announcing rare and ancient vintages immediately catch the eye. There is too an inner sanctum which only a privileged few are invited to visit. This is the Lions' Cellar, in the bottom of the building, where the vast barrels are named after the master coopers who rebuilt them. 'You had to have the strength of a lion to lift such a barrel,' said one of the Blandy directors when they were last moved.

A staggering 800,000 litres of fine and improving wine are stored in the Blandy Wine Lodge. Madeira wine improves in the wood. When down to sixty bottles of any one wine Blandy's cease to sell it, transferring it to a reserve collection used for special tastings.

One of the big surprises of recent years in Madeira

has been the runaway success of the cable car ascending from the Funchal seafront to Monte, a hillside suburb of lush, almost tropical gardens. Next to the lower station on the seafront is the Madeira Story Centre built by Blandy's.

A potentially new point of interest is John Blandy's town house which still stands in a remarkable state of preservation overlooking a large public garden. The stone entrance portal is set a little incongruously in the glass front of a real-estate agent but, above, a handsome row of four balconies with lacy ironwork announce grand salons within. The house until recently has been used as a series of staff flats. The entrance passage leads to a splendid dark wooden staircase rising around the walls to airy landings on the first and second floors. The style is that of England in the first half of the eighteenth century, with a broad handrail, a pair of wooden columns

Richly carved 17th century gateway at Quinta Santa Luzia

to each step and stouter columns at the corners. The ceiling above the open stairwell is adorned with a large oval medallion in decorative plasterwork displaying the Blandy lion and family motto, Ex Urna Resurgam ('I arise out of the ashes'), with three urns all framed by stylised leaves and branches. In Madeira it seems doubly appropriate in view of the forest fire said to have consumed the island for seven years after it was discovered by João Gonçalves Zarco.

The doorways on the landing are surmounted by fanlights with emphatic keystones, still baroque in style. Original sash windows survive, with hinged shutters below allowing you to walk out on to the balconies when the lower sash is raised. The rooms here have more ceiling medallions – the whole arrangement recalls that described by Isabel de França on her visit to Madeira in 1853: 'The best rooms are generally on the second floor … These rooms are all lofty, with coved ceilings beautifully ornamented in stucco. The windows and doors are large and there is always a glazed space above the latter, which adds much to the lightness of the room.'

John Blandy, like merchants and sea captains in England and New England, wanted to keep an eye on the harbour to see what ships were arriving and departing, and his house retains a tower projecting two storeys above the rooftops – like several others in the town. This is approached by a second timber stair.

Richard Blandy's son Andrew has recently returned to Madeira to start a new enterprise at Quinta Santa Luzia, replanting the upper terraces with vines and organising regular tours and tastings. These are arranged through the Blandy Wine Lodge in town, with tours taken by the same well-trained and lively guides. Visitors enter the quinta down the pebbled drive constructed by John Burden Blandy in the early twentieth century. Roses are planted at the end of each row of vines. They are susceptible to the same diseases such as fungus or mildew which show up on the roses first.

The top terrace is now planted with the Terrantez

grape, others with Malvasia Candida, Verdelho, which originated from Italy, Bual from France and Sercial, a Riesling. Tastings are held in a vaulted chamber beneath one of the terraces. Nearby is another Blandy house, Quinta das Malvas, a quinta within a quinta, secluded in its own garden beneath a spreading jacaranda tree.

Andrew, who was educated at Gordonstoun and then Newcastle University, became interested in environmental issues and wrote his dissertation on an experimental community on the north-west coast of Scotland, where he lived for six weeks. He then moved to Edinburgh and began to do some work as a landscape gardener, which is when his interest in tree surgery began. Following the difficult time around his father's illness and subsequent death, Andrew took a Masters at Edinburgh University in Natural Resource Management, in some ways to help with the responsibility of looking after Santa Luzia and with the aim of perhaps moving to Madeira one day.

'I want to see if I can bring to life a lot of the experience I have had outside the island as well as to guide Santa Luzia into its next phases of development,' he says. 'I would love to maintain this beautiful property as an essentially green space and encourage activities that would complement this vision. The concept of having visitors come to view the vineyard and other traditional aspects of the quinta is a beginning; let's see how it unfolds.'

At Palheiro, the latest venture has been a new spa at Casa Velha which opened in the summer of 2009. By contrast to the colonial feel of the hotel, this has a fashionable minimalist aura. Panels of floor-to-ceiling glass alternate with massive walls built of large random stones set in irregular courses like traditional drystone walls around fields. The stone walls are without windows, increasing the sense of a building where you come to commune with nature. Inside it has its own distinct set of proportions, with tall doors and lofty ceilings creating a temple-like calmness.

The treatment rooms look out on to small gardens planted with ferns, enclosed monastically by high

The spa at Casa Velha opened in May 2009

walls with barely a glimpse of sky or trees, all creating a sense of timelessness and separation from everyday cares. The palette is predominantly shades of grey ranging from silver to dove, matching the natural stone. In the bathrooms all the surfaces – walls, showers and basin surrounds – are in matching pale marble, highly polished and gently veined. A spa is a major investment, which more and more country-house hotels feel they cannot be without. 'The aim is to increase occupancy by 5 per cent a year,' explains Luciano, the financial director.

Meanwhile the family retain ambitious long-term plans for the Palheiro estate and discussions with the Funchal planning authorities are already underway for further development.

Adam's eldest son Jonathan took over as chairman of Palheiro Golf and Casa Velha in 2004–5. Jonathan's background was a far cry from the more conservative social atmosphere of Madeira. His mother was Rita Fletcher, the wife of Ronald Fletcher, and Jonathan grew up in the Fletchers' home in Richmond-upon-Thames, with the Royal Mid Surrey Golf Club becoming his nursery and school. During his Latymers schooldays, he would often come out to Madeira to join his half sisters

and brother at Palheiro and Porto Santo.

He arrived in Madeira after university in Brighton to work at the newly opened Palheiro golf course. Twenty years later, Jonathan is still smiling and still at Palheiro – where he has taken over many of Adam's executive functions. 'At the end of the day I would have preferred to be a DJ,' he jokes.

Jonathan became managing director of Palheiro Real Estate in 2008, assisted closely by Dr Luciano Homen de Gouveia and engineer Gonçalo Câmara. Adam remains chairman of the holding company, keeping out of the day-to-day running of the business but retaining ultimate control. His daughter Louisa, married to Philippe Moreau, joined Jonathan's team in 2008. She helps to run property rentals and is responsible for owner and guest relations for the village; she is passionate about Palheiro, having spent her childhood there, and can often be seen accompanying visiting VIPs and journalists round the estate.

Jonathan pays tribute to Adam's thoroughness, old-school punctuality and minute-taking, all a contrast to more relaxed Portuguese business practices. 'The Palheiro way tends to be more structured and we do minutes stating action deadlines and responsibilities,' he says. 'Some of the managers find this unnecessary and situations are resolved by their ability to be more flexible and desenrascar (literally translated as "solve by disentangling") at the last moment.'

Adam's latest boat, the Balancal, owned by Hotel Casa Velha, was built in Essex in 1999 by Lochin Marine, and arrived in Madeira in September 2000. It is a traditional Thames estuary pilot boat adapted for big-game fishing, with the addition of a fly bridge. The co-pilot's chair can be spun round to look back at the fishing lines. The deck has been reinforced for the fighting chair which came from Florida.   This is like a dentist's chair with rod holders for lines on either side and a central rod holder for fighting the fish as soon as the line is taken. The boat is used by the hotel guests and is available for charter in the summer.

In Madeira large game fish can be caught close to the harbour thanks largely to the sudden drop in the sea floor. Elsewhere it's necessary to sail 40–50 miles to the fishing ground. The bait is mackerel or plastic lures – there are up to six arching rods with lines running out behind the boat which, when stationary, looks like a giant bewhiskered cat.

The main quarry are blue marlin and tuna. Balancal, says Jonathan, has 'proved herself as a fishraiser'. Major catches include a fish of over 1,000 lbs, hooked and lost in September 2003, a giant fish estimated at over 1,100 lbs caught and released in September 2004, a double hook-up with two fish estimated at 700 and 1,000 lbs in June 2005 and in July 2006 the successful catch and release of three marlin in one day.

The captain, Anibal Fernandes, usually sees the fish chasing the lures even before they take the line. When they bite he powers forward while the line spins out. The rule is that no one but the angler can touch the rod. The angler is in a harness – some fight the fish standing up, others in the chair. The aim is to bring in fish within twenty minutes so a blue marlin can be released before it is exhausted.

Today the number of Blandys in business in Funchal is on the increase again. Adam's second son Christopher is managing director of the travel agency and the shipping agencies and a director of the Madeira Wine Company. Previously he worked for two years in Oporto with the Symingtons in the wine trade and played rugby for the leading team there. He left speaking fluent Portuguese and worked for a further two years at the Willard Hotel in Washington. Michael's son John has been studying hotel and catering management in Manchester and in 2009 spent several months working at the company's hotels in Brazil and Madeira as part of his course. Whether this will lead him to one day

'The light of four tall candles was reflected in the polished table, the gleaming silver and the crystal. To all intents and purposes it was a regular meeting of Savannah's select Madeira Club: six men in black tie, two white-gloved butlers to serve them, great wines on the sideboard and all of it taking place in a magnificently restored historic Savannah mansion, the Ward-Anderson House.

But not everything is what it seems. Surrounding the six as they chatted and tried to look natural was a film crew equipped with what looked like enough lights, microphones and cameras for a remake of Gone With the Wind. For this was no ordinary meeting of the Madeira Club. This one was being filmed for a series on wine with Hugh Johnson, the English wine authority, as host.

He had come to Savannah – from Madeira itself – to recapture a bit of American history and wine lore unknown to most Americans … The wines served at the Madeira Club dinner here were a 1915 Bual, a 1906 Malvasia, an 1885 Malmsey, an 1884 Campanario, an 1870 Terrantez and an 1838 Verdelho. The first two wines came from Mr Johnson's cellar; the last four from the collection of Dr Bernard Rhodes, a California vineyard owner and wine collector.'

Article in New York Times, 20 April 1988

Adam and Christina Blandy with their expanding family at Palheiro

The Savannah home of Isaiah Davenport, now open to the public, provides abundant evidence of the taste for fine Madeira wines in Georgia. His inventory lists '4 doz cut and plain wineglasses', '3 pair decanters', '1 pr decanter slides' and '3 demijohn jugs'. 'Decanter slides' were wine coasters on which the decanters were slid as they circled clockwise round the table. Langdon Mitchell wrote, 'These parties began at 4.30 pm and lasted two to three hours. There were usually eight men at table, and five wines were tasted and discussed.

Captain James Cook called at Madeira in the summer of 1768 in the Endeavour on his famous voyage to explore the Pacific. He took on onions and 3,032 gallons of wine, as part of his continuing efforts to ensure his crew remained healthy and free from scurvy. He rounded Cape Horn and reached Tahiti in April 1769 (according to one report he supplied each crewman with a gallon of Madeira per month).

working with the group is too early to say.

Since John Blandy established the family business in 1811, seven generations of Blandys have worked in Madeira. Such an enduring bond between the family and the island is remarkable. At times, of course, Blandys have thought of moving to England, to America and to South Africa, but the island with its majestic scenery has continued to cast a spell. No less remarkable is that through famine, war, recession and revolution, the Blandys have remained welcome in Madeira, continuing to build ever stronger ties with the island.

This in turn reflects the way the Madeirans themselves have constantly gone in search of fortune, finding work and establishing strong Madeira communities in Venezuela, South Africa and Brazil, in Toronto, Macau and the English Channel Islands of Jersey and Guernsey.

The Madeirans are hardworking, energetic and resourceful people with as strong an ideal of family loyalty as is to be found anywhere in Europe. Today the Blandys speak fluent Portuguese, they are acquiring and opening hotels in Portugal itself and in Brazil. Their keen sense of both family and company is evident in the regard they have paid the great anniversaries in Blandy history: the 150th in 1961 and the 200th in 2011. The island itself, its people, landscape and traditions are celebrated in exhibitions at Casa Velha at Palheiro and the Story Centre in Funchal.

The Blandys' pride in Madeira is manifest in the way family homes and gardens as well as the wine lodge now rank among the leading sights of the island. Guides at the wine lodge engage visitors' attention with charm and wit, leaving no one unmarked by their enthusiasm for Madeira wines.

For decades tourism in Madeira was almost synonymous with Reid's Hotel. Today, while Reid's still retains its legendary glamour and style, there is an equal band of regular visitors at the Blandy Porto Bay hotels and Casa Velha — returning year after year to enjoy good food in breathtaking surroundings. The greatest continuing challenge will always be the wine, constantly assaulted by changing fashions and tastes. Yet enthusiasts and connoisseurs around the world increasingly recognise that no one has ever produced a wine to rival the distinctive and fascinating qualities of Madeira. There were imitations in the past — as of port and sherry — including Madeira from the Crimea. But from Savannah to Stockholm Madeira is written into the lore of great wine.

The bicentenary of 2011 — preceded by the worst global economic crisis of modern times — sees the Blandy businesses in good health, poised for another century of continuing enterprise, involving both family members and Madeirans at every level.

In 1974 John Reeder Blandy, faced with unfolding Communist revolution, had suitcases packed ready for an instant departure. Today no Blandy young or old would conceive of leaving the island without a return ticket.

The Inspira Santa Marta Hotel in Lisbon, which opened in 2010. The aim of the Inspira brand of hotels — the next one is due to open in Oporto in 2012 — is to create an oasis of quiet in bustling cities.

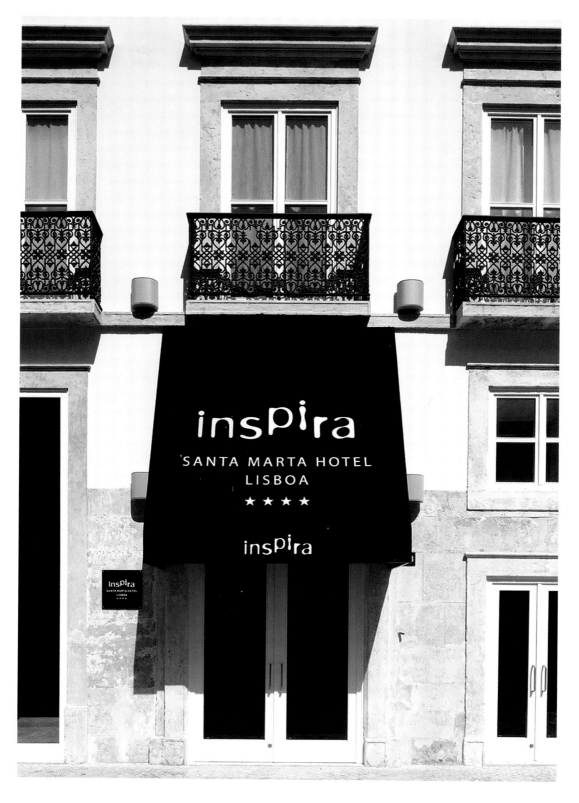

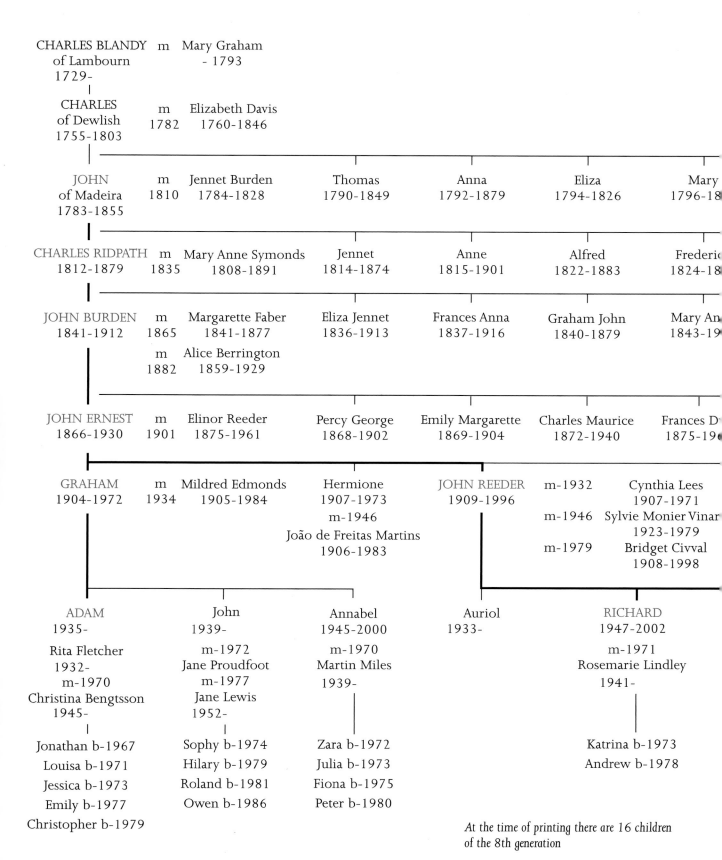

CHARLES BLANDY m Mary Graham
of Lambourn   - 1793
1729-

CHARLES   m   Elizabeth Davis
of Dewlish   1782   1760-1846
1755-1803

JOHN   m   Jennet Burden   Thomas   Anna   Eliza   Mary
of Madeira   1810   1784-1828   1790-1849   1792-1879   1794-1826   1796-18
1783-1855

CHARLES RIDPATH m Mary Anne Symonds   Jennet   Anne   Alfred   Frederic
1812-1879   1835   1808-1891   1814-1874   1815-1901   1822-1883   1824-18

JOHN BURDEN   m   Margarette Faber   Eliza Jennet   Frances Anna   Graham John   Mary An
1841-1912   1865   1841-1877   1836-1913   1837-1916   1840-1879   1843-19

            m   Alice Berrington
         1882   1859-1929

JOHN ERNEST   m   Elinor Reeder   Percy George   Emily Margarette   Charles Maurice   Frances D
1866-1930   1901   1875-1961   1868-1902   1869-1904   1872-1940   1875-19

GRAHAM   m   Mildred Edmonds   Hermione   JOHN REEDER   m-1932   Cynthia Lees
1904-1972   1934   1905-1984   1907-1973   1909-1996   1907-1971
                                   m-1946
                                   João de Freitas Martins   m-1946   Sylvie Monier Vinar
                                   1906-1983   1923-1979

                                                             m-1979   Bridget Civval
                                                                       1908-1998

ADAM   John   Annabel   Auriol   RICHARD
1935-   1939-   1945-2000   1933-   1947-2002

Rita Fletcher   m-1972   m-1970   m-1971
1932-   Jane Proudfoot Martin Miles   Rosemarie Lindley
m-1970   m-1977   1939-   1941-
Christina Bengtsson   Jane Lewis
1945-   1952-

Jonathan b-1967   Sophy b-1974   Zara b-1972   Katrina b-1973
Louisa b-1971   Hilary b-1979   Julia b-1973   Andrew b-1978
Jessica b-1973   Roland b-1981   Fiona b-1975
Emily b-1977   Owen b-1986   Peter b-1980
Christopher b-1979

*At the time of printing there are 16 children
of the 8th generation*

The Blandys
of Madeira

Company heads shown in red

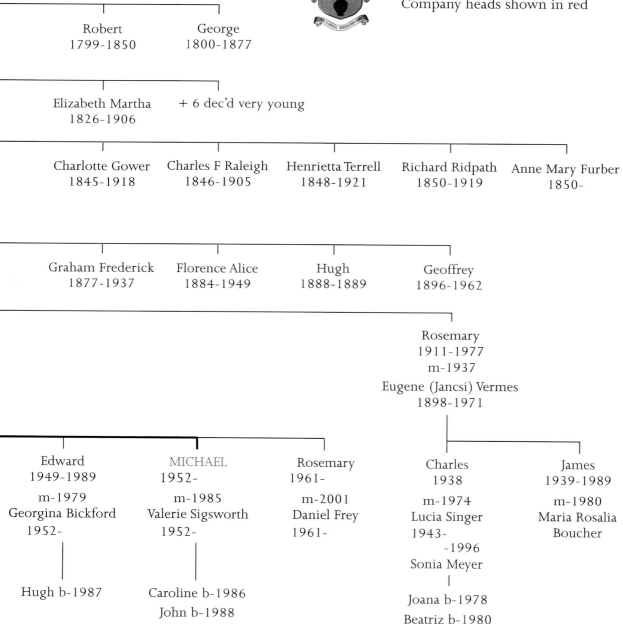

Robert
1799-1850

George
1800-1877

Elizabeth Martha
1826-1906

+ 6 dec'd very young

Charlotte Gower
1845-1918

Charles F Raleigh
1846-1905

Henrietta Terrell
1848-1921

Richard Ridpath
1850-1919

Anne Mary Furber
1850-

Graham Frederick
1877-1937

Florence Alice
1884-1949

Hugh
1888-1889

Geoffrey
1896-1962

Rosemary
1911-1977
m-1937
Eugene (Jancsi) Vermes
1898-1971

Edward
1949-1989
m-1979
Georgina Bickford
1952-

MICHAEL
1952-
m-1985
Valerie Sigsworth
1952-

Rosemary
1961-
m-2001
Daniel Frey
1961-

Charles
1938
m-1974
Lucia Singer
1943-
-1996
Sonia Meyer

James
1939-1989
m-1980
Maria Rosalia
Boucher

Hugh b-1987

Caroline b-1986
John b-1988

Joana b-1978
Beatriz b-1980

Notes on Sources

This book is based principally on the archives built up by the Blandy family. Graham Blandy's researches into the family and firm are contained in numerous manuscript and typed notes, covering every aspect of the business, including wine, shipping, coaling and banking, with memoirs on his father, grandfather and business colleagues. Today one archive is maintained by Michael Blandy at the Blandy office in Funchal. Here there are four large photographic albums containing not only numerous fascinating old photographs of the town and the harbour but also numerous clippings about the firm and the family members who ran it. At Palheiro Adam Blandy's archive contains a large number of family trees (the basis for the family tree he has compiled which is illustrated on p174-5) and extensive correspondence with other branches of the family, notably in North America and Australia. A good deal of research on 19th-century Blandys was done by the late Murray Symonds, of Adelaide, South Australia, a descendant of Richard Symonds, the brother-in-law of Charles Ridpath Blandy. Both archives contain the extensive material compiled by Graham Blandy.

The more recent chapters are based on interviews, principally with Adam and Michael Blandy and also on written memoirs they have provided, in best Blandy tradition, about themselves and their families. I have also talked to past and present members of the family firm, and have had interviews with successive members of the firm, including João Carlos Rodrigues on the Shipping business and Teotónio Rodrigues and Maria Augusta on the electronics business.

I have had extensive tours in the Blandy Wine Lodge and winery in Funchal and learnt much about Madeira wine from Franciso Albuquerque, Blandys wine maker who took me on a tour of the island's vineyards during the September harvest. I have also talked to José Câmara, the managing director of the Diário da Notícias and to Antonio Trindade whose

family have been involved in joint hotel ventures with the Blandys. Christina Blandy has illuminated the beauties of the Blandy gardens at Palheiro during the changing seasons as well as the restoration of Casa Velha as a hotel. John Blandy has directed me towards key items in the Madeira literature and has provided vivid descriptions of the island and his family.

The Man with the Big Cigar
Graham Blandy left a lively and detailed account of Churchill's visit, to which his wife Mildred added further details in a separate note. The visit is also described by Churchill's granddaughter Celia Sandys in *Chasing Churchill: The Travels of Winston Churchill* London 2003

1 A Poor Young Man In Search of a Fortune
The principal source is a typescript entitled 'Letters Written or Concerning Thomas Blandy From His Family in Madeira 1811-1846' which contains transcriptions of letters between John and Thomas Blandy, their sisters and other members of the family.

2 Rich Harvest, Bitter Legacy
The main sources for Charles Ridpath Blandy's childhood are the letters cited above. Further material on his family life comes in correspondence with the Symonds family. The dispute at the Anglican church in Madeira is well documented in Roy Nash's *Scandal in Madeira*: the Story of Richard Thomas Lowe, Lewes 1990. Material on the Blandys and the American Civil War is included in the Blandy albums. André Simon's assessment is taken from his book *Madeira*, Constable's Wine Library 1933.

3 Crisis Turned to Grand Advantage
Extensive material on John Burden Blandy was assembled by Graham Blandy. Henry Vizetelly's description of the Blandy wine lodge is taken from his Facts about Port and Madeira 1880. John Burden's correspondence about the acquisition of the Palheiro estate, and the building of his new

house is in the archive at Palheiro. At National Archives in London there are files on the controversy over German plans to build sanitoria and hotels in Madeira FO63/1442. Copies and transcripts of the letters between Raleigh Blandy and Floss Berrington are in the Blandy Office archive.

4 War, Retrenchment and Hard Times
The material assembled by Graham Blandy provides extensive insights into his father John Ernest's role in the firm. Further recollections have come from Michael Blandy.

5 Riots and Revolution
Graham Blandy left numerous notes of the firm's activities. Additional vivid details of the Madeira Revolution of 1931 were provided on an almost daily basis by the firm's redoubtable manager Major Shaw. Background on the Blandy business in Lisbon has come from Rupert Mullins.

6 A Sense of the Old Order
Jean Burca's autobiography *Call the Manager! From the Diaries of a Hotelier* London 1996 provides a wealth of lively and amusing insights into life at Reid's in the 1950s on which I have drawn extensively by kind permission of his widow Elizabeth. Further material has come from The Reid's Hotel minute books 1949-51 which I studied at the hotel.

7 Soldier, Builder and Mountain Climber
Michael Blandy provided me with a note about his father John Reeder and his family. Further details come from Graham Blandy.

8 Youth in Charge Again
Adam Blandy provided details of his life and career. For the Revolution of 1974 I have also drawn on interviews with one of the managers of Blandy's electronics business, Teotónio Rodrigues, and his colleague, Maria Augusta.

9 Boom Times, Big Decisions
Michael Blandy, in notes and discussions, has provided details of his brother Richard's life and career. Richard's description of the sinking of the *Lakonia*, written aged 16, is preserved in the Blandy Office archives.

10 New Investments and New Ways
Michael Blandy has provided extensive detail on the Blandy businesses in both Tenerife and Grand Canary as well as the expansion of the hotel business. Further details on the expansion of the hotel business has come from their joint venture partner Antonio Trindade. José Câmara who has managed the Diário de Notícias for 20 years, provided background on the newspaper.

11 Palheiro Moves into the Twenty-first Century
Information has come from discussions with Adam and Christina Blandy, and Jonathan Fletcher. Michael Brown and Roger Still have provided background on Palheiro Village. The quotes from Cabell Robinson are from an article by Colm Gill in *Golf Europe* August 25, 2004 'Design master Jones had great impact on Cabell Robinson'.

12 Champions of Madeira Wine
This chapter is based on talks with James Symington, Dominic Symington, Francisco Albuquerque, Michael Blandy, Mannie Berk and Richard Mayson.

13 The Adventure Continues
This is based on discussions with Michael Blandy, Richard Blandy's son Andrew, Adam Blandy and his eldest son Jonathan Fletcher.

Further Reading

Biddle, A J Drexel, *The Madeira Islands* 2 vols, London 1900

Bryans, Robin, *Madeira – Pearl of the Atlantic* London, 1959

Burca, Jean *Call the Manager! From the Diaries of a Hotelier* London 1996

Cane, Florence Du, *The Flowers and Gardens of Madeira* London 1909

Croft-Cooke, Rupert *Madeira* London 1961

Cossart, Noel, *Madeira – the Island Vineyard* London 1984

Duncan, Thomas Bentley, *Atlantic Islands in the Seventeenth Century* London 1972

De Faria e Castro, Padre Carlos Jorge, *Homens do Mar*, Funchal, 1963

Ferreira de Castro, José Maria, *Eternidade*, Lisbon 1933

França, Isabella de, *Journal of a Visit to Madeira and Portugal* (1853-1854) Funchal 1970

Gregory, Desmond, *The Beneficient Usurpers: A History of the British in Madeira* London 1988

Hancock, David, *Oceans of Wine: Madeira and the emergence of American trade and taste* London 2009

Harcourt, Edward Vernon, *A Sketch of Madeira* London 1880

Hoare, Marjorie, *The Quintas of Madeira* Funchal 2004

Hoe, Susanna, *Madeira – Islands and Women series*, Oxford, 2004

Johnson, Donald S, *Phantom Islands of the Atlantic*, New Brunswick 1988

Kinder, Thomas, *War, revolution & society in the Rio de la Plata, 1808-1810 : Thomas Kinder's narrative of a journey to Madeira, Montevideo and Buenos Aires* Oxford 2010

Koebel *Madeira Old and New* London 1908

Leitão Cristina, *Madeira and Porto Santo* Funchal 2004

Leitão Cristina, *Madeira: the book* Funchal 2007

Lethbridge Alan *Madeira Impressions and Associations* London 1924

Liddell, Alex, *Madeira* London 1998

Lowe, Richard Thomas, *Manual of Flora of Madeira* London 1881

Lowe, Richard Thomas, *The Fishes of Madeira* London 1843

Lyall, Alfred, *Rambles in Madeira and Portugal* London 1827

Lysons, Rev Samuel, *Machin and Madeira* London 1861

Macaulay, Rose, *They Went to Portugal* London 1990 (including the second part of *They Went to Portugal*, not published with the 1946 edition because of paper restrictions)

Mayson, Richard, *Portugal's Wines and Wine Makers* London 1992

Mayson, Richard, *The Wines & Vineyards of Portugal* London 2003

De Menezes, Charles Azevedo, and Da Silva, Padre Fernando Augusto, *Elucidario Madeirense*, 2 vols, Funchal 1922

Miles, Cecil, *A Glimpse of Madeira* London 1949

Mitchell, Silas Weir *A Madeira Party* New York 1902

Nash, Roy, *Scandal in Madeira: the story of Richard Thomas Lowe* Lewes 1990

Newall, H A *The English Church in Madeira* Oxford 1931

Parkinson, C N, *Trade in the Eastern Seas* Cambridge 1937

Pitta, N C, *An Account of the Island of Madeira* London 1812

Silva, J Donald, *An Annotated Bibliography and Internet Guide to the Madeira Islands* Lampeter 2005

Simon, André L, *Madeira* London 1951

Simon, André L, and Craig, Elizabeth, *Madeira Wine, Cakes and Sauces* London 1933

Sitwell, Sacheverell, *Portugal and Madeira* London 1954

Taylor, Ellen M, *Madeira, Its Scenery and How to See It* London 1882

Transportes na Madeira, Funchal, 1983

Underwood, John and Pat, *Madeira* – London 2010

Varvara, *Madère* (photographs), Geneva 1955

Vieira, Alberto, and Palma, Constantino, *Madeira Wine* Lisbon 1998

Vizetelly, Henry, *Facts about Port and Madeira* London 1880

Weaver, H J, *Reid's Hotel Jewel of the Altantic* London 1991

White, Robert, *Madeira: its Climate and Scenery* London 1851

Wortley Lady Emmeline, *A Visit to Portugal and Madeira* London 1854

Acknowledgements

This book tells the story of 200 years of the Blandy family and their businesses. Adam and Michael Blandy both felt that unless this story was told now, a wealth of material might be easily be lost. It is a story written from a Blandy perspective, set against the background of historical events, extensively based on archives and first hand recollections.

On visits to Madeira I have received unrivalled help and hospitality from Adam and Michael Blandy, including guided tours round Blandy properties, the island and its vineyards. These have been supplemented by numerous lengthy discussions in which they have described the family, the business and their own careers, often over congenial meals. They have arranged further interviews with people who have worked with the firm, both now and in the past, as well as introductions to their joint venture partners, notably the Symingtons in the Madeira wine business and Antonio Trindade in the new hotels in Madeira, mainland Portugal and Brazil. Christina Blandy has provided a wealth of observations about the Palheiro gardens and the Casa Velha hotel.

At the Blandy Office Simon Zino has organised photography and developed an online photographic gallery, an enormous boon given the distance between the publisher in London and Madeira.

Special photography has been undertaken by Henrique Seruca, covering houses and gardens, the wine lodge, the hotels and the vineyards. Images in the Blandy archives have been copied to a very high standard by the Vicentes Photography Museum in Funchal where Dra. Maria Helena Araújo and her team have also been tireless in finding and identifying period photographs from the collections at the Museum which date back to the 1870s. Dra Ana Margarida Araújo Camacho kindly provided us with high quality digital versions of period drawings and etchings of Madeira from the wonderful collection at Casa-Museu Frederico de Freitas'. In Madeira I have received valuable help from Doris Fabris at Reid's Hotel, Dra Teresa Pais of the Cruzes Museum and Cristina Leitão. I have also drawn on Dr Paulo Rodrigues's historical accounts of the British occupation of Madeira.

John Blandy, who first put my name forward as a potential author of this book, has generously helped me at every stage in providing vivid observations on the family and business and the history of the island where he grew up – on which I have freely drawn.

At Frances Lincoln, the publishers, Sarah Jane Forder has edited the text and Jessica Halliwell and John Nicoll have played a crucial role in shaping the book and piloting it through all stages of editing and production. Design and layouts are the work of Frank Lee and Robin Ollington.

On visits to Madeira my wife Anne has helped me extensively in noting and copying the Blandy archives, as well as transcribing documents and texts, and sharing her extensive knowledge of gardens and plants.

Picture Credits

Blandy Archive:
8, 15, 18, 35 middle (Raleigh Blandy), 35 bottom (Raleigh Blandy), 36, 39, 43 right, 44 top, middle & bottom, 45, 46, 47, 50 top and bottom, 53 right, 54, 55 top and bottom, 60 top, 64, 68, 70, 71, 86, 92 left, 102, 103, 104 top, 105, 107 left and right, 110, 117, 120, 121 (LIFE Magazine 03.01.1964), 121 top, 124, 125.

Casa-Museu Frederico de Freitas:
9 - Johan Frederik Eckersberg (drawing) T. Picken (lithograph), 12 - W. S. Pitt Springett (drawing) T. Picken (lithograph), 13 - John R. Isac, (engraving), 23 right, 24 bottom - Isabella Hurst de França, 25 top - W. S. Pitt Springett (drawing) T. Picken (lithograph), 25 bottom - Isabella Hurst de França, 28 - Frank Dillon (drawing) T. Picken (lithograph), 29 - Lady Susan Vernon Harcourt (drawing and lithograph), 33 - W. S. Pitt Springett (drawing) T. Picken (lithograph).

Dimas Almada:
99 top, 100 top and bottom, 114, 122.

Henrique Seruca Photography:
Inside Cover, 34, 56, 13 left, 130 right, 140 top and bottom, 142, 143, 144, 145, 146, 147, 148, 153, 154, 155, 157, 164, 167, 171.

Madeira Wine Company:
40 bottom, 97, 123, 152, 159, 160.

Michael Blandy:
106 top.

Michael Brown:
141 bottom.

Mount Vernon Ladies' Association:
161, 162.

Museu Quinta das Cruzes:
51 'Piquenique' (Painting by Tomás José da Anunciação) photograph by Henrique Seruca Photography.

Photographia Museu Vicentes:
4 right, 5, 6, 10, 11, 16, 23 left, 24 top, 27, 32, 35 top, 38 top, 40 top, 42, 43 left, 53 left, 58, 60 bottom, 61, 62, 63, 67, 72 right and left, 73 left and right, 74, 75, 76, 78, 79 left and right, 80 top and bottom, 81 top and bottom, 82, 83, 84, 85, 91 top, 92 right, 93, 94, 96, 99 bottom, 104 bottom, 106 bottom, 115, 150.

Porto Bay Hotels & Resorts:
136.

Palheiro Estate:
138, 139,141 top, 169.

Quinta Jardins do Lago:
129.

Reid's Palace Hotel:
4 left, 88 – (Max Römer), 89, 90 top - (Max Römer), 91 bottom - (Max Römer), 95 bottom - (Max Römer), 98 - (Max Römer).

Sérgio Santos:
142 bottom right.

Simon Zino:
66, 118, 128, 134, 156, 165, 166.

Union League Philadelphia:
38 bottom.

'Madeira M'Dear' (page 149) reproduced by permission of the Estates of Michael Flanders & Donald Swann 2010. Any use of Flanders & Swann material, large or small, should be referred to the Estates at leonberger@donaldswann.co.uk

Index

Page numbers in bold indicate chapters and longer accounts of particular subjects; stars (*) indicate text panels at the bottom of pages.